2023 SCOTT STAMP VALUES
U.S. SPECIALIZED BY GRADE

EDITOR-IN-CHIEF ....Jay Bigalke
EDITOR EMERITUS... James E. Kloetzel
EDITOR-AT-LARGE .... Donna Houseman
CONTRIBUTING EDITOR..Charles Snee
SENIOR EDITOR/NEW ISSUES & VALUING..........................Martin J. Frankevicz
ADMINISTRATIVE ASSISTANT/CATALOGUE LAYOUT .... Eric Wiessinger
PRINTING AND IMAGE COORDINATOR ....Stacey Mahan
SENIOR GRAPHIC DESIGNER .... Cinda McAlexander
GRAPHIC DESIGNER...Angela Kiser
ADVERTISING/SALES ....David Pistello, Eric Roth, Brenda Wyen,
Julie Dalhstrom
PRESIDENT ....Rick Amos

Copyright 2022 by

AMOS MEDIA

1660 Campbell Road, Suite A, Sidney, Ohio 45365

Publishers of
Linn's Stamp News, Linn's Stamp News Monthly,
Coin World, and *Coin World Monthly*

ADVERTISING INDEX

2023 SCOTT STAMP VALUES

U.S. SPECIALIZED BY GRADE

Extended Values in Eight Different Grades for Selected United States Stamps

This is the twenty-seventh edition of *Scott Stamp Values: U.S. Specialized by Grade.* Editions before 2011 had been issued as stand-alone pamphlets, the 2011 through 2021 editions appeared as part of the *Scott Specialized Catalogue of United States Stamps and Covers*, and the 2022 and this 2023 edition resume the stand-alone booklet tradition. Scott Stamp Values lists values for sound stamps in eight different grades and, in addition, numerical grades are assigned to the verbal grades commonly used. Thus, all stamps are now valued in the grades of Gem-100, Superb-98, Extremely Fine-Superb-95, Extremely Fine-90, Very Fine-Extremely Fine-85, Very Fine-80, Fine-Very Fine-75 and Fine-70.

The stamps listed are generally those with higher catalog values and greater susceptibility to value differentials based on grade changes. They consist of Scott 1 through 715 (including coil pairs, coil guide line and joint line pairs, and booklet panes), 720b, 832-834a, 1053, C1-C31, E1-E14, F1, J1-J86, K1-K18, O1-O126 (including the special printings), PR1-PR125, Q1-Q12, JQ1-JQ5, QE1-QE4a and RW1-RW88A.

This publication is designed to fill the needs of collectors who want to know what they might expect to pay for stamps in grades other than Scott's benchmark grade of Very Fine. You will note that the values for Very Fine in *Scott Stamp Values* are the same as they are in the corresponding sections of the U.S. Specialized catalog. *Scott Stamp Values* should aid those who want to buy higher-grade stamps and need to know what kinds of premiums over the benchmark Very Fine value they might be required to pay. It also will aid budget-conscious collectors who want to know what discounts they might expect to receive when buying stamps in grades lower than Very Fine. And for those interested in selling stamps, this important valuing information should help form more realistic expectations.

All the stamps valued herein are sound stamps. Stamps with faults will sell for less, no matter what grade they would fall into if sound. Different collectors rate faults in different ways. A small margin tear is very significant to some, less so to others. If a stamp has somewhat short perforations but has extremely fine or superb centering, some collectors will shy away from paying a high price, while others seem quite content to overlook the perforations and will pay a very high price. Similarly, some collectors tend to accept a beautiful stamp with a small thin at only a slight discount (especially if it's a very scarce item), while others would shy away at the same price, holding out for a faultless gem.

The description of stamp grades on the following page notes that stamps valued in *Scott Stamp Values* are assumed to have margins of a normal size for the issue. For Gem stamps, margins will be slightly larger than normal, and for Superb or Extremely Fine stamps, the margins may be normal or slightly larger than normal. But the values shown are NOT for large-margined, "jumbo" examples of Very Fine or higher-grade stamps. A Very Fine "jumbo" stamp will sell for more than the value shown here for a Very Fine stamp, and "jumbo" stamps in higher grades will sell for more than the respective non-"jumbo" stamps of the same grades. In grades lower than Very Fine, the fact that a stamp has "jumbo" margins has little influence on the stamp's value.

For stamps in unused, original-gum (OG) condition, the illustrated gum chart will be helpful in assessing value based on the condition of the gum and the degree of hinging. This chart was developed in conjunction with Robert A. Siegel Auction Galleries and has become the standard concise reference on this subject in the stamp marketplace as well as in the Scott catalog.

Used stamps present the challenge of assessing cancellations as well as centering, perforations and freshness. It may be assumed that as a stamp's grade ascends from Very Good through Superb, its cancellation will become neater, cleaner and less defacing of the design. A fresh, superbly centered stamp with a heavy blob of a cancel directly on the vignette cannot be considered a Superb used stamp. The value of such a stamp will be determined in the marketplace based on the preferences of individual collectors. Similarly, while a stamp with perforations cutting into the design may in all cases be considered to fall into the Very Good grade, a stamp with this centering but with a very neat and non-defacing cancel will sell for more than the same stamp with a heavier cancel.

Just as "jumbo" margins enhance the values of higher-grade stamps, so do scarcer color cancels and fancy cancels enhance the values of used stamps. The values in *Scott Stamp Values* represent used stamps with normal cancels. Stamps with scarcer color cancels and fancy cancels may be expected to sell for more, often much more.

We believe that a generally common and appropriate system for grading the highest-grade stamps is being consistently adhered to by all the main participants who are in the businesses of publishing valuing guides and/or actually grading stamps. Those participants are Amos Media Co., Professional Stamp Experts in Nevada, The Philatelic Foundation in New York, and Philatelic Stamp Authentication and Grading,

Inc. in Florida. While many collectors and dealers desire a certificate from one of these organizations attesting to the authenticity and grade of a stamp, the values in *Scott Stamp Values* are not tied to any expertizing body. Many expert collectors and dealers are capable of exercising their own judgment on matters of grading, and as long as their grading is consistent with the standards set forth within these pages, the values shown will serve as an accurate guide to value.

Warning: Collectors should be cautious of United States stamps graded by other than a recognized expertizing service that are offered with the grade descriptions and/or prices that are tied to the grades and values listed in *Scott Stamp Values: U.S. Specialized by Grade*. It is strongly recommended that such stamps be subject to examination by a recognized third-party expertizing service.

See pages 8, 9 and 10 for definitions of grade, an illustrated gum chart and illustrations of representative stamps in each of the eight grades that are valued herein for each stamp. Please study both definitions and illustrations carefully. The values in this publication match the grades described and illustrated. Descriptions used by some buyers and sellers of stamps may not match the grades described and illustrated in this Scott Stamp Values publication. We believe strongly that the Scott standards and definitions match most accurately the traditional marketplace uses. Therefore, in order to accurately judge a stamp's value, it is essential that users match values and grades accurately in accordance with the strict standards of *Scott Stamp Values*.

A Description of Stamp Grades for Sound United States Stamps (excluding the 1857-61 Issue and the 1875 Reprints thereof)*

GEM-100: The stamp is perfectly centered within four equal margins that are slightly larger than normal for the issue. Stamps that are perfectly centered within very large "jumbo" margins may be expected to sell for even more than the listed values for the gem grade. Color, impression and freshness will be noticeably excellent. Essentially, this will be a perfect stamp.

SUPERB-98: The stamp is almost perfectly centered within margins of a normal size or margins somewhat larger than normal. Stamps that are almost perfectly centered within very large "jumbo" margins may be expected to sell for even more than the listed values for the superb grade. Color, impression and freshness will be excellent. Essentially, this will be an almost perfect stamp.

EXTREMELY FINE-SUPERB-95: Extremely well centered within margins that are at least of normal size or perhaps slightly larger than normal. Close examination by unaided normal eyesight will reveal that the stamp is not perfectly centered. Extremely well-centered stamps with very large "jumbo" margins may be expected to sell for even more than the listed values for the extremely fine-superb grade. Color, impression and freshness will be very nice. All in all, an extremely choice example of the stamp.

EXTREMELY FINE-90: A very well-centered stamp within margins that are normal or slightly larger than normal. A discerning collector will be able to tell rather easily that the stamp is a little bit off in one or two directions. As with the preceding grades, good color, impression and freshness should be evident. And, again, stamps with "jumbo" margins will sell for more than the values shown. This will be a premium example of the stamp.

VERY FINE-EXTREMELY FINE-85: A well-centered stamp with margins of a normal size. In all respects an excellent example of the issue.

VERY FINE-80: The stamp is just slightly off-center on one or two sides. All frame lines will be well clear of the perforations (except for the 1857-61 first perforated issue (Scott 18-39) and most of the 1875 Reprints of the 1857-61 issue (Scott 41-46). With exceptions as noted in the catalogs, Very Fine is the benchmark grade valued in the Scott Standard Volume 1 and the *Scott Specialized Catalogue of United States Stamps and Covers.* A Very Fine stamp is, in all cases, a very desirable example of the issue.

FINE-VERY FINE-75: The stamp is noticeably off-center, with the perforations close to the design on one or two sides, resulting in margins that are narrow but with some white space between the perforations and the design. In this and lower grades, the color, impression and freshness may be somewhat below the levels of the higher grades.

FINE-70: The stamp is quite off-center, with the perforations on one or two sides very close to the design but not quite touching it. There is white space between the perforations and the design that is minimal but evident to the unaided eye.

*See the Illustrated Gum Chart on page 9 and also the introduction to the *Scott Specialized Catalogue of United States Stamps and Covers* for additional information concerning gum.

Illustrated Gum Chart

For purposes of helping to determine the gum condition and value of an unused stamp, Scott Publishing Co. presents the following chart which details different gum conditions and indicates how the conditions correlate with the Scott values for unused stamps. Used together, the Illustrated Grading Chart on the next page and this Illustrated Gum Chart should allow catalog users to better understand the grade and gum condition of stamps valued in the Scott catalogs.

Gum Categories:	MINT N.H.	ORIGINAL GUM (O.G.)					NO GUM
	Mint Never Hinged *Free from any disturbance*	Lightly Hinged *Faint impression of a removed hinge over a small area*	Hinge Mark or Remnant *Prominent hinged spot; may have part or all of the hinge remaining*	Large part o.g. *Approximately half or more of the gum intact*	Small part o.g. *Approximately less than half of the gum intact*		No gum *Only if issued with gum*
Commonly Used Symbol:	★ ★	★	★	★	★		(★)
PRE-1879 ISSUES	*Very fine pre-1879 stamps in these categories trade at a premium over Scott value*		Scott Value for "Unused" (Actual value will be affected by the degree of hinging and completeness of the gum.)				Scott "No Gum" Values thru No. 218
1879-1935 ISSUES	Scott "Never Hinged" Values for Nos. 182-771	Scott Value for "Unused" (Actual value will be affected by the degree of hinging of the full o.g.)					
1935 TO DATE	Scott Value for "Unused"						

Never Hinged (NH; ★★): A never-hinged stamp will have full original gum that will have no hinge mark or disturbance. The presence of an expertizer's mark does not disqualify a stamp from this designation.

Original Gum (OG; ★): Pre-1879 stamps should have approximately half or more of their original gum. On rarer stamps, it may be expected that the original gum will be somewhat more disturbed that it will be on more common issues. From 1879, stamps should have full original gum. Original gum will show some disturbance caused by a previous hinge(s) which may be present or entirely removed. The actual value of an 1879 or later stamp will be affected by the degree of hinging of the full original gum.

Disturbed Original Gum: –Gum showing noticeable effects of humidity, climate or hinging over more than half of the gum. The significance of gum disturbance in valuing a stamp in any of the Original Gum categories depends on the degree of disturbance, the rarity and normal gum condition of the issue and other variables affecting quality.

Regummed (RG; (★)): A regummed stamp is a stamp without gum that has had some type of gum privately applied at a time after it was issued. This normally is done to deceive collectors and/or dealers into thinking that the stamp has original gum and therefore has a higher value. A regummed stamp is considered the same as a stamp with none of its original gum for purposes of grading.

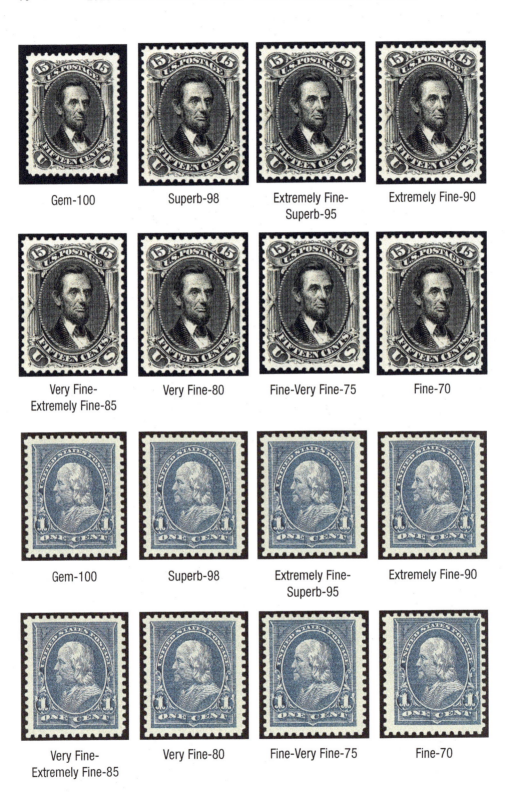

Gem-100

Superb-98

Extremely Fine-
Superb-95

Extremely Fine-90

Very Fine-
Extremely Fine-85

Very Fine-80

Fine-Very Fine-75

Fine-70

Gem-100

Superb-98

Extremely Fine-
Superb-95

Extremely Fine-90

Very Fine-
Extremely Fine-85

Very Fine-80

Fine-Very Fine-75

Fine-70

Trust Scott to protect and display your most valued collection

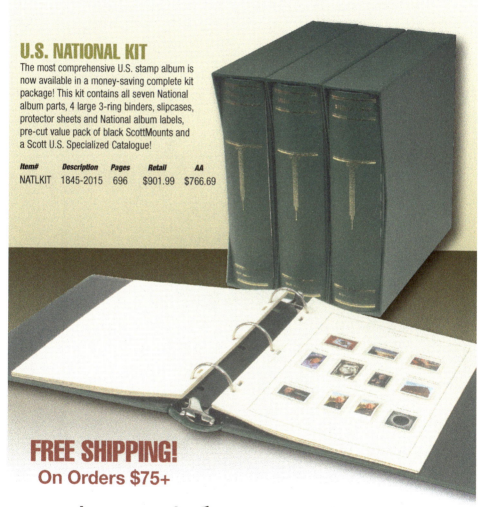

U.S. NATIONAL KIT

The most comprehensive U.S. stamp album is now available in a money-saving complete kit package! This kit contains all seven National album parts, 4 large 3-ring binders, slipcases, protector sheets and National album labels, pre-cut value pack of black ScottMounts and a Scott U.S. Specialized Catalogue!

Item#	Description	Pages	Retail	AA
NATLKIT	1845-2015	696	$901.99	$766.69

FREE SHIPPING!
On Orders $75+

AmosAdvantage.com
1-800-572-6885

SCT#	DENOM	COLOR	CONDITION	F 70	F-VF 75	VF 80	VF-XF 85	XF 90	XF-SUP 95	SUP 98	GEM 100

1847 REGULAR ISSUES

SCT#	DENOM	COLOR	CONDITION	F 70	F-VF 75	VF 80	VF-XF 85	XF 90	XF-SUP 95	SUP 98	GEM 100
1	5¢	red	Used	200	300	425	500	650	1,200	3,850	7,500
		brown	Unused NG	825	1,400	2,100	2,400	3,500	5,000	—	—
			Unused OG	2,650	4,250	6,000	9,000	12,500	17,500	29,000	—
1a	5¢	dark	Used	225	360	525	650	1,150	2,250	4,500	—
		brown	Unused NG	950	1,600	2,400	2,750	3,400	4,600	7,000	—
			Unused OG	2,700	4,400	7,000	9,000	14,500	22,500	35,000	—
1b	5¢	orange	Used	290	435	675	800	1,100	2,100	4,250	—
		brown	Unused NG	1,700	2,500	3,500	4,000	4,750	6,250	—	—
			Unused OG	4,000	6,900	10,000	12,000	16,000	29,000	—	—
1c	5¢	red	Used	4,000	6,000	8,500	10,500	15,000	25,000	—	—
		orange	Unused NG	4,500	7,000	9,500	—	—	—	—	—
			Unused OG	10,000	15,500	25,000	—	—	—	—	—
1d	5¢	brown	Used	425	750	1,000	1,300	2,150	4,750		
		orange	Unused NG	—	—	4,500	—				
			Unused OG	—	—	—	—				
2	10¢	black	Used	450	625	900	1,175	1,600	3,000	6,000	—
			Unused NG	6,500	11,000	16,000	18,500	22,500	32,500	—	—
			Unused OG	14,000	25,000	37,500	47,500	80,000	—	—	—

1875 REPRODUCTIONS OF 1847 ISSUE

SCT#	DENOM	COLOR	CONDITION	F 70	F-VF 75	VF 80	VF-XF 85	XF 90	XF-SUP 95	SUP 98	GEM 100
3	5¢	red brown	Unused NGAI	450	725	1,000	1,175	1,450	1,900	3,000	5,000
4	10¢	black	Unused NGAI	625	900	1,250	1,500	1,900	2,600	4,750	—

1851-57 REGULAR ISSUE (IMPERFORATE)

SCT#	DENOM	COLOR	CONDITION	F 70	F-VF 75	VF 80	VF-XF 85	XF 90	XF-SUP 95	SUP 98	GEM 100
5	1¢	blue	Used	50,000	75,000	115,000	175,000	275,000			
		type I	Unused OG	115,000	—	—					
5A	1¢	blue	Used	6,500	8,500	10,000	13,250	17,500	26,500	45,000	
		type Ib	Unused NG	12,000	14,000	16,500	20,000	32,500	—	—	
			Unused OG	35,000	40,000	45,000	55,000	77,500		—	
6	1¢	blue	Used	5,250	7,000	9,250	12,250	20,000	35,000	75,000	
		type Ia	Unused NG	12,000	14,000	20,000	26,000	35,000	—	—	
			Unused OG	22,500	32,500	45,000	72,500	115,000	—	—	
6b	1¢	blue	Used	1,600	2,250	3,500	4,500	7,250	18,000	—	
		type Ic	Unused NG	1,500	2,100	3,000	3,500	4,000	6,000	—	
		E relief	Unused OG	3,500	5,000	7,000	9,000	14,000	—	—	
		type Ic	Used	4,500	5,750	9,000	11,750	20,000	31,500	—	
		F relief pos.	Unused NG	6,000	8,500	12,500	15,500	22,500	—	—	
		91 & 96 R4	Unused OG	15,000	22,500	27,500	40,000	—	—	—	
7	1¢	blue	Used	60	100	150	200	300	800	2,100	3,500
		type II	Unused NG	150	250	375	450	550	850	1,400	2,500
			Unused OG	475	750	1,000	1,325	2,200	4,500	9,250	17,500

SCT#	DENOM	COLOR	CONDITION	F 70	F-VF 75	VF 80	VF-XF 85	XF 90	XF-SUP 95	SUP 98	GEM 100
8	1¢	blue	Used	750	1,125	1,500	2,500	4,250	7,750	17,500	—
		type III	Unused NG	3,000	5,000	7,500	9,000	15,000	—	—	—
			Unused OG	9,500	13,750	25,000	37,500	62,500	—	—	—
(8)	1¢	blue	Used	2,000	3,350	5,250	8,750	12,500	19,500	—	—
(99R2)		type III	Unused NG	4,600	7,100	10,000	15,000	22,500	—	—	—
			Unused OG	14,500	25,000	35,000	50,000	—	—	—	—
8A	1¢	blue	Used	375	500	800	1,125	2,000	4,250	9,000	—
		type IIIa	Unused NG	775	1,475	2,250	2,750	3,500	5,000	—	—
			Unused OG	1,800	3,600	6,000	8,000	17,500	—	—	—
9	1¢	blue	Used	40	70	100	160	275	700	1,400	2,800
		type IV	Unused NG	110	175	260	300	400	650	950	—
			Unused OG	290	405	725	950	1,500	3,000	6,250	9,750
10	3¢	orange	Used	87.50	130	190	300	700	2,250	3,500	—
		brown	Unused NG	575	950	1,500	1,700	2,000	2,700	4,000	—
		type I	Unused OG	1,325	2,350	4,000	5,000	7,500	13,750	—	—
10A	3¢	orange	Used	65	100	150	250	400	1,125	2,650	5,250
		brown	Unused NG	625	975	1,600	1,750	1,900	2,500	—	—
		type II	Unused OG	1,125	2,000	3,250	4,200	6,000	11,500	—	—
11	3¢	dull	Used	6	12.50	17.50	45	85	250	500	1,000
		red	Unused NG	45	70	100	125	175	300	450	—
		type I	Unused OG	90	135	250	350	500	900	1,450	4,850
11A	3¢	dull	Used	5	10	15	42.50	82.50	225	525	1,050
		red	Unused NG	37.50	60	85	100	130	225	375	—
		type II	Unused OG	110	145	250	375	525	1,000	1,600	2,000
12	5¢	red	Used	325	550	775	900	1,350	2,000	4,250	—
		brown	Unused NG	4,000	7,000	11,000	12,500	15,000	19,000	—	—
		type I	Unused OG	10,000	19,000	30,000	40,000	55,000	—	—	—
13	10¢	green	Used	375	525	750	1,050	1,400	2,500	6,000	—
		type I	Unused NG	3,700	5,400	8,500	9,750	12,500	—	—	—
			Unused OG	8,000	12,000	19,000	27,500	45,000	—	—	—
14	10¢	green	Used	62.50	110	145	180	325	625	1,200	6,000
		type II	Unused NG	725	1,175	1,800	2,000	2,300	3,000	—	—
			Unused OG	2,200	3,250	5,000	6,750	8,750	16,500	32,500	60,000
15	10¢	green	Used	62.50	110	145	180	350	700	1,250	2,800
		type III	Unused NG	725	1,175	1,800	2,000	2,300	3,000	4,250	—
			Unused OG	2,200	3,200	5,000	6,000	8,750	16,500	32,500	—
16	10¢	green	Used	850	1,200	1,700	2,200	2,850	6,500	13,000	—
		type IV	Unused NG	12,750	18,500	27,500	37,500	70,000	—	—	—
			Unused OG	30,000	40,000	50,000	62,500	100,000	—	—	—
17	12¢	gray	Used	105	145	260	325	500	1,100	2,500	5,500
		black	Unused NG	950	1,500	2,100	2,400	2,900	4,000	—	—
			Unused OG	2,750	4,000	6,250	9,000	12,000	21,500	45,000	—

1857-61 REGULAR ISSUE (PERFORATED)

SCT#	DENOM	COLOR	CONDITION	F 70	F-VF 75	VF 80	VF-XF 85	XF 90	XF-SUP 95	SUP 98	GEM 100
18	1¢	blue	Used	170	340	500	725	1,000	6,250	—	—
		type I	Unused NG	320	490	800	1,000	1,200	1,900	2,500	—
			Unused OG	850	1,325	2,100	3,000	6,000	9,000	14,500	—
19	1¢	blue	Used	9,500	11,000	13,000	21,000	30,000	80,000	240,000	—
		type Ia	Unused NG	20,000	25,000	30,000	37,500	45,000	—	—	—
			Unused OG	42,500	47,500	55,000	65,000	80,000	—	—	—
19b	1¢	blue	Used	3,750	4,250	5,000	6,500	9,000	27,500	—	—
		type Ic	Unused NG	1,750	2,150	3,000	3,500	5,500	—	—	—
		E relief	Unused OG	4,250	5,500	7,000	9,000	14,000	—	—	—
		type Ic	Used	7,250	9,500	11,000	12,500	20,000	—	—	—
		F relief pos.	Unused NG	9,000	10,250	11,500	13,000	21,000	—	—	—
		91 & 96 R4	Unused OG	20,000	22,500	25,000	30,000	52,500	—	—	—
20	1¢	blue	Used	100	175	275	425	825	2,500	—	—
		type II	Unused NG	140	260	375	475	750	1,250	—	—
			Unused OG	325	525	850	1,450	3,000	5,250	—	—

SCT#	DENOM	COLOR	CONDITION	F 70	F-VF 75	VF 80	VF-XF 85	XF 90	XF-SUP 95	SUP 98	GEM 100
21	1¢	blue	Used	625	950	1,400	2,000	4,000	8,500	15,500	—type III
		type III	Unused NG	2,500	3,700	6,000	7,000	8,750	—	—	—
			Unused OG	7,250	10,500	17,500	24,000	37,500	—	—	—
(21) (99R2)	1¢	blue type III	Used	3,650	5,000	7,250	—	—			
22	1¢	blue	Used	170	315	475	800	1,700	4,500	—	—
		type IIIa	Unused NG	325	550	850	1,050	1,400	2,500	—	—
			Unused OG	875	1,525	2,200	3,250	5,500	12,000	—	—
23	1¢	blue	Used	550	900	1,200	1,500	3,000	7,500	—	—
		type IV	Unused NG	4,250	5,000	6,250	7,000	8,000	—	—	—
			Unused OG	10,000	12,500	16,500	20,000	27,500	—	—	—
24	1¢	blue	Used	14	25	40	140	350	850	2,500	—
		type V	Unused NG	27.50	40	60	72.50	87.50	130	190	—
			Unused OG	60	95	140	200	375	675	1,100	—
25	3¢	rose	Used	190	225	250	575	1,300	2,400	5,000	—
		type I	Unused NG	1,050	1,150	1,250	1,500	2,000	—	—	—
			Unused OG	3,000	3,500	4,000	6,000	9,000	—	—	—
25A	3¢	rose	Used	900	1,025	1,200	2,500	5,500	—	—	—
		type II	Unused NG	4,000	5,000	6,000	7,250	9,000	—	—	—
			Unused OG	9,000	10,250	11,500	13,000	21,000	—	—	—
26	3¢	dull red	Used	3.25	5	10	40	130	400	800	—
		type III	Unused NG	9.75	16.50	27.50	37.50	65	120	—	—
			Unused OG	30	40	65	85	125	260	475	—
26A	3¢	dull red	Used	60	97.50	150	260	460	1,400	5,500	8,750
		type IV	Unused NG	115	180	260	320	400	600	—	—
			Unused OG	190	360	600	900	1,250	2,600	—	—
27	5¢	brick red	Used	575	925	1,450	2,500	4,750	13,500	—	—
		type I	Unused NG	7,750	13,000	20,000	25,000	—	—	—	—
			Unused OG	35,000	60,000	80,000	120,000	—	—	—	—
28	5¢	red brown	Used	500	700	1,100	1,750	3,000	9,500	25,000	—
		type I	Unused NG	6,100	9,500	15,000	17,250	21,500	—	—	—
			Unused OG	21,000	36,000	60,000	75,000	90,000	—	—	—
28b	5¢	bright red brown	Used	875	1,675	2,250	3,150	4,750	9,500	—	—
		type I	Unused NG	9,250	12,250	20,000	22,500	—	—	—	—
			Unused OG	25,000	42,500	70,000	90,000	—	—	—	—
28A	5¢	Indian red	Used	1,775	2,500	3,750	4,850	6,000	20,500		
		type I	Unused NG	18,000	28,000	40,000	—				
			Unused OG	160,000							
29	5¢	brown	Used	140	240	325	550	950	4,250	10,000	—
		type I	Unused NG	750	1,175	1,750	2,250	3,000	—	—	—
			Unused OG	2,000	3,250	5,500	8,250	12,500	—	—	—
30	5¢	orange brown	Used	500	825	1,300	1,850	3,250	9,750	—	—
		type II	Unused NG	210	340	500	600	750	1,175	1,650	—
			Unused OG	575	800	1,200	2,000	3,150	8,250	—	—
30A	5¢	brown	Used	125	175	280	450	825	2,600	8,500	20,000
		type II	Unused NG	375	550	825	975	1,200	2,000	—	—
			Unused OG	900	1,500	2,250	2,850	5,000	12,000	—	—
31	10¢	green	Used	460	725	1,100	1,650	4,250	11,000	—	—
		type I	Unused NG	3,750	7,250	11,500	14,500	18,500	26,000	—	—
			Unused OG	12,000	22,000	35,000	57,500	90,000	—	—	—
32	10¢	green	Used	84.50	130	190	275	700	2,750	10,000	—
		type II	Unused NG	800	1,175	2,000	2,450	3,100	4,400	—	—
			Unused OG	2,100	3,350	5,750	10,000	15,000	22,500	—	—
33	10¢	green	Used	85	130	190	285	725	2,750	15,000	—
		type III	Unused NG	800	1,175	2,000	2,450	3,100	4,400	—	—
			Unused OG	2,100	3,350	5,750	10,000	15,000	22,500	—	—
34	10¢	green	Used	900	1,450	2,200	3,250	5,500	12,000	—	—
		type IV	Unused NG	8,500	11,000	20,000	25,000	33,500	—	—	—
			Unused OG	16,000	27,500	50,000	72,500	110,000	—	—	—
35	10¢	green	Used	25	40	55	85	160	475	1,450	—
		type V	Unused NG	37.50	62.50	95	115	140	210	—	—
			Unused OG	75	135	210	325	675	1,500	2,250	—
36	12¢	black	Used	125	185	300	460	800	2,400	8,500	—
		plate 1	Unused NG	210	325	600	725	900	1,550	—	—
			Unused OG	725	1,150	1,700	3,000	5,650	9,000	—	—
36B	12¢	black	Used	110	175	275	400	775	2,000	6,500	—
		plate 3	Unused NG	175	240	375	475	600	1,050	—	—
			Unused OG	275	525	775	1,100	1,800	3,750	7,000	—

SCT#	DENOM	COLOR	CONDITION	F 70	F-VF 75	VF 80	VF-XF 85	XF 90	XF-SUP 95	SUP 98	GEM 100
37	24¢	gray	Used	150	265	400	550	1,050	3,650	7,500	—
		lilac	Unused NG	180	300	500	600	750	1,250	2,000	—
			Unused OG	575	1,025	1,450	2,000	3,750	6,500	—	—
37a	24¢	gray	Used	140	250	375	525	1,025	3,650	7,500	—
			Unused NG	180	300	500	600	750	1,250	2,000	—
			Unused OG	550	1,025	1,450	2,000	3,150	6,500	—	—
38	30¢	orange	Used	190	325	500	800	1,250	4,000	10,000	—
			Unused NG	210	440	700	800	1,000	1,800	2,500	—
			Unused OG	825	1,225	1,900	3,000	5,250	11,000	—	—
39	90¢	blue	Used	4,500	7,250	10,000	16,000	25,000	47,500	—	—
			Unused NG	525	950	1,400	1,700	2,150	3,250	4,500	—
			Unused OG	1,300	2,100	3,000	4,000	6,500	15,000	—	—

1875 REPRINTS OF THE 1857-61 ISSUE

SCT#	DENOM	COLOR	CONDITION	F 70	F-VF 75	VF 80	VF-XF 85	XF 90	XF-SUP 95	SUP 98	GEM 100
40	1¢	bright blue	Unused NGAI	235	385	600	700	850	1,650	5,000	—
41	3¢	scarlet	Unused NGAI	2,850	3,500	4,800	5,750	8,750	12,500	—	—
42	5¢	orange brown	Unused NGAI	1,200	1,850	2,500	3,750	5,750	12,000	—	—
43	10¢	blue green	Unused NGAI	2,500	2,700	3,850	5,000	9,000	13,000	—	—
44	12¢	greenish black	Unused NGAI	2,750	3,250	4,150	5,500	9,500	—	—	—
45	24¢	blackish violet	Unused NGAI	3,000	3,600	4,600	5,750	9,750	—	—	—
46	30¢	yellow orange	Unused NGAI	3,000	3,600	4,600	5,500	9,000	—	—	—
47	90¢	deep blue	Unused NGAI	1,750	2,600	3,750	6,000	10,500	15,000	—	—

1861-66 REGULAR ISSUES

SCT#	DENOM	COLOR	CONDITION	F 70	F-VF 75	VF 80	VF-XF 85	XF 90	XF-SUP 95	SUP 98	GEM 100
62B	10¢	dark	Used	925	1,375	1,750	2,600	4,250	11,500	—	—
		green	Unused NG	1,500	2,250	3,600	4,750	6,500	8,750	—	—
			Unused OG	4,750	6,500	8,500	13,000	22,000	50,000	—	—
63	1¢	blue	Used	17.50	30	45	100	170	575	2,250	—
			Unused NG	42.50	65	100	120	145	240	380	—
			Unused OG	97.50	170	275	365	650	1,500	2,500	—
63a	1¢	ultramarine	Used	850	1,200	1,900	2,650	4,000	—	—	—
			Unused NG	390	625	1,000	1,200	1,500	2,750	—	—
			Unused OG	975	1,600	2,500	3,250	4,750	8,500	—	—
63b	1¢	dark	Used	380	550	875	1,250	2,000	4,000	—	—
		blue	Unused NG	135	200	300	375	500	900	—	—
			Unused OG	330	525	800	1,025	1,400	3,150	—	—
64	3¢	pink	Used	300	425	575	1,100	3,000	6,000	—	—
			Unused NG	2,250	3,200	5,000	5,500	6,500	—	—	—
			Unused OG	5,500	8,500	14,000	17,000	23,500	—	—	—
64a	3¢	pigeon	Used	2,000	2,850	4,250	5,600	8,250	21,000	—	—
		blood	Unused NG	7,250	10,500	17,500	21,000	25,000	—	—	—
		pink	Unused OG	22,000	37,500	55,000	72,500	90,000	—	—	—
64b	3¢	rose	Used	75	105	140	250	400	1,350	4,000	—
		pink	Unused NG	110	160	250	300	360	600	950	—
			Unused OG	240	375	600	800	1,200	2,500	4,800	—
65	3¢	rose	Used	1.10	2	3	22.50	75	250	1,000	—
			Unused NG	20	32.50	50	60	80	125	—	—
			Unused OG	47.50	72.50	125	175	290	575	1,150	—
67	5¢	buff	Used	375	550	750	1,350	2,750	6,000	—	—
			Unused NG	5,750	8,250	12,500	15,000	18,000	—	—	—
			Unused OG	14,500	20,000	30,000	42,500	—	—	—	—

SCT#	DENOM	COLOR	CONDITION	F 70	F-VF 75	VF 80	VF-XF 85	XF 90	XF-SUP 95	SUP 98	GEM 100
67a	5¢	brown yellow	Used	575	800	1,100	1,900	3,000	7,250	—	—
			Unused NG	5,500	8,000	11,500	13,500	17,000	—		
			Unused OG	14,000	20,000	30,000	—	—			
67b	5¢	olive yellow	Used	2,000	3,250	4,850	7,500	14,000	—		
68	10¢	green	Used	25	40	60	130	300	800	2,500	7,500
			Unused NG	150	225	375	525	750	1,150	—	—
			Unused OG	360	625	950	1,525	2,400	5,250	11,000	—
68a	10¢	dark green	Used	35	47.50	90	140	260	1,000	2,500	—
			Unused NG	220	335	500	600	750	1,250	1,950	—
			Unused OG	480	825	1,350	2,050	3,150	6,500	13,500	—
69	12¢	black	Used	42.50	62.50	95	230	325	750	2,850	—
			Unused NG	300	475	675	800	1,000	1,600	2,750	—
			Unused OG	650	1,050	1,700	2,450	4,000	9,000	—	—
70	24¢	red lilac	Used	115	180	300	600	1,000	4,000	—	—
			Unused NG	450	750	1,100	1,450	1,900	3,250	—	—
			Unused OG	1,250	2,000	2,900	4,150	8,000	16,000	—	—
70a	24¢	brown lilac	Used	125	190	325	525	850	2,650	6,500	—
			Unused NG	575	850	1,250	1,500	2,000	3,250	—	—
			Unused OG	1,450	2,100	3,250	4,500	7,000	14,000	—	—
70b	24¢	steel blue	Used	370	525	825	1,300	2,750	9,000	—	—
			Unused NG	2,650	4,100	6,250	7,250	8,750	—	—	—
			Unused OG	7,000	10,500	16,500	21,500	32,500	—	—	—
70c	24¢	violet	Used	975	1,475	2,250	3,250	4,750	12,500	—	—
			Unused NG	6,750	10,500	13,500	15,500	20,000	—	—	—
			Unused OG	15,000	22,500	35,000	42,500	55,000	100,000	—	—
70d	24¢	pale gray violet	Used	1,300	2,400	3,000	4,250	6,750	18,000	—	—
			Unused NG	2,250	4,000	6,000	7,000	8,500	13,000	—	—
			Unused OG	7,750	17,500	25,000	35,000	55,000	—	—	—
71	30¢	orange	Used	110	165	250	375	650	2,000	5,500	—
			Unused NG	400	625	900	1,100	1,550	2,750	—	—
			Unused OG	950	1,550	2,600	4,000	7,500	—	—	—
72	90¢	blue	Used	265	400	575	875	1,350	4,500	11,500	21,500
			Unused NG	500	775	1,200	1,350	1,700	2,750	4,000	—
			Unused OG	1,100	1,850	3,000	4,250	6,750	13,500	22,500	—
72a	90¢	pale blue	Used	300	450	675	950	1,350	4,500	11,500	—
			Unused NG	500	775	1,200	1,350	1,675	2,500	3,650	—
			Unused OG	1,100	1,850	3,000	4,150	6,500	12,500	21,000	—
72b	90¢	dark blue	Used	450	625	950	1,250	1,850	6,750	14,000	—
			Unused NG	650	975	1,500	1,700	2,100	2,750	4,500	—
			Unused OG	1,325	2,100	3,750	5,000	8,000	14,500	26,000	—
73	2¢	black	Used	22.50	45	65	120	260	750	2,750	—
			Unused NG	52.50	90	150	175	225	500	900	—
			Unused OG	150	250	350	575	1,150	2,750	—	—
75	5¢	red brown	Used	210	300	425	675	1,200	4,250	—	—
			Unused NG	850	1,350	2,000	2,300	2,750	4,250	—	—
			Unused OG	2,250	3,750	5,500	7,250	11,000	—	—	—
76	5¢	brown	Used	52.50	77.50	125	200	385	1,400	3,250	7,500
			Unused NG	260	375	550	750	950	1,400	2,000	—
			Unused OG	575	875	1,400	2,150	3,500	6,250	—	—
76a	5¢	black brown	Used	150	230	400	625	1,150	3,000	8,500	—
			Unused NG	375	525	850	1,000	1,250	2,000	—	—
			Unused OG	825	1,300	2,250	3,250	4,750	10,000	—	—
77	15¢	black	Used	82.50	120	175	285	550	2,250	5,250	—
			Unused NG	800	1,150	1,900	2,250	2,750	3,750	6,000	—
			Unused OG	1,750	3,000	5,000	6,750	10,500	20,000	—	—
78	24¢	lilac	Used	170	255	400	600	1,000	3,750	7,250	—
			Unused NG	400	625	950	1,150	1,500	2,450	—	—
			Unused OG	1,000	1,750	2,750	4,000	6,250	12,000	—	—
78a	24¢	grayish lilac	Used	185	255	425	650	1,100	3,850	7,750	—
			Unused NG	350	575	950	1,150	1,525	2,450	—	—
			Unused OG	950	1,800	2,750	4,000	7,250	—	—	—
78b	24¢	gray	Used	200	275	450	675	1,200	4,000	—	—
			Unused NG	360	575	950	1,150	1,475	2,400	—	—
			Unused OG	925	1,700	2,750	4,000	6,750	12,500	—	—
78c	24¢	blackish violet	Used	8,000	11,500	16,000	25,000	42,500	60,000		
			Unused NG	—	30,000						
			Unused OG	72,500	95,000						

1867-68 GRILLED ISSUES

SCT#	DENOM	COLOR	CONDITION	F 70	F-VF 75	VF 80	VF-XF 85	XF 90	XF-SUP 95	SUP 98	GEM 100
79	3¢	rose	Used	1,000	1,300	4,600	9,000	16,000	—		
			Unused NG	1,750	2,750	5,000	9,000	—	—		
			Unused OG	5,500	8,500	17,000	27,500	—	—		
80	5¢	brown	Used	400,000							
80a	5¢	dark brown	Used	400,000							
81	30¢	orange	Used	225,000							
82	3¢	rose	Used	900,000							
83	3¢	rose	Used	440	625	1,100	1,500	2,750	8,500	—	
			Unused NG	825	1,300	2,000	2,500	3,250	5,250	—	
			Unused OG	2,100	3,550	5,500	7,500	13,000	27,500	50,000	—
84	2¢	black	Used	5,250	6,250	8,000	10,750	18,500	40,000	77,500	
			Unused NG	6,250	8,000	10,000	—	—	—		
			Unused OG	16,000	23,000	32,500	—	—			
85	3¢	rose	Used	500	775	1,100	1,525	2,600	8,000	22,500	
			Unused NG	1,125	1,575	2,400	3,250	5,000	7,250	—	
			Unused OG	3,500	5,250	8,000	12,500	20,000	—	—	
85A	1¢	blue	Used					3,000,000			
85B	2¢	black	Used	525	725	1,100	1,750	3,500	10,500	28,500	
			Unused NG	3,000	4,600	6,750	7,500	8,750	12,500	—	
			Unused OG	8,500	12,000	17,500	21,000	27,500	55,000		
85C	3¢	rose	Used	1,850	2,350	3,500	5,500	9,000	21,000	32,500	
			Unused NG	4,750	6,500	9,000	15,000	—			
			Unused OG	10,000	16,000	25,000	40,000	65,000			
85D	10¢	green	Used	475,000	600,000	750,000	1,200,000				
85E	12¢	black	Used	875	1,450	2,250	3,250	5,000	17,000	37,500	
			Unused NG	4,250	6,250	8,500	11,500	15,000	—		
			Unused OG	10,000	17,000	25,000	35,000	47,500			
85F	15¢	black	Used	two known, one in VG grade, value thus 1,600,000				2,000,000			
86	1¢	blue	Used	190	300	450	750	1,450	4,750	13,500	
			Unused NG	550	725	1,100	1,400	1,850	—		
			Unused OG	1,200	2,100	3,000	4,750	7,500	—		
86a	1¢	dull blue	Used	170	275	400	750	1,300	4,250	12,500	
			Unused NG	550	725	1,100	1,400	1,900	3,000	—	
			Unused OG	1,200	2,100	3,000	4,750	7,750	16,500	—	
87	2¢	black	Used	82.50	125	200	325	600	1,900	4,250	—
			Unused NG	275	435	650	775	975	1,600	2,400	—
			Unused OG	825	1,075	1,700	3,500	4,750	—	—	
88	3¢	rose	Used	12	18	30	55	175	750	—	
			Unused NG	160	220	350	450	625	950	—	
			Unused OG	400	700	1,050	1,850	2,750	4,850	9,000	
88a	3¢	lake red	Used	30	45	75	135	265	1,250	—	
			Unused NG	210	300	475	575	725	1,100	1,625	
			Unused OG	450	800	1,250	1,750	2,750	5,500	10,500	
89	10¢	green	Used	120	200	350	575	875	2,250	7,000	
			Unused NG	800	1,275	2,000	2,500	3,100	5,250	7,250	
			Unused OG	2,000	3,200	5,000	7,500	12,500	24,000		
90	12¢	black	Used	150	240	400	650	1,150	3,250	9,500	
			Unused NG	750	1,200	1,900	2,250	2,750	—		
			Unused OG	2,000	3,500	4,750	6,250	11,500	—		
91	15¢	black	Used	250	400	575	800	1,450	5,750	—	
			Unused NG	1,900	3,000	4,500	5,250	6,500	—		
			Unused OG	4,750	7,500	12,500	17,500	25,000	—		
92	1¢	blue	Used	180	285	425	700	1,450	4,750	13,000	—
			Mint NG	425	600	900	1,225	1,950	3,250	4,250	—
			Unused OG	1,125	1,725	2,800	4,250	7,500	16,500	—	—

SCT#	DENOM	COLOR	CONDITION	F 70	F-VF 75	VF 80	VF-XF 85	XF 90	XF-SUP 95	SUP 98	GEM 100
92a	1¢	pale	Used	140	250	375	575	1,250	4,500	11,500	—
		blue	Unused NG	300	475	700	925	1,250	2,150	3,250	—
			Unused OG	950	1,450	2,300	3,750	6,000	11,000	—	—
93	2¢	black	Used	22.50	35	55	100	250	2,600	6,000	—
			Unused NG	70	110	155	220	300	750	1,250	—
			Unused OG	205	340	450	800	1,750	4,500	8,000	—
94	3¢	red	Used	4.50	7	12.50	45	95	500	1,250	—
			Mint NG	70	100	150	185	260	500	—	—
			Unused OG	130	240	350	575	950	2,500	4,750	—
94a	3¢	rose	Used	4.50	7	12.50	40	90	300	800	—
			Unused NG	72.50	105	155	200	270	525	875	—
			Unused OG	130	240	350	575	950	2,500	4,500	—
95	5¢	brown	Used	450	625	850	1,325	2,150	9,500	—	—
			Unused NG	500	775	1,250	1,575	2,100	3,000	—	—
			Unused OG	1,300	2,100	3,250	5,500	9,500	18,500	—	—
95a	5¢	black	Used	1,000	1,600	2,400	3,750	9,000	40,000	—	—
		brown	Unused NG	775	1,175	1,750	2,000	2,650	3,500	—	—
			Unused OG	1,900	3,000	5,000	6,500	10,000	—	—	—
96	10¢	yellow	Used	120	165	250	375	725	2,500	—	—
		green	Mint NG	360	525	825	1,050	1,500	2,150	3,250	—
			Unused OG	900	1,550	2,500	3,750	6,000	12,500	—	—
97	12¢	black	Used	115	165	250	375	675	2,250	8,500	—
			Unused NG	475	650	1,000	1,250	1,700	3,000	4,250	—
			Unused OG	1,025	1,725	2,800	4,250	6,750	13,000	23,000	—
98	15¢	black	Used	140	200	275	525	825	3,000	10,000	20,000
			Unused NG	675	1,025	1,600	1,875	2,500	4,500	7,000	—
			Unused OG	1,750	2,850	4,250	7,250	11,500	22,500	42,500	—
99	24¢	gray	Used	625	1,025	1,600	2,150	3,500	10,000	—	—
		lilac	Unused NG	1,450	2,100	3,250	3,750	4,750	7,500	—	—
			Unused OG	3,000	5,750	8,500	12,500	18,500	35,000	—	—
100	30¢	orange	Used	500	700	1,050	1,350	2,250	10,000	—	—
			Unused NG	1,800	2,800	4,500	5,250	6,750	—	—	—
			Unused OG	4,850	8,250	12,500	16,000	22,500	—	—	—
101	90¢	blue	Used	1,000	1,675	2,500	3,750	5,250	14,000	22,500	37,500
			Unused NG	2,500	3,750	5,750	6,750	8,000	12,000	—	—
			Unused OG	5,500	8,750	14,500	22,500	37,500	70,000	—	—

1875 RE-ISSUES OF THE 1861-66 ISSUES

SCT#	DENOM	COLOR	CONDITION	F 70	F-VF 75	VF 80	VF-XF 85	XF 90	XF-SUP 95	SUP 98	GEM 100
102	1¢	blue	Used	900	1,225	1,700	1,950	2,750	5,000	10,000	—
			Unused NG	145	245	350	425	625	875	1,150	—
			Unused OG	375	575	750	975	1,850	2,750	5,650	—
103	2¢	black	Used	6,000	8,000	10,500	22,000	27,500	—	—	—
			Unused NG	650	975	1,600	2,150	3,000	4,250	6,250	—
			Unused OG	1,750	2,500	3,500	5,000	7,750	10,000	—	—
104	3¢	brown	Used	7,750	11,000	13,000	20,000	35,000	—	—	—
		red	Unused NG	775	1,125	1,700	2,150	3,000	5,500	—	—
			Unused OG	1,875	2,650	3,750	5,500	8,500	15,000	—	—
105	5¢	brown	Used	2,600	4,250	6,000	7,750	10,500	19,000	55,000	—
			Unused NG	500	750	1,150	1,600	2,100	3,250	—	—
			Unused OG	1,250	1,800	2,500	4,750	7,500	12,500	—	—
106	10¢	green	Used	60,000	77,500	100,000	120,000	150,000	—	—	—
			Unused NG	575	875	1,400	2,250	4,000	5,250	—	—
			Unused OG	1,200	1,900	2,900	3,750	6,500	10,000	20,000	—
107	12¢	black	Used	7,500	9,250	12,000	16,750	27,500	52,500	—	—
			Unused NG	775	1,125	1,750	2,250	3,750	6,500	—	—
			Unused OG	1,750	2,650	3,750	5,250	9,000	13,000	19,000	—

SCT#	DENOM	COLOR	CONDITION	F 70	F-VF 75	VF 80	VF-XF 85	XF 90	XF-SUP 95	SUP 98	GEM 100
108	15¢	black	Used	15,000	21,000	30,000	40,000	55,000	—		—
			Unused NG	900	1,325	2,100	2,650	3,500	5,000	—	—
			Unused OG	2,250	3,300	4,500	6,250	10,000	17,000		—
109	24¢	deep	Used	8,750	12,500	17,500	27,500	45,000	—	—	
		violet	Unused NG	1,200	1,775	2,750	3,500	4,500	6,500	10,500	—
			Unused OG	3,000	4,500	6,000	8,500	12,500	21,000	—	
110	30¢	brownish	Used	8,750	12,500	17,500	27,500	45,000	—	—	
		orange	Unused NG	1,100	1,800	2,800	3,400	4,250	6,000	10,000	—
			Unused OG	2,800	3,700	5,750	8,000	11,000	20,000	—	
111	90¢	blue	Used	160,000	190,000	225,000		275,000			
			Unused NG	1,600	2,250	3,500	4,250	5,500	7,500	—	—
			Unused OG	3,500	5,250	7,000	11,500	15,500	—	—	

1869 PICTORIAL ISSUE											
112	1¢	buff	Used	67.50	110	140	200	325	1,300	3,250	
			Unused NG	92.50	130	210	260	350	700	1,000	—
			Unused OG	260	425	575	875	2,250	4,500	7,000	—
113	2¢	brown	Used	32.50	60	80	135	275	1,000	2,150	
			Unused NG	85	135	190	230	300	450	700	—
			Unused OG	190	310	500	750	1,600	3,250		—
114	3¢	ultramarine	Used	7	11	18	65	300	1,100	2,500	
			Unused NG	37.50	65	90	120	145	225	325	—
			Unused OG	80	140	225	350	800	1,450	—	—
115	6¢	ultramarine	Used	90	135	225	325	600	2,500	5,250	
			Unused NG	420	675	1,050	1,275	1,550	2,350	3,350	—
			Unused OG	925	1,700	2,600	3,400	5,500	12,500	20,000	—
116	10¢	yellow	Used	35	67.50	110	175	325	850	2,750	
			Unused NG	300	475	750	875	1,150	1,700	2,250	—
			Unused OG	700	1,200	1,850	2,800	4,500	11,500	19,500	—
117	12¢	green	Used	37.50	80	130	200	375	875	2,150	
			Unused NG	300	460	725	850	1,075	1,650	—	—
			Unused OG	900	1,200	1,850	3,000	4,650	10,250	19,000	—
118	15¢	brown	Used	350	550	850	1,050	1,650	4,250	11,000	
		& blue	Unused NG	1,400	2,200	3,250	3,700	4,400	6,250	—	—
		type I	Unused OG	3,600	5,750	9,000	13,000	20,000	35,000	—	—
119	15¢	brown	Used	75	120	190	300	650	2,200	5,000	
		& blue	Unused NG	375	600	925	1,075	1,300	2,250	3,150	—
		type II	Unused OG	1,100	1,800	2,600	4,500	7,500	12,000	—	—
119b	15¢	invert	Used	22,500	45,000						
			Unused NG	700,000							
			Unused OG	1,000,000							
120	24¢	green	Used	250	410	650	900	1,750	4,500	15,000	—
		& violet	Unused NG	1,250	1,950	3,000	3,750	4,250	6,750	—	—
			Unused OG	2,750	5,000	8,000	13,000	19,750	38,500	—	—
120b	24¢	invert	Used	37,500	75,000	100,000					
			Unused NG	750,000							
121	30¢	ultramarine	Used	180	310	450	800	1,400	3,750	—	—
		& carmine	Unused NG	575	875	1,450	1,800	2,350	4,500	—	—
			Unused OG	1,425	2,650	4,000	6,250	16,500	32,000	47,500	—
121b	30¢	invert	Used	65,000	80,000	90,000	120,000	150,000			
			Unused NG	180,000	240,000	300,000					
			Unused OG	—	—	750,000					
122	90¢	carmine	Used	900	1,300	1,900	3,000	4,250	8,750	20,000	—
		& black	Unused NG	1,600	2,750	4,000	4,750	6,250	10,500	—	—
			Unused OG	3,250	7,000	11,000	17,500	27,500	77,500	—	—

SCT#	DENOM	COLOR	CONDITION	F 70	F-VF 75	VF 80	VF-XF 85	XF 90	XF-SUP 95	SUP 98	GEM 100

1875-81 RE-ISSUES OF THE 1869 ISSUE

SCT#	DENOM	COLOR	CONDITION	F 70	F-VF 75	VF 80	VF-XF 85	XF 90	XF-SUP 95	SUP 98	GEM 100
123	1¢	buff	Used	170	265	425	650	1,075	3,000	5,250	—
			Unused NG	100	160	220	300	450	700	—	—
			Unused OG	200	335	525	825	1,300	2,750	—	—
124	2¢	brown	Used	375	550	750	1,150	2,000	4,250	—	—
			Unused NG	105	170	250	350	475	775	1,750	4,000
			Unused OG	210	360	600	1,000	1,850	4,500	—	—
125	3¢	blue	Used	18,500	25,000	40,000	55,000	80,000	—	—	—
			Unused NG	1,150	1,650	2,500	3,000	4,000	6,500	—	—
			Unused OG	2,000	3,500	5,000	7,750	13,500	22,500	—	—
126	6¢	blue	Used	1,525	2,100	3,000	4,250	650	15,000	32,500	—
			Unused NG	425	575	900	1,150	1,400	2,100	—	—
			Unused OG	625	1,150	1,900	2,650	3,750	7,000	—	—
127	10¢	yellow	Used	1,000	1,350	1,800	3,250	5,250	9,500	—	—
			Unused NG	325	500	750	950	1,250	2,750	—	—
			Unused OG	575	1,000	1,600	2,250	3,000	6,000	10,000	—
128	12¢	green	Used	1,650	2,200	3,000	4,250	6,250	14,000	—	—
			Unused NG	450	675	1,000	1,400	2,100	4,000	—	—
			Unused OG	900	1,250	2,000	3,000	4,750	9,000	19,000	—
129	15¢	brown & blue type III	Used	600	750	1,000	1,600	2,350	5,250	—	—
			Unused NG	300	450	625	850	1,050	1,850	—	—
			Unused OG	650	900	1,300	1,850	3,250	6,500	—	—
130	24¢	green & violet	Used	800	1,150	1,600	2,100	3,250	7,500	—	—
			Unused NG	450	675	1,000	1,325	1,750	2,600	4,250	—
			Unused OG	725	1,200	2,000	3,000	6,000	8,750	15,500	—
131	30¢	ultramarine & carmine	Used	1,275	1,900	2,750	3,750	5,750	11,500	19,500	—
			Unused NG	475	725	1,100	1,375	1,800	3,250	4,500	—
			Unused OG	800	1,300	2,250	3,250	6,000	8,500	15,000	—
132	90¢	carmine & black	Used	3,200	4,250	6,000	7,500	11,500	22,500	—	—
			Unused NG	850	1,150	1,750	2,250	3,250	4,500	7,250	—
			Unused OG	1,500	2,600	3,750	5,000	7,750	17,500	27,500	—
133	1¢	buff	Used	285	415	550	825	1,350	2,250	—	—
			Unused NG	70	100	150	190	280	425	—	—
			Unused OG	150	220	350	500	800	1,450	—	—
133a	1¢	brown orange	Used	275	425	650	775	1,200	1,650	—	—
			Unused NGAI	180	260	400	575	900	1,350	2,650	3,500

1870-71 NATIONAL BANK NOTE ISSUE (WITH "H" GRILL)

SCT#	DENOM	COLOR	CONDITION	F 70	F-VF 75	VF 80	VF-XF 85	XF 90	XF-SUP 95	SUP 98	GEM 100
134	1¢	ultramarine	Used	90	125	200	250	425	1,600	4,500	—
			Unused NG	310	460	700	850	1,100	1,750	2,750	—
			Unused OG	700	1,150	2,000	3,250	5,250	10,000	—	—
135	2¢	red brown	Used	35	55	80	110	190	650	1,600	—
			Unused NG	160	230	360	450	575	825	—	—
			Unused OG	375	625	1,000	1,500	2,250	4,500	—	—
136	3¢	green	Used	11.50	20	32.50	55	140	550	1,500	—
			Unused NG	85	120	190	275	350	475	775	—
			Unused OG	220	375	575	950	1,500	2,750	5,750	—
137	6¢	carmine	Used	225	300	425	650	1,000	2,750	8,250	—
			Unused NG	825	1,225	1,750	2,150	2,650	3,650	—	—
			Unused OG	2,000	3,150	5,000	7,150	10,500	19,000	—	—

SCT#	DENOM	COLOR	CONDITION	F 70	F-VF 75	VF 80	VF-XF 85	XF 90	XF-SUP 95	SUP 98	GEM 100
138	7¢	vermilion	Used	260	380	525	675	1,000	3,250	11,000	—
			Unused NG	725	1,025	1,550	1,875	2,350	3,150	—	—
			Unused OG	1,600	2,650	4,250	6,150	9,250	12,500	—	—
139	10¢	brown	Used	330	550	800	1,100	1,500	5,250	13,500	—
			Unused NG	1,200	1,800	2,700	3,200	3,750	5,500	—	—
			Unused OG	2,750	4,500	7,500	10,000	14,000	27,500	—	—
140	12¢	dull violet	Used	2,000	2,850	3,750	5,500	8,750	—	—	—
			Unused NG	8,250	12,500	17,500	21,500	26,000	—	—	—
			Unused OG	13,500	21,000	32,500	40,000	50,000	—	—	—
141	15¢	orange	Used	700	1,050	1,500	2,250	3,500	6,000	15,000	—
			Unused NG	1,125	1,700	2,500	3,150	4,000	5,500	—	—
			Unused OG	2,800	5,000	7,500	11,000	18,000	30,000	—	—
142	24¢	purple	Used	3,850	5,250	6,500	9,000	15,000	17,500	—	—
143	30¢	black	Used	1,875	2,700	3,750	5,000	8,500	18,500	—	—
			Unused NG	3,650	5,250	7,500	9,250	12,000	—	—	—
			Unused OG	8,500	13,250	20,000	26,500	37,500	—	—	—
144	90¢	carmine	Used	1,025	1,525	2,250	3,250	5,250	13,500	—	—
			Unused NG	3,900	6,500	10,000	12,000	16,000	—	—	—
			Unused OG	8,750	16,250	25,000	40,000	65,000	—	—	—

1870-71 NATIONAL BANK NOTE ISSUE (WITH "I" GRILL)

SCT#	DENOM	COLOR	CONDITION	F 70	F-VF 75	VF 80	VF-XF 85	XF 90	XF-SUP 95	SUP 98	GEM 100
134A	1¢	ultramarine	Used	180	260	400	525	1,050			
			Unused NG	355	525	800	975	1,600			
			Unused OG	975	1,575	2,750	4,450	8,250			
135A	2¢	red brown	Used	130	200	300	425	650	1,150	2,250	
			Unused NG	425	750	1,000	1,200				
			Unused OG	850	1,350	2,000	3,250	7,500			
136A	3¢	green	Used	42.50	67.50	100	130	250	1,150	1,900	—
			Unused NG			—	—	400			
			Unused OG	300	460	800	1,200	1,800			
137A	6¢	carmine	Used	370	625	950	1,400	2,900			
			Unused NG			—					
			Unused OG	3,000	4,850	8,500	10,500	16,000	—		
138A	7¢	vermilion	Used	375	525	800	1,450	2,750	—		
			Unused NG	1,000	1,500	2,200	3,200	4,500	6,500	9,000	—
			Unused OG	2,250	3,850	6,500	9,000	15,000			
139A	10¢	brown	Used	3,750	6,750	10,000	13,000	22,500			
			UnusedOG		—	17,500	27,500	40,000			
140A	12¢	dull violet	Unused OG	7,750	—	30,000					
141A	15¢	orange	Used	3,750	5,500	8,500	9,750	—	12,500		
			Unused OG	7,500	—	16,500					
143A	30¢	black	Unused OG		75,000						
144A	90¢	carmine	Used	8,000	—	15,000					
			Unused OG			—					

1870-71 NATIONAL BANK NOTE ISSUE (WITHOUT GRILL)

SCT#	DENOM	COLOR	CONDITION	F 70	F-VF 75	VF 80	VF-XF 85	XF 90	XF-SUP 95	SUP 98	GEM 100
145	1¢	ultramarine	Used	7.50	11.50	20	55	175	500	1,000	—
			Unused NG	95	160	240	310	400	650	900	1,500
			Unused OG	240	435	650	1,050	2,250	4,500	—	—
146	2¢	red brown	Used	7	10.50	17.50	50	170	600	1,250	—
			Unused NG	60	105	160	190	240	350	—	—
			Unused OG	110	220	350	550	925	1,900	—	—
147	3¢	green	Used	0.90	1.25	1.80	8	37.50	250	550	—
			Unused NG	32.50	50	80	100	150	200	—	—
			Unused OG	70	130	200	425	950	—	—	—

SCT#	DENOM	COLOR	CONDITION	F 70	F-VF 75	VF 80	VF-XF 85	XF 90	XF-SUP 95	SUP 98	GEM 100
148	6¢	carmine	Used	8.50	14.50	22.50	65	275	675	1,300	2,600
			Unused NG	120	190	290	375	500	800	—	—
			Unused OG	300	550	900	1,450	2,250	5,000	9,000	—
149	7¢	vermilion	Used	45	75	100	150	275	800	1,900	4,250
			Unused NG	120	190	290	375	525	850	—	—
			Unused OG	315	550	900	1,850	3,000	4,750	—	—
150	10¢	brown	Used	12.50	20	35	70	200	600	1,250	2,500
			Unused NG	400	550	800	950	1,200	1,500	2,250	—
			Unused OG	800	1,250	2,000	2,750	4,250	—	—	—
151	12¢	dull	Used	77.50	130	200	275	550	1,450	3,500	—
		violet	Unused NG	450	725	1,050	1,250	1,650	2,250	—	—
			Unused OG	1,050	1,900	2,850	3,900	6,500	—	—	—
152	15¢	bright	Used	90	145	225	300	625	1,700	4,000	—
		orange	Unused NG	525	850	1,300	1,450	1,600	2,200	—	—
			Unused OG	1,225	2,150	3,500	4,750	6,750	13,500	—	—
153	24¢	purple	Used	90	145	225	325	500	1,500	3,500	—
			Unused NG	300	425	650	850	1,000	1,450	2,250	—
			Unused OG	575	1,025	1,700	2,850	4,750	9,250	—	—
154	30¢	black	Used	120	200	300	425	700	2,000	5,250	—
			Unused NG	1,175	1,725	2,600	3,000	4,000	5,000	—	—
			Unused OG	2,600	4,350	7,000	8,750	14,000	37,500	—	—
155	90¢	carmine	Used	150	230	350	475	750	2,400	6,500	—
			Unused NG	750	1,200	1,800	2,150	2,600	3,100	—	—
			Unused OG	1,825	3,200	5,000	7,000	11,000	19,000	—	—

1873 CONTINENTAL BANK NOTE ISSUE

SCT#	DENOM	COLOR	CONDITION	F 70	F-VF 75	VF 80	VF-XF 85	XF 90	XF-SUP 95	SUP 98	GEM 100
156	1¢	ultramarine	Used	2	3.25	5.75	12	45	260	600	—
			Unused NG	37.50	62.50	90	110	145	—	—	—
			Unused OG	70	120	200	300	600	1,200	—	—
157	2¢	brown	Used	10	16	25	37.50	100	350	950	—
			Unused NG	55	85	125	150	205	—	—	—
			Unused OG	130	210	325	500	950	1,750	—	—
158	3¢	green	Used	0.25	0.40	1	8	32.50	110	400	—
			Unused NG	18	27.50	40	52.50	77.50	100	—	—
			Unused OG	40	70	110	170	275	500	1,250	—
159	6¢	dull	Used	7.75	12.50	18	27.50	75	225	800	—
		pink	Unused NG	52.50	85	120	150	210	300	—	—
			Unused OG	130	230	375	600	925	1,700	3,250	—
160	7¢	orange	Used	35	57.50	85	125	200	850	2,250	4,250
		vermilion	Unused NG	160	230	350	415	600	850	—	—
			Unused OG	370	625	1,000	1,500	2,850	5,250	8,750	—
161	10¢	brown	Used	9	15	25	37.50	100	350	950	—
			Unused NG	125	185	275	325	500	750	—	—
			Unused OG	300	465	800	1,100	1,650	4,250	8,250	—
162	12¢	black	Used	67.50	95	140	190	300	775	2,000	—
		violet	Unused NG	325	550	775	925	1,300	1,850	—	—
			Unused OG	875	1,425	2,200	3,500	5,500	10,500	—	—
163	15¢	yellow	Used	62.50	100	160	225	375	1,100	—	—
		orange	Unused NG	350	550	775	950	1,350	2,150	3,250	—
			Unused OG	800	1,450	2,250	3,400	6,000	9,750	—	—
164	24¢	purple	Used	One known, VG grade, value $357,500.							
165	30¢	gray	Used	60	87.50	140	190	300	825	2,500	—
		black	Unused NG	625	925	1,300	1,500	2,000	3,250	—	—
			Unused OG	1,500	2,450	4,000	5,500	8,750	18,000	—	—
166	90¢	rose	Used	140	190	300	450	750	2,000	—	—
		carmine	Unused NG	325	500	700	850	1,025	1,500	—	—
			Unused OG	875	1,400	2,100	3,000	4,750	8,250	17,500	—

SCT#	DENOM	COLOR	CONDITION	F 70	F-VF 75	VF 80	VF-XF 85	XF 90	XF-SUP 95	SUP 98	GEM 100

1875 SPECIAL PRINTINGS OF THE 1873 ISSUE

SCT#	DENOM	COLOR	CONDITION	F 70	F-VF 75	VF 80	VF-XF 85	XF 90	XF-SUP 95	SUP 98	GEM 100
167	1¢	ultramarine	Unused NGAI	8,500	11,250	14,000	23,500	45,000			
168	2¢	dark brown	Unused NGAI	3,900	4,650	6,000	15,000	—			
169	3¢	blue green	Unused NGAI	12,750	17,250	21,500	—				
170	6¢	dull rose rose	Unused NGAI	13,500	15,500	20,000	29,000	50,000			
171	7¢	reddish vermilion	Unused NGAI	3,000	3,600	4,250	8,500	16,000	29,000		
172	10¢	pale brown	Unused NGAI	13,000	15,000	19,000	30,000	47,500			
173	12¢	dark violet	Unused NGAI	3,750	4,400	5,500	10,000	19,000	27,500		
174	15¢	bright orange	Unused NGAI	13,000	15,000	19,000	30,000	47,500			
175	24¢	dull purple	Used	One known, VG grade, value $22,500.							
			Unused NGAI	2,500	2,800	3,500	8,000	14,000	22,500		
176	30¢	greenish black	Unused NGAI	9,000	10,000	12,000	20,000	32,500			
177	90¢	violet carmine	Unused NGAI	13,500	15,500	18,000	32,500	57,500			

1875 CONTINENTAL BANK NOTE & SPECIAL PRINTINGS

SCT#	DENOM	COLOR	CONDITION	F 70	F-VF 75	VF 80	VF-XF 85	XF 90	XF-SUP 95	SUP 98	GEM 100
178	2¢	vermilion	Used	6	9	15	27.50	75	375	850	—
			Unused NG	47.50	72.50	100	125	145	225	325	—
			Unused OG	115	210	325	420	600	1,300	2,500	—
179	5¢	blue	Used	11	16.50	27.50	42.50	110	350	1,000	—
			Unused NG	85	145	225	270	330	470	700	—
			Unused OG	240	450	700	950	1,400	3,000	6,000	—

1875 Special Printings of the 1875 Issue

SCT#	DENOM	COLOR	CONDITION	F 70	F-VF 75	VF 80	VF-XF 85	XF 90	XF-SUP 95	SUP 98	GEM 100
180	2¢	carmine vermilion	Unused NGAI	36,000	55,000	70,000	92,500	135,000			
181	5¢	bright blue	Unused NGAI	210,000	310,000	450,000	550,000	775,000			

1879 AMERICAN BANK NOTE ISSUE

SCT#	DENOM	COLOR	CONDITION	F 70	F-VF 75	VF 80	VF-XF 85	XF 90	XF-SUP 95	SUP 98	GEM 100
182	1¢	dark ultramarine	Used	2.30	3.40	6	12.50	67.50	210	625	—
			Unused NG	35	52.50	80	100	135	230	—	—
			Unused OG	80	125	200	325	525	1,100	2,100	—
			Mint NH	120	270	675	1,250	2,750	7,250	—	—

SCT#	DENOM	COLOR	CONDITION	F 70	F-VF 75	VF 80	VF-XF 85	XF 90	XF-SUP 95	SUP 98	GEM 100
183	2¢	vermilion	Used	2.40	3.50	5	11	50	175	550	—
			Unused NG	17	25	40	47.50	60	92.50	—	—
			Unused OG	45	67.50	100	140	225	625	1,025	—
			Mint NH	62.50	160	370	650	1,250	4,000	6,000	—
184	3¢	green	Used	0.30	0.70	1	15	55	125	475	925
			Unused NG	14.50	22	35	45	57.50	95	—	—
			Unused OG	35	57.50	90	140	190	375	800	—
			Mint NH	62.50	150	325	525	800	2,250	7,500	—
185	5¢	blue	Used	6.75	10	16	32.50	92.50	300	950	1,900
			Unused NG	72.50	105	155	180	220	300	450	—
			Unused OG	210	335	500	700	1,050	1,750	4,500	—
			Mint NH	295	750	1,600	2,250	4,000	11,500	—	—
186	6¢	pink	Used	9	15	22.50	50	100	375	1,150	—
			Unused NG	130	190	275	310	360	500	800	—
			Unused OG	375	625	900	1,200	1,900	3,150	6,250	—
			Mint NH	625	1,425	3,100	4,500	7,750	18,500	—	—
187	10¢	brown (no mark)	Used	18.50	27.50	45	70	170	550	2,500	—
			Unused NG	450	675	1,000	1,200	1,500	1,900	—	—
			Unused OG	1,200	2,000	3,000	4,000	6,000	10,000	—	—
			Mint NH	2,100	5,750	10,000	13,500	20,000	45,000	—	—
188	10¢	brown (mark)	Used	12	18.50	30	70	140	400	1,400	2,750
			Unused NG	300	415	650	825	975	1,350	—	—
			Unused OG	725	1,150	1,800	2,300	3,850	6,500	12,500	20,000
			Mint NH	1,275	2,850	6,000	8,500	14,000	33,500	—	—
189	15¢	red orange	Used	12	18.50	27.50	45	160	375	1,050	2,750
			Unused NG	35	47.50	70	82.50	100	140	220	—
			Unused OG	80	120	180	250	425	1,000	1,750	—
			Mint NH	140	350	600	900	1,750	4,250	8,750	17,000
190	30¢	full black	Used	32.50	52.50	90	140	325	700	2,000	—
			Unused NG	150	210	300	350	425	525	825	1,600
			Unused OG	350	600	850	1,150	1,700	3,500	7,000	—
			Mint NH	550	1,250	2,800	4,500	7,250	17,500	—	—
191	90¢	carmine	Used	160	235	375	525	1,000	3,250	7,500	—
			Unused NG	325	500	700	775	1,000	1,350	2,000	—
			Unused OG	800	1,575	2,100	3,000	4,500	8,750	14,500	—
			Mint NH	1,700	4,750	7,250	10,500	16,500	40,000	—	—

1880 SPECIAL PRINTINGS OF THE 1879 ISSUE

SCT#	DENOM	COLOR	CONDITION	F 70	F-VF 75	VF 80	VF-XF 85	XF 90	XF-SUP 95	SUP 98	GEM 100
192	1¢	dark ultramarine	Unused NGAI	45,000	65,000	77,500	105,000	120,000	—	—	
193	2¢	black brown	Unused NGAI	9,500	12,500	16,000	26,500	37,500			
194	3¢	blue green	Unused NGAI	120,000	150,000	185,000	210,000	290,000			
195	6¢	dull rose	Unused NGAI	42,500	57,500	67,500	82,500	105,000			
196	7¢	scarlet vermilion	Unused NGAI	4,500	5,650	6,750	12,000	19,000	—		
197	10¢	deep brown	Unused NGAI	24,000	30,000	37,500	60,000	77,500			
198	12¢	blackish purple	Unused NGAI	6,050	7,500	9,500	14,000	19,000	29,000		
199	15¢	orange	Unused NGAI	15,000	21,500	30,000	42,500	60,000	95,000		
200	24¢	dark violet	Unused NGAI	4,950	6,750	9,000	13,000	19,000			
201	30¢	greenish black	Unused NGAI	11,750	17,000	22,500	30,000	45,000	60,000		
202	90¢	dull carmine	Unused NGAI	15,000	21,500	30,000	42,500	60,000			
203	2¢	scarlet vermilion	Unused NGAI	60,000	77,500	100,000	145,000	180,000			
204	5¢	deep blue	Unused NGAI	135,000	185,000	240,000	300,000	350,000	425,000	525,000	

SCT#	DENOM	COLOR	CONDITION	F 70	F-VF 75	VF 80	VF-XF 85	XF 90	XF-SUP 95	SUP 98	GEM 100
1881-1885 AMERICAN BANK NOTE ISSUES & SPECIAL PRINTINGS											
205	5¢	yellow brown	Used	5.50	9	15	30	130	300	825	2,400
			Unused NG	37.50	62.50	90	110	130	185	290	—
			Unused OG	115	175	240	400	600	1,150	2,000	5,750
			Mint NH	250	485	775	1,200	1,950	5,500	10,500	—
205C	5¢	gray brown	Unused NGAI	30,000	38,500	50,000	57,500	65,000	100,000		
206	1¢	gray blue	Used	0.35	0.60	1	10	37.50	225	450	—
			Unused NG	11	17	25	32.50	42.50	60	—	—
			Unused OG	30	47.50	70	110	190	500	800	2,250
			Mint NH	90	140	225	350	550	2,250	—	—
207	3¢	blue green	Used	0.30	0.55	0.80	10	32.50	125	750	—
			Unused NG	12.50	18	27.50	37.50	60	87.50	—	—
			Unused OG	35	52.50	80	105	170	325	675	—
			Mint NH	92.50	150	250	600	1,000	3,750	7,250	—
208	6¢	rose	Used	50	77.50	110	175	425	1,150	2,250	—
			Unused NG	105	165	250	275	325	425	625	—
			Unused OG	350	550	825	1,050	1,450	2,750	7,000	—
			Mint NH	950	1,650	2,600	3,500	5,250	9,250	—	—
208a	6¢	deep brown red	Used	90	135	190	260	425	1,250	3,000	—
			Unused NG	77.50	115	170	200	240	350	475	—
			Unused OG	250	375	600	775	1,125	1,850	4,250	—
			Mint NH	700	1,175	1,900	2,850	4,100	7,750	—	—
209	10¢	brown	Used	2.75	4.25	6	12.50	45	200	500	—
			Unused NG	32.50	50	65	72.50	82.50	115	—	—
			Unused OG	70	100	160	250	450	800	1,500	—
			Mint NH	170	300	500	675	1,100	3,250	12,750	—
209b	10¢	black brown	Used	140	245	375	480	800	2,250	5,000	—
			Unused NG	375	550	950	1,100	1,350	—		
			Unused OG	1,100	1,750	3,000	4,000	5,250	7,500		
			Mint NH	2,250	4,000	6,000	8,000	11,000			
210	2¢	red brown	Used	0.40	0.55	0.75	10	45	110	350	1,000
			Unused NG	7.50	11	17	22.50	35	55	—	—
			Unused OG	21	29	45	62.50	87.50	180	425	—
			Mint NH	50	90	135	275	525	1,200	3,500	—
211	4¢	blue green	Used	11	17	25	37.50	120	300	850	—
			Unused NG	30	50	80	100	125	200	—	—
			Unused OG	100	150	225	340	850	1,300	2,500	—
			Mint NH	300	500	800	1,200	2,500	5,250	11,500	—
211B	2¢	pale red brown	Unused NG	62.50	95	140	155	170	200	260	—
			Unused OG	190	275	400	525	800	1,250	2,150	—
			Mint NH	375	625	1,000	1,350	2,350	5,250	—	—
211D	4¢	deep blue green	Unused NGAI	27,000	35,500	47,500	57,500	75,000			

SCT#	DENOM	COLOR	CONDITION	F 70	F-VF 75	VF 80	VF-XF 85	XF 90	XF-SUP 95	SUP 98	GEM 100
1887-88 AMERICAN BANK NOTE ISSUES											
212	1¢	ultramarine	Used	1.05	1.70	2.50	12.50	32.50	140	425	900
			Unused NG	14.50	22.50	35	42.50	52.50	75	110	—
			Unused OG	40	60	90	145	275	—	—	—
			Mint NH	110	180	290	450	725	2,250	6,500	16,500

SCT#	DENOM	COLOR	CONDITION	F 70	F-VF 75	VF 80	VF-XF 85	XF 90	XF-SUP 95	SUP 98	GEM 100
213	2¢	green	Used	0.25	0.45	0.60	10	50	200	750	2,100
			Unused NG	6.50	10	15	20	35	55	—	—
			Unused OG	18	25	40	55	80	170	350	—
			Mint NH	47.50	77.50	120	185	375	950	3,750	10,500
214	3¢	vermilion	Used	20	35	50	80	175	475	1,200	—
			Unused NG	10	15	25	35	52.50	75	—	—
			Unused OG	25	40	60	80	115	210	500	—
			Mint NH	67.50	130	190	275	450	1,400	4,750	10,500
215	4¢	carmine	Used	13.50	20	30	47.50	100	300	1,000	—
			Unused NG	25	40	60	70	82.50	130	—	—
			Unused OG	90	135	180	260	400	700	1,350	—
			Mint NH	190	335	525	800	1,500	4,000	10,000	—
216	5¢	indigo	Used	9.50	13.50	20	45	125	300	700	1,400
			Unused NG	35	50	75	90	120	165	—	—
			Unused OG	110	145	220	350	600	1,100	1,950	—
			Mint NH	250	425	675	1,100	2,500	6,500	10,000	—
217	30¢	orange	Used	40	62.50	90	120	175	775	1,600	—
		brown	Unused NG	40	60	90	105	125	185	280	—
			Unused OG	140	210	300	450	650	1,250	2,500	8,000
			Mint NH	375	675	1,075	1,500	2,500	6,250	17,500	—
218	90¢	purple	Used	100	160	225	325	550	1,500	—	—
			Unused NG	120	160	250	290	375	500	900	—
			Unused OG	375	550	800	1,100	1,750	3,500	8,750	—
			Mint NH	900	1,600	2,500	3,750	6,500	26,500	—	—

1890-93 AMERICAN BANK NOTE ISSUE

SCT#	DENOM	COLOR	CONDITION	F 70	F-VF 75	VF 80	VF-XF 85	XF 90	XF-SUP 95	SUP 98	GEM 100
219	1¢	dull	Used	0.35	0.50	0.75	8	30	125	350	775
		blue	Unused OG	8.50	12.50	20	27.50	45	100	180	325
			Mint NH	22.50	40	65	120	240	875	3,500	—
219D	2¢	lake	Used	2.50	4	5.75	12.50	50	225	650	—
			Unused OG	72	105	160	225	350	850	1,400	3,250
			Mint NH	190	325	500	825	1,400	4,250	17,500	—
220	2¢	carmine	Used	0.30	0.50	0.70	8	30	105	275	850
			Unused OG	8.50	12.50	20	30	45	130	275	—
			Mint NH	17.50	37.50	60	100	250	800	2,400	—
220a	2¢	cap	Used	5.75	9.75	12.50	25	67.50	210	650	—
		left 2	Unused OG	65	100	150	200	350	550	1,050	—
			Mint NH	160	275	450	625	1,100	2,500	—	—
220c	2¢	cap	Used	15	25	35	60	170	475	1,200	—
		both 2s	Unused OG	250	460	650	850	1,750	2,500	—	—
			Mint NH	575	1,000	1,800	2,750	5,000	11,000	—	—
221	3¢	purple	Used	4	6	9	15	55	225	750	—
			Unused OG	22.50	37.50	55	75	130	400	625	—
			Mint NH	67.50	105	175	300	650	1,800	7,000	—
222	4¢	dark	Used	1.90	3.25	4.75	12.50	47.50	185	500	—
		brown	Unused OG	35	50	80	110	160	375	1,200	—
			Mint NH	87.50	150	240	400	700	2,400	7,500	—
223	5¢	chocolate	Used	1.90	3.25	4.75	12.50	47.50	225	825	—
			Unused OG	26	40	60	85	140	280	500	900
			Mint NH	70	110	185	300	550	1,825	5,750	14,000
224	6¢	brown	Used	10	18	25	40	120	275	775	—
		red	Unused OG	21	33.50	50	75	120	275	575	2,250
			Mint NH	60	97.50	160	250	475	1,800	5,000	11,500
225	8¢	lilac	Used	7.25	11.50	17	35	100	325	650	—
			Unused OG	19	30	45	65	115	225	425	—
			Mint NH	42.50	85	135	325	475	1,500	4,250	—
226	10¢	green	Used	2.20	3.60	5	12.50	40	175	525	1,200
			Unused OG	70	105	160	225	300	550	1,200	2,300
			Mint NH	165	295	475	800	1,400	4,250	11,250	—

SCT#	DENOM	COLOR	CONDITION	F 70	F-VF 75	VF 80	VF-XF 85	XF 90	XF-SUP 95	SUP 98	GEM 100
227	15¢	indigo	Used	11	17.50	25	45	115	325	800	—
			Unused OG	82.50	125	180	250	450	800	1,650	—
			Mint NH	200	365	550	950	2,000	5,500	—	
228	30¢	black	Used	12.50	20	30	52.50	175	425	1,100	—
			Unused OG	140	190	300	400	650	1,150	2,500	—
			Mint NH	350	600	900	1,175	2,750	7,250	17,500	—
229	90¢	orange	Used	65	92.50	140	190	300	850	1,750	—
			Unused OG	200	325	475	650	1,100	1,650	2,750	—
			Mint NH	575	1,050	1,600	2,300	3,900	10,000	19,000	—

1893 COLUMBIAN EXPOSITION ISSUE

SCT#	DENOM	COLOR	CONDITION	F 70	F-VF 75	VF 80	VF-XF 85	XF 90	XF-SUP 95	SUP 98	GEM 100
230	1¢	deep	Used	0.25	0.30	0.40	5	30	130	450	950
		blue	Unused OG	6	9.25	14	20	30	60	145	350
			Mint NH	12	22.50	32.50	55	100	400	1,450	—
231	2¢	brown	Used	0.25	0.25	0.30	4	32.50	120	375	—
		violet	Unused OG	5.50	8.25	12.50	17.50	27.50	50	125	350
			Mint NH	11.50	22.50	31	50	125	450	1,300	3,150
231 var	2¢	broken hat	Used	1.60	2.40	3.50	17.50	110	400	1,000	—
			Unused OG	25	37.50	55	70	120	225	500	—
			Mint NH	57.50	115	160	220	350	850	3,000	—
232	3¢	green	Used	7.25	10.25	15	30	77.50	260	650	—
			Unused OG	14	25	35	42.50	60	120	300	—
			Mint NH	32.50	65	97.50	140	225	625	2,050	4,750
233	4¢	ultramarine	Used	3.50	5.50	8	15	50	200	525	—
			Unused OG	22.50	37.50	55	72.50	110	250	500	1,000
			Mint NH	57.50	100	150	210	350	925	2,250	5,500
233a	4¢	blue (error)	Used	6,750	10,500	15,000	—	—			
			Unused OG	10,000	15,000	20,000	27,500	37,500			
			Mint NH	14,000	24,000	35,000	—	—			
234	5¢	chocolate	Used	3.75	5.75	8.50	17.50	52.50	225	775	1,750
			Unused OG	22.50	37.50	55	72.50	110	250	500	1,400
			Mint NH	57.50	100	150	230	450	950	2,500	9,000
235	6¢	purple	Used	10	16	22.50	40	95	280	725	1,800
			Unused OG	22	38.50	55	75	115	265	550	—
			Mint NH	57.50	100	150	220	425	1,050	5,000	13,000
235a	6¢	red violet	Used	10	16	22.50	40	95	280	725	—
			Unused OG	27.50	45	65	82.50	110	300	750	—
			Mint NH	67.50	115	175	290	425	1,050	4,250	—
236	8¢	magenta	Used	4.50	7.25	10	22.50	60	240	600	1,500
			Unused OG	20	35	50	60	80	175	425	—
			Mint NH	52.50	92.50	140	200	325	1,500	5,750	13,000
237	10¢	black brown	Used	3.75	5.50	8	22.50	100	350	700	1,650
			Unused OG	42.50	62.50	95	120	170	600	900	—
			Mint NH	87.50	170	265	375	575	2,250	7,250	—
238	15¢	dark green	Used	35	57.50	80	120	275	825	2,000	—
			Unused OG	90	140	200	260	375	700	1,600	—
			Mint NH	240	385	600	850	1,850	5,750	14,000	50,000
239	30¢	orange brown	Used	42.50	62.50	90	140	250	1,000	2,000	—
			Unused OG	105	150	225	280	400	550	1,500	—
			Mint NH	270	450	675	850	1,250	2,650	7,500	35,000
240	50¢	slate blue	Used	95	140	200	300	600	1,500	3,250	—
			Unused NG	80	130	200	235	400	950	—	—
			Unused OG	190	290	450	550	750	1,750	3,500	8,500
			Mint NH	550	950	1,400	2,000	3,600	10,500	38,500	70,000
241	$1	salmon	Used	250	365	525	675	900	2,400	—	—
			Unused NG	240	340	500	600	725	1,000	1,450	—
			Unused OG	450	675	1,000	1,350	2,000	5,000	7,500	—
			Mint NH	1,350	2,250	3,400	5,250	12,000	34,000	—	—

SCT#	DENOM	COLOR	CONDITION	F 70	F-VF 75	VF 80	VF-XF 85	XF 90	XF-SUP 95	SUP 98	GEM 100
242	$2	brown	Used	250	365	525	675	1,050	3,250	10,000	—
		red	Unused NG	265	375	550	650	775	1,150	1,850	
			Unused OG	475	725	1,100	1,400	2,000	4,500	9,250	18,500
			Mint NH	1,450	2,400	3,600	6,000	15,000	55,000	85,000	
243	$3	yellow	Used	300	550	775	1,250	1,750	4,750	10,000	—
		green	Unused NG	300	525	750	850	1,000	1,500	2,350	5,750
			Unused OG	700	1,025	1,500	1,800	3,000	5,500	8,500	
			Mint NH	1,900	3,000	4,750	7,250	12,000	65,000	—	
243a	$3	olive	Used	300	525	750	1,000	1,600	4,750	11,500	
		green	Unused NG	270	475	675	800	1,000	1,500	2,050	
			Unused OG	625	925	1,350	1,550	2,250	4,500	8,000	
			Mint NH	1,700	2,700	4,250	7,250	12,000	65,000	—	
244	$4	crimson	Used	450	700	975	1,500	2,000	6,500	15,000	
		lake	Unused NG	450	725	1,000	1,150	1,350	2,250	3,000	
			Unused OG	900	1,400	2,100	2,500	4,000	7,000	14,500	
			Mint NH	2,600	4,750	7,250	11,500	18,500	55,000	—	
244a	$4	rose	Used	450	700	975	1,500	1,900	6,000	15,000	
		carmine	Unused NG	425	700	950	1,100	1,300	1,850	2,600	
			Unused OG	875	1,325	2,000	2,500	3,500	6,750	13,250	
			Mint NH	2,500	4,500	7,000	11,500	16,500	55,000	—	
245	$5	black	Used	550	875	1,200	1,650	2,750	6,000	12,500	
			Unused NG	625	850	1,250	1,500	1,750	2,150	3,000	
			Unused OG	975	1,625	2,400	3,000	4,000	8,000	15,000	
			Mint NH	3,750	6,250	9,750	17,500	30,000	85,000	—	

1894 FIRST BUREAU OF ENGRAVING AND PRINTING ISSUE (UNWATERMARKED)

SCT#	DENOM	COLOR	CONDITION	F 70	F-VF 75	VF 80	VF-XF 85	XF 90	XF-SUP 95	SUP 98	GEM 100
246	1¢	ultramarine	Used	3	4.50	7	15	57.50	240	1,025	—
			Unused OG	13.50	20	30	45	62.50	125	250	575
			Mint NH	27.50	60	90	145	240	850	2,900	—
247	1¢	blue	Used	1.60	2.75	4	12.50	55	220	850	1,750
			Unused OG	27.50	45	62.50	82.50	115	260	525	—
			Mint NH	65	115	180	325	500	2,100	—	
248	2¢	pink	Used	4	6.75	10	24	70	300	1,000	—
		type I	Unused OG	14	21	32.50	45	70	115	260	575
			Mint NH	35	60	97.50	160	300	1,400	4,250	—
249	2¢	carmine	Used	2.90	4.50	7	17.50	65	250	950	—
		lake	Unused OG	80	125	175	235	325	750	1,200	2,500
		type I	Mint NH	220	335	500	750	1,500	4,750	16,000	35,000
250	2¢	carmine	Used	1.20	2.10	3	12.50	65	200	725	1,800
		type I	Unused OG	11.50	19.50	29	42.50	67.50	125	240	—
			Mint NH	28.50	52.50	85	150	325	1,350	4,000	—
250a	2¢	rose	Used	4	6	8.50	22.50	90	210	750	—
		type I	Unused OG	17.50	27.50	40	57.50	92.50	165	275	—
			Mint NH	40	75	115	180	350	1,300	—	
250b	2¢	scarlet	Used	1.10	1.90	2.75	11.50	57.50	200	725	—
		type I	Unused OG	10.50	17.50	26	40	61.50	120	235	—
			Mint NH	27.50	50	80	135	290	1,050	—	
251	2¢	carmine	Used	7	11.50	17.50	35	95	380	—	
		type II	Unused OG	185	265	400	500	650	1,350	2,200	
			Mint NH	550	800	1,200	1,800	3,500	10,000	—	
251a	2¢	scarlet	Used	6.25	10.50	15	32.50	92.50	360	—	
		type II	Unused OG	170	245	375	475	625	1,300	—	
			Mint NH	430	750	1,125	1,775	3,100	9,750	—	
252	2¢	carmine	Used	5.50	9	13	32.50	90	375	1,250	—
		type III	Unused OG	60	90	135	155	225	485	925	—
			Mint NH	160	260	400	650	1,200	5,250	12,500	—

SCT#	DENOM	COLOR	CONDITION	F 70	F-VF 75	VF 80	VF-XF 85	XF 90	XF-SUP 95	SUP 98	GEM 100
252a	2¢	scarlet type III	Used	6.25	10.75	15	37.50	100	450	1,400	—
			Unused OG	55	85	120	150	220	475	900	—
			Mint NH	130	240	360	550	950	3,750	10,000	—
253	3¢	purple	Used	4.75	8.25	12	30	95	340	1,200	—
			Unused OG	55	85	120	160	275	550	—	—
			Mint NH	130	240	360	550	950	4,250	1,700	—
254	4¢	dark brown	Used	5	7.50	11	25	70	300	1,250	3,250
			Unused OG	87.50	125	200	240	300	500	—	—
			Mint NH	225	375	600	850	1,275	4,250	11,500	—
255	5¢	chocolate	Used	4	6	9	22.50	90	260	1,100	—
			Unused OG	55	85	120	150	240	525	1,000	—
			Mint NH	130	240	360	550	1,000	2,750	9,000	—
256	6¢	dull brown	Used	12	18.50	27.50	60	160	525	1,400	—
			Unused OG	70	110	160	200	260	575	1,150	—
			Mint NH	150	300	475	650	1,150	3,750	15,000	—
257	8¢	violet brown	Used	9	13.25	20	40	110	425	1,400	—
			Unused OG	67.50	110	160	200	260	600	1,150	—
			Mint NH	150	300	475	700	1,100	3,500	12,500	—
258	10¢	dark green	Used	9	13.25	20	40	125	425	1,400	—
			Unused OG	130	190	275	360	650	1,250	2,000	—
			Mint NH	300	550	850	1,500	3,250	6,750	20,000	—
259	15¢	dark blue	Used	30	45	65	130	300	850	2,900	—
			Unused OG	130	190	275	360	480	1,050	2,050	—
			Mint NH	300	550	850	1,275	2,750	7,250	20,000	—
260	50¢	orange	Used	67.50	105	140	235	400	1,450	4,250	—
			Unused OG	220	320	475	700	1,750	2,500	4,250	—
			Mint NH	550	925	1,425	2,100	3,500	11,000	28,500	—
261	$1	black type I	Used	160	240	350	550	1,000	3,250	7,750	—
			Unused NG	185	270	400	475	600	800	—	—
			Unused OG	425	675	1,000	1,250	1,750	4,000	6,500	—
			Mint NH	1,125	1,925	3,200	5,500	8,500	22,500	37,500	90,000
261A	$1	black type II	Used	375	550	800	1,200	1,900	6,250	15,500	—
			Unused NG	365	575	850	950	1,125	1,500	—	—
			Unused OG	950	1,475	2,100	3,000	4,250	7,250	10,500	—
			Mint NH	2,150	4,000	6,500	8,500	13,500	31,000	—	—
262	$2	bright blue	Used	575	900	1,200	1,900	3,000	9,000	—	—
			Unused NG	500	700	1,100	1,250	1,475	2,000	3,000	—
			Unused OG	1,275	1,900	2,750	3,600	5,500	8,500	17,500	—
			Mint NH	3,750	6,000	9,000	12,500	20,000	—	—	—
263	$5	dark green	Used	1,200	1,800	2,600	3,600	6,000	17,500	40,000	—
			Unused NG	925	1,400	2,100	2,400	2,850	4,000	7,500	—
			Unused OG	1,875	3,000	4,000	5,250	7,250	12,500	21,000	—
			Mint NH	5,250	9,500	15,000	26,500	—	—	—	—

1895 BUREAU ISSUE (DOUBLE LINE WATERMARK)

SCT#	DENOM	COLOR	CONDITION	F 70	F-VF 75	VF 80	VF-XF 85	XF 90	XF-SUP 95	SUP 98	GEM 100
264	1¢	blue	Used	0.30	0.40	0.60	8	30	95	475	—
			Unused OG	3	4.25	6	8.25	13.50	30	75	—
			Mint NH	5	11	17.50	30	60	375	1,250	3,000
265	2¢	carmine type I	Used	1	2.10	3.50	13.50	50	200	875	—
			Unused OG	15	22.50	35	55	80	125	230	—
			Mint NH	35	70	105	175	325	1,000	3,000	6,250
266	2¢	carmine type II	Used	5.50	9.50	15	35	75	240	950	—
			Unused OG	17	26	40	57.50	85	170	300	650
			Mint NH	42.50	77.50	120	210	425	1,200	4,000	—
267	2¢	carmine type III	Used	0.30	0.40	0.60	8	35	135	400	850
			Unused OG	2.50	3.75	5.50	8.75	14	32.50	72.50	—
			Mint NH	5.75	10	16	27.50	60	350	950	2,000
267a	2¢	pink	Used	2.20	3.50	5	22.50	90	350	—	—
			Unused OG	9.50	14	20	35	60	120	260	—
			Mint NH	22.50	37.50	60	150	325	1,250	2,250	—

SCT#	DENOM	COLOR	CONDITION	F 70	F-VF 75	VF 80	VF-XF 85	XF 90	XF-SUP 95	SUP 98	GEM 100
267b	2¢	vermilion	Used	7.50	11.25	15	40	135	400	—	—
		type III	Unused OG	21	32.50	50	85	170	800	—	—
267c	2¢	rose	Used	—	—	—	—	—	—	—	—
		carmine	Unused OG	—	—	—	—	—	—	—	—
		type III	Mint NH	—	—	3,500	5,000	7,500	—	—	—
268	3¢	purple	Used	1	1.55	2.25	14	55	175	725	—
			Unused OG	17.50	25	37.50	50	67.50	110	250	—
			Mint NH	40	67.50	115	175	275	1,800	8,500	—
269	4¢	dark	Used	2.15	2.80	3.50	20	65	210	925	—
		brown	Unused OG	19	28	42.50	55	75	150	300	650
			Mint NH	45	75	125	190	375	1,500	6,500	—
270	5¢	chocolate	Used	2	2.45	3.50	16	60	200	850	1,700
			Unused OG	17	24	35	45	60	125	260	—
			Mint NH	37	62	105	165	300	850	3,000	—
271	6¢	dull	Used	4	6	8.50	25	75	350	1,100	—
		brown	Unused OG	50	70	110	145	200	425	900	—
			Mint NH	105	200	325	450	800	4,000	13,500	—
272	8¢	violet	Used	1	1.75	2.75	15	45	150	600	1,150
		brown	Unused OG	32.50	47	70	95	135	275	600	1,200
			Mint NH	70	130	210	325	700	2,250	7,500	—
273	10¢	dark	Used	0.80	1.45	2.25	11	45	180	675	—
		green	Unused OG	42.50	67.50	95	130	175	385	775	—
			Mint NH	100	190	280	500	775	3,250	13,500	—
274	15¢	dark	Used	8	12	17.50	55	105	425	1,450	—
		blue	Unused OG	87.50	140	200	260	360	950	1,600	—
			Mint NH	210	380	625	925	1,350	5,250	16,500	25,000
275	50¢	orange	Used	16	26	40	85	225	725	1,950	—
			Unused OG	115	155	240	325	675	1,200	2,000	—
			Mint NH	260	450	725	1,150	2,500	8,000	22,500	—
275a	50¢	red	Used	20	33	47.50	95	250	800	2,250	10,500
		orange	Unused OG	140	210	325	400	550	1,200	2,100	—
			Mint NH	350	600	975	1,400	2,500	8,000	22,500	—
276	$1	black	Used	42.50	65	95	150	325	950	2,500	—
		type I	Unused NG	110	165	250	300	400	525	—	—
			Unused OG	275	400	600	750	1,100	2,750	5,250	—
			Mint NH	650	1,100	1,800	2,750	4,250	14,000	—	—
276A	$1	black	Used	85	135	200	300	450	1,250	4,000	—
		type II	Unused NG	200	350	500	575	675	975	—	—
			Unused OG	525	825	1,250	1,500	2,400	5,500	—	—
			Mint NH	1,400	2,400	3,750	5,750	9,500	25,000	—	—
277	$2	bright	Used	190	280	400	525	725	2,500	7,500	—
		blue	Unused NG	175	250	375	435	525	725	—	—
			Unused OG	375	600	900	1,150	1,500	3,000	5,750	12,500
			Mint NH	1,100	1,825	2,900	4,500	8,000	22,000	—	—
277a	$2	dark	Used	190	280	400	525	775	2,500	7,500	—
		blue	Unused NG	175	250	375	435	525	725	—	—
			Unused OG	375	600	900	1,150	1,600	3,250	5,750	—
			Mint NH	1,100	1,825	2,900	4,500	7,250	22,000	—	—
278	$5	dark	Used	280	420	600	775	1,000	3,750	10,000	—
		green	Unused NG	350	550	800	900	1,025	1,225	—	—
			Unused OG	950	1,325	2,000	2,400	3,250	5,000	9,500	—
			Mint NH	2,500	4,150	6,250	8,750	15,000	38,500	70,000	—

1897-1903 REGULAR ISSUE

SCT#	DENOM	COLOR	CONDITION	F 70	F-VF 75	VF 80	VF-XF 85	XF 90	XF-SUP 95	SUP 98	GEM 100
279	1¢	deep	Used	0.25	0.40	0.50	10	25	90	325	750
		green	Unused OG	4	6	9	12	18	47.50	125	350
			Mint NH	9.75	16	25	42.50	85	400	1,200	4,000
279B	2¢	red	Used	0.25	0.30	0.40	8	25	95	500	—
		type IV	Unused OG	4	6	9	12	18	45	100	—
			Mint NH	9.75	16	25	45	110	350	1,250	—

SCT#	DENOM	COLOR	CONDITION	F 70	F-VF 75	VF 80	VF-XF 85	XF 90	XF-SUP 95	SUP 98	GEM 100
279Bc	2¢	rose	Used	77.50	160	230	340	575	1,450	3,650	—
		carmine	Unused OG	120	195	275	375	500	1,000	1,600	3,750
		type IV	Mint NH	340	575	850	1,250	2,250	7,500	15,000	30,000
279Bd	2¢	orange	Used	0.90	1.65	2	15	50	150	450	—
		red	Unused OG	5.25	8	11.50	17.50	27.50	65	150	—
		type IV	Mint NH	12	20	32.50	60	110	400	1,500	—
279Bf	2¢	carmine	Used	1	1.60	2	22.50	90	250	550	—
		type IV	Unused OG	4	6.75	10	14	25	60	125	—
			Mint NH	11	17	27.50	47.50	90	600	1,750	—
279Bg	2¢	pink	Used	2.55	4.30	7.50	32.50	115	310	700	—
		type IV	Unused OG	25	40	55	82.50	130	275	—	—
			Mint NH	65	105	165	300	600	2,200	—	—
279Bh	2¢	vermilion	Used	1.35	2.45	3	30	165	650	2,000	—
		type IV	Unused OG	5.75	8.75	12.50	17.50	27.50	65	150	—
			Mint NH	13.50	22.50	35	60	100	375	—	—
279Bi	2¢	brown	Used	50	70	100	230	575	1,300	—	—
		orange	Unused OG	175	285	400	600	—	—	—	—
		type IV	Mint NH	400	650	950	1,450	—	—	—	—
279Bj	2¢	red type IV	Used	1,800	2,300	3,000	3,500	—			
Booklet Pane of 6			Unused OG	320	400	500	575	675	900	—	—
Horiz. wmk.			Mint NH	600	800	1,000	1,175	1,500	2,500	—	—
279Bk	2¢	red type IV	Used	—	—	—	—	—			
Booklet Pane of 6			Unused OG	320	400	500	575	675	900	—	—
Vert. wmk.			Mint NH	900	1,200	1,500	1,775	2,250	3,750	—	—
280	4¢	rose	Used	1.25	1.90	3.25	12.50	65	325	900	—
		brown	Unused OG	13.50	21	30	42.50	57.50	125	—	—
			Mint NH	27.50	47.50	80	125	225	1,250	3,000	—
280a	4¢	lilac	Used	1.25	1.90	3.25	12.50	120	1,000	1,500	—
		brown	Unused OG	13.50	21	30	42.50	57.50	125	—	—
			Mint NH	27.50	47.50	80	125	225	1,250	3,650	—
280b	4¢	orange	Used	0.95	1.75	3	10	55	260	700	—
		brown	Unused OG	13.50	21	30	42.50	57.50	125	—	—
			Mint NH	27.50	47.50	80	125	300	1,500	4,500	—
281	5¢	dark	Used	0.85	1.40	2.25	14	42.50	160	850	1,750
		blue	Unused OG	14	21	32.50	45	57.50	125	240	—
			Mint NH	37.50	62.50	100	180	375	1,500	5,250	—
282	6¢	lake	Used	3	4.50	6.50	20	75	425	800	—
			Unused OG	21	32	45	55	75	160	325	—
			Mint NH	48	87.50	140	225	500	1,400	4,000	12,000
282a	6¢	purple	Used	9	13.50	20	40	100	—	—	—
		lake	Unused OG	35	55	80	100	140	300	650	—
			Mint NH	77.50	150	240	400	725	1,850	6,250	—
282C	10¢	brown	Used	2.50	4	6.50	12.50	70	350	1,200	—
		type I	Unused OG	77.50	115	175	230	350	625	1,200	—
			Mint NH	200	350	525	825	1,425	4,750	17,500	—
283	10¢	orange	Used	3.25	4.25	6	11	65	250	850	—
Horiz. wmk.		brown	Unused OG	65	105	150	225	325	700	1,000	—
		type II	Mint NH	155	260	450	725	1,250	3,850	13,500	—
283a	10¢	orange	Used	7	9.50	15	40	115	575	1,500	—
Vert. wmk.		brown	Unused OG	100	160	250	350	500	1,000	2,000	—
		type II	Mint NH	275	500	775	1,100	2,000	7,000	16,500	32,500
284	15¢	olive	Used	6	9	13	37.50	115	450	1,500	—
		green	Unused OG	65	100	150	200	275	600	1,200	—
			Mint NH	170	310	475	750	1,500	4,750	15,000	—

1898 TRANS-MISSISSIPPI EXPOSITION ISSUE

SCT#	DENOM	COLOR	CONDITION	F 70	F-VF 75	VF 80	VF-XF 85	XF 90	XF-SUP 95	SUP 98	GEM 100
285	1¢	dark	Used	3.50	5	7	30	75	300	900	—
		yellow	Unused OG	12	18.50	27.50	37.50	60	110	230	—
		green	Mint NH	27.50	47.50	75	120	225	625	1,900	3,750

SCT#	DENOM	COLOR	CONDITION	F 70	F-VF 75	VF 80	VF-XF 85	XF 90	XF-SUP 95	SUP 98	GEM 100
286	2¢	copper red	Used	1	2	2.75	15	60	375	800	1,600
			Unused OG	11	17	25	32.50	55	105	220	—
			Mint NH	30	47.50	72.50	125	325	700	2,500	5,000
287	4¢	orange	Used	11.75	17.50	25	50	130	625	1,500	—
			Unused OG	45	77.50	110	150	220	425	850	—
			Mint NH	105	220	330	475	750	2,250	10,000	—
288	5¢	dull blue	Used	11	17	25	45	120	425	1,150	—
			Unused OG	42.50	70	100	135	210	415	850	—
			Mint NH	95	190	300	500	850	2,250	10,500	30,000
289	8¢	violet brown	Used	21	35	47.50	75	180	625	1,800	—
			Unused OG	57.50	90	140	180	350	750	1,450	7,000
			Mint NH	145	260	425	650	1,100	5,250	19,500	40,000
290	10¢	gray violet	Used	15	24	35	50	165	575	1,800	—
			Unused OG	62.50	92.50	140	180	325	525	1,250	4,750
			Mint NH	140	260	425	625	975	5,000	11,500	—
291	50¢	sage green	Used	75	125	175	260	475	1,100	3,400	—
			Unused OG	280	450	600	725	1,000	2,000	4,500	—
			Mint NH	650	1,225	1,750	3,000	6,000	12,500	57,500	—
292	$1	black	Used	315	575	700	875	1,650	5,000	12,000	23,000
			Unused NG	400	575	850	925	1,025	1,175	1,325	—
			Unused OG	650	1,000	1,500	1,700	2,500	4,500	11,500	18,000
			Mint NH	1,450	2,450	3,750	5,750	10,000	18,500	75,000	—
293	$2	orange brown	Used	475	725	1,000	1,375	2,750	87,500	—	—
			Unused NG	400	600	950	1,075	1,300	1,750	—	—
			Unused OG	825	1,275	1,900	2,250	3,000	7,000	18,000	—
			Mint NH	2,000	3,800	5,750	8,000	15,500	57,500	—	—
285-293 Set		9 stamps	Used	950	1,551	2,067	2,850	5,705	17,725	23,400	—
			Unused OG	1,986	3,091	4,543	5,390	7,970	15,055	37,600	—
			Mint NH	4,650	8,505	12,883	19,245	35,385	107,575	188,400	—

1901 PAN-AMERICAN EXPOSITION ISSUE

SCT#	DENOM	COLOR	CONDITION	F 70	F-VF 75	VF 80	VF-XF 85	XF 90	XF-SUP 95	SUP 98	GEM 100
294	1¢	green & black	Used	1.20	2.10	3	17.50	70	260	875	—
			Unused OG	6.25	10	16	20.50	27.50	52.50	110	—
			Mint NH	14	25	40	60	125	475	2,000	4,500
294a	1¢	invert	Used	16,500	21,000	25,000	33,500	42,500			
			Unused OG	7,000	10,500	12,500	20,000	40,000			
			Mint NH	—	—	22,500	27,500	45,000			
295	2¢	carmine & black	Used	0.45	0.75	1	8	45	125	625	1,500
			Unused OG	6	9.75	15	20	30	50	90	—
			Mint NH	14	23.50	37.50	55	105	350	1,100	—
295a	2¢	invert	Used	27,500	35,000	50,000	75,000	—			
			Unused OG	35,000	47,500	55,000	90,000	110,000	—	220,000	
296	4¢	deep red brown & black	Used	8.50	13.50	18	25	110	350	1,250	—
			Unused OG	30	50	70	80	100	200	350	—
			Mint NH	67.50	110	170	230	450	1,200	4,750	21,500
296a	4¢	invert	Unused OG	52,500	67,500	80,000	175,000	600,000	—		
297	5¢	ultramarine & black	Used	7.50	12	17	35	110	425	1,700	4,750
			Unused OG	32.50	50	75	90	120	190	375	—
			Mint NH	75	120	180	230	375	1,150	3,750	9,000
298	8¢	brown violet & black	Used	22.50	37.50	50	77.50	125	500	1,750	—
			Unused OG	45	62.50	90	105	140	225	400	750
			Mint NH	97.50	150	230	300	500	1,350	5,500	—
299	10¢	yellow brown & black	Used	12	21	30	57.50	140	525	1,500	—
			Unused OG	52.50	80	115	135	175	275	500	—
			Mint NH	115	200	325	450	800	2,750	8,500	—
294-299 Set		6 stamps	Used	52	86.85	119	220.50	600	2,190	5,950	—
			Unused OG	170	262.25	381	450.50	592.50	992.50	1,800	—
			Mint NH	385	623.50	957.50	1,325	2,355	7,025	26,100	—

SCT#	DENOM	COLOR	CONDITION	F 70	F-VF 75	VF 80	VF-XF 85	XF 90	XF-SUP 95	SUP 98	GEM 100

1902-03 REGULAR ISSUE

SCT#	DENOM	COLOR	CONDITION	F 70	F-VF 75	VF 80	VF-XF 85	XF 90	XF-SUP 95	SUP 98	GEM 100
300	1¢	blue	Used	0.25	0.25	0.25	8	25	100	300	725
		green	Unused OG	5.50	8.50	12	17.50	25	50	110	—
			Mint NH	13	20	30	45	80	300	1,100	1,800
300b Booklet Pane of 6	1¢	blue green	Used		9,000	11,500					
			Unused OG	325	500	600	675	750	1,100		
			Mint NH	575	950	1,150	1,350	1,600	3,000		
301	2¢	carmine	Used	0.25	0.40	0.50	10	30	140	475	—
			Unused OG	6.50	10	15	19	26	47.50	105	—
			Mint NH	15	25	37.50	60	100	425	1,850	5,000
301c Booklet Pane of 6	2¢	carmine	Used	—	—	6,000					
			Unused OG	260	400	500	575	700	1,050		
			Mint NH	420	775	950	1,150	1,400	2,750		
302	3¢	bright violet	Used	1.90	2.80	3.75	14	65	225	750	—
			Unused OG	22.50	37.50	55	67.50	87.50	200	325	550
			Mint NH	57.50	95	140	200	375	850	2,600	—
303	4¢	brown	Used	0.90	1.65	2.25	11.25	22.50	150	550	—
			Unused OG	25	40	55	67.50	90	150	325	—
			Mint NH	52.50	87.50	140	250	400	1,650	3,250	6,000
304	5¢	blue	Used	0.90	1.40	2	11	60	225	650	1,000
			Unused OG	27.50	42.50	60	75	100	150	350	650
			Mint NH	55	95	150	210	350	1,250	3,250	—
305	6¢	claret	Used	2.20	3.85	5.50	14.50	40	145	800	—
			Unused OG	27	40	60	75	95	175	350	625
			Mint NH	57.50	97.50	150	275	600	1,200	4,000	—
306	8¢	violet black	Used	1.65	2.80	3.25	11.50	32.50	150	425	1,000
			Unused OG	20	32.50	45	55	67.50	125	260	—
			Mint NH	42.50	72.50	110	160	300	875	3,500	—
307	10¢	pale red brown	Used	1.45	2	3	22.50	55	210	550	—
			Unused OG	27.50	40	60	75	100	180	400	650
			Mint NH	57.50	100	150	230	350	1,500	4,500	—
308	13¢	purple black	Used	4.50	7	10	17.50	67.50	210	675	1,350
			Unused OG	17.50	27	40	55	70	100	225	—
			Mint NH	37.50	62.50	100	170	300	825	2,400	10,000
309	15¢	olive green	Used	4.50	8	12.50	22.50	55	210	800	—
			Unused OG	80	120	185	225	280	525	1,100	1,900
			Mint NH	200	325	475	775	1,250	3,700	11,000	—
310	50¢	orange	Used	15	22.50	35	47.50	110	325	—	—
			Unused OG	190	290	425	475	625	1,025	2,000	—
			Mint NH	525	850	1,225	1,750	2,250	8,500	27,000	—
311	$1	black	Used	40	62.50	90	115	215	550	1,050	2,250
			Unused NG	100	170	240	275	400	—	—	—
			Unused OG	280	425	600	650	800	1,650	2,500	—
			Mint NH	650	1,100	1,800	2,250	3,750	9,500	34,000	—
312	$2	dark blue	Used	90	140	200	290	460	1,200	3,250	—
			Unused NG	155	225	325	370	465	700	—	—
			Unused OG	380	525	825	950	1,500	2,750	4,500	15,000
			Mint NH	950	1,750	2,500	3,500	5,750	20,000	—	—
313	$5	dark green	Used	350	525	700	875	1,100	3,500	7,750	—
			Unused NG	375	575	800	875	950	1,050	—	—
			Unused OG	950	1,375	2,100	2,450	2,900	4,500	7,000	14,000
			Mint NH	2,250	3,750	6,500	8,250	14,000	—	—	—
300-313 Set	14 stamps		Used	525	780.15	1,068	1,470	2,338	7,325	17,975	
			Unused OG	2,050	3,013	4,537	5,257	6,766	11,328	19,550	
			Mint NH	4,950	8,430	13,508	18,125	29,730	46,250	98,450	
314	1¢	blue green	Used	8	12.50	17.50	22.50	32.50	70	200	600
			Unused OG	6.50	9.50	14	16	19	25	40	70
			Mint NH	11	18.50	30	35	42.50	77.50	180	400

SCT#	DENOM	COLOR	CONDITION	F 70	F-VF 75	VF 80	VF-XF 85	XF 90	XF-SUP 95	SUP 98	GEM 100
314A Sgl.	4¢	brown	Used	30,000	40,000	45,000	52,500	75,000			
			Unused OG	42,500	60,000	85,000	—				
			Mint NH			200,000	240,000				
314A Pair	4¢	brown	Unused OG	122,500	177,500	250,000		500,000			
314A LP	4¢	brown	Unused OG		375,000			460,000			
315	5¢	blue	Used	575	900	1,250	1,500	2,150	3,250	—	—
			Unused OG	150	245	350	400	450	525	650	—
			Mint NH	210	425	600	650	750	800	950	2,250
316 Sgl.	1¢	blue green	Unused OG	—	150,000						
316 Pair	1¢	blue green	Unused OG	225,000	375,000						
316 LP	1¢	blue green	Unused OG	325,000	500,000						
317 Sgl.	5¢	blue	Used	—	—	—	—	—			
			Unused OG	—	—	6,000	11,500	26,500	—		
			Mint NH	—	—	12,000	20,000	—			
317 Pair	5¢	blue	Unused OG	9,500	12,500	15,000	18,000	25,000			
			Mint NH	—	—	45,000	—	—			
317 LP	5¢	blue	Unused OG		55,000	70,000					
			Mint NH		160,000						
318 Sgl.	1¢	blue green	Unused OG	4,500	5,000	6,150	10,000	—			
			Mint NH	9,500							
318 Pair	1¢	blue green	Unused OG	6,250	8,000	11,000	12,000	14,000			
318 LP	1¢	blue green	Unused OG		27,500	35,000					
319	2¢	carmine type I	Used	0.25	0.25	0.25	8	40	100	325	600
			Unused OG	2.75	4.25	6	9	12.50	25	50	—
			Mint NH	5.75	9.50	15	27.50	50	425	950	2,100
319b	2¢	carmine rose type I	Used	0.25	0.30	0.40	9	25	125	325	—
			Unused OG	6.75	10	15	17.50	22.50	40	100	—
			Mint NH	17.50	30	45	70	100	800	1,750	—
319c	2¢	scarlet type I	Used	0.25	0.25	0.30	8	27.50	90	300	—
			Unused OG	4.50	6.75	10	12.50	16	40	95	—
			Mint NH	9.50	16	25	50	125	900	—	—
319g Booklet Pane of 6	2¢	carmine type I	Used	250	340	450	525	675	—		
			Unused OG	75	95	125	145	180	350		
			Mint NH	125	175	240	300	400	850		
319n Booklet Pane of 6	2¢	carmine rose type I	Used	400	525	700	850	1,100	—		
			Unused OG	160	210	275	350	475	950		
			Mint NH	220	335	500	725	1,000	2,750		
319p Booklet Pane of 6	2¢	scarlet type I	Used	325	455	625	750	1,000	—		
			Unused OG	105	140	185	240	325	850		
			Mint NH	160	270	350	500	750	2,250		
319F	2¢	lake type II	Used	0.25	0.25	0.30	8	22.50	90	300	—
			Unused OG	4.50	6.75	10	12.50	16	40	95	—
			Mint NH	9.50	16	25	45	75	750	3,000	—
319Fi	2¢	carmine type II	Used	22.50	35	50	70	110	275	900	—
			Unused OG	27.50	45	65	78	97.50	165	—	—
			Mint NH	60	100	150	225	350	900	2,400	—
319Fj	2¢	carmine rose type II	Used	0.80	1.20	1.75	20	100	225	—	—
			Unused OG	45	67.50	100	125	175	240	425	—
			Mint NH	90	145	225	340	600	2,000	3,750	—
319Fk	2¢	scarlet type II	Used	0.90	1.50	2	7	20	55	150	—
			Unused OG	30	47.50	70	85	115	210	350	—
			Mint NH	65	105	160	240	440	1,200	—	—
319Fh Booklet Pane of 6	2¢	carmine type II	Unused OG	550	675	900	1,100	1,250	2,000		
			Mint NH	825	1,150	1,500	1,750	2,400	4,500		
319Fq Booklet Pane of 6	2¢	lake type II	Used	450	625	800	950	1,150	—		
			Unused OG	185	235	300	375	500	1,250		
			Mint NH	350	440	575	800	1,250	2,500		

SCT#	DENOM	COLOR	CONDITION	F 70	F-VF 75	VF 80	VF-XF 85	XF 90	XF-SUP 95	SUP 98	GEM 100
320	2¢	carmine	Used	9	14	19	22.50	30	65	175	300
		type I	Unused OG	6.50	10	15	16.50	19	27.50	45	90
			Mint NH	12.50	21	32.50	37.50	45	67.50	140	375
320b	2¢	scarlet	Used	7	10	15	22.50	37.50	90	240	—
		type I	Unused OG	8	11.75	17.50	19	22.50	27.50	42.50	—
			Mint NH	14	22.50	37.50	42.50	50	95	200	650
320c	2¢	carmine	Used	18.50	27.50	42.50	52.50	67.50	120	310	—
		rose	Unused OG	32	47	75	80	90	105	140	—
		type I	Mint NH	58	100	150	165	180	200	325	575
320A	2¢	lake	Used	22	32.50	50	60	75	160	900	—
		type II	Unused OG	20	32.50	45	50	57.50	70	95	—
			Mint NH	37.50	65	100	115	135	180	325	850
320Ad	2¢	carmine	Used	—	—	—	—	—	—		
		type II	Unused OG	55	97.50	135	175	—	—		
			Mint NH	105	135	200	235	—	—		
321 Pair	2¢	carmine type I	Unused OG	475,000	1,000,000	--					
322 Sgl.	2¢	carmine	Unused OG	4,250	5,500	7,000	8,250	10,000	12,500	16,000	
		type II	Mint NH	—	—	15,000	—	—			
322 Pair	2¢	carmine type II	Unused OG	11,750	14,500	17,500	20,000	25,000			
322 LP	2¢	carmine type II	Unused OG			35,000					

1904 LOUISIANA PURCHASE EXPOSITION ISSUE

SCT#	DENOM	COLOR	CONDITION	F 70	F-VF 75	VF 80	VF-XF 85	XF 90	XF-SUP 95	SUP 98	GEM 100
323	1¢	green	Used	2.20	3.50	4.75	20	40	200	575	—
			Unused OG	10	15.50	22.50	30	40	85	180	—
			Mint NH	21	40	60	90	175	650	2,200	3,250
324	2¢	carmine	Used	1	1.40	2	12	32.50	140	475	—
			Unused OG	10	15.50	22.50	30	40	87.50	175	—
			Mint NH	21	40	60	100	175	850	1,950	3,000
325	3¢	violet	Used	11.50	19.50	27.50	50	115	280	900	—
			Unused OG	30	47.50	65	80	110	190	400	—
			Mint NH	65	105	170	225	450	1,250	3,650	—
326	5¢	dark	Used	10.25	15.50	22.50	42.50	90	250	700	—
		blue	Unused OG	32.50	50	70	85	120	210	475	—
			Mint NH	60	115	180	300	525	1,700	4,850	—
327	10¢	red	Used	11	20	27.50	47.50	97.50	325	950	—
		brown	Unused OG	60	82.50	125	160	240	350	700	—
			Mint NH	110	185	300	425	750	2,500	6,750	12,750
323-327 Set	5 stamps		Used	36	59.90	84.25	172	375	1,195	3,600	
			Unused OG	145	211	305	385	550	922.50	1,930	
			Mint NH	275	485	770	1,140	2,025	6,250	19,400	

1907 JAMESTOWN EXPOSITION ISSUE

SCT#	DENOM	COLOR	CONDITION	F 70	F-VF 75	VF 80	VF-XF 85	XF 90	XF-SUP 95	SUP 98	GEM 100
328	1¢	green	Used	2.15	3.40	4.50	16	50	275	800	—
			Unused OG	12.50	17.50	30	45	75	180	350	—
			Mint NH	25	45	75	130	250	1,100	2,500	—
329	2¢	carmine	Used	1.85	2.90	4	15	50	240	650	—
			Unused OG	13	20	32.50	47.50	80	165	300	—
			Mint NH	25	50	85	140	375	2,500	7,500	13,500

SCT#	DENOM	COLOR	CONDITION	F 70	F-VF 75	VF 80	VF-XF 85	XF 90	XF-SUP 95	SUP 98	GEM 100
330	5¢	blue	Used	13	20	30	55	125	400	1,150	—
			Unused OG	70	97.50	150	170	225	400	800	—
			Mint NH	120	190	375	500	1,100	4,250	11,500	—
328-330	3 stamps		Used	17	26.30	38.50	86	225	915	2,600	
Set			Unused OG	95.50	135	212.50	262.50	380	745	1,450	
			Mint NH	170	285	535	770	1,725	7,150	25,400	

1908-09 WASHINGTON-FRANKLIN ISSUE
(DOUBLE LINE WATERMARK)

SCT#	DENOM	COLOR	CONDITION	F 70	F-VF 75	VF 80	VF-XF 85	XF 90	XF-SUP 95	SUP 98	GEM 100
331	1¢	green	Used	0.25	0.30	0.40	8	17.50	55	170	450
			Unused OG	3	4.75	6.50	8.50	12	22.50	65	—
			Mint NH	6.75	11	16.50	30	60	170	600	1,300
331a	1¢	green	Used	425	550	700	800	1,000	1,300	—	—
Booklet			Unused OG	89	115	150	190	250	525	—	—
Pane of 6			Mint NH	155	220	300	420	600	1,150	—	—
332	2¢	carmine	Used	0.25	0.25	0.35	8	20	60	180	480
			Unused OG	2.75	4	6	7.75	11	22.50	52.50	100
			Mint NH	5.75	9.50	14.50	26	38.50	160	500	1,100
332a	2¢	carmine	Used	290	390	500	600	800	1,050	—	—
Booklet			Unused OG	75	100	135	160	200	475	—	—
Pane of 6			Mint NH	120	170	240	340	490	1,250	—	—
333	3¢	deep	Used	1.40	2.10	3	12.50	32.50	125	425	—
		violet	Unused OG	14	20	30	37.50	47.50	85	225	—
			Mint NH	30	45	75	110	170	825	1,725	—
334	4¢	orange	Used	0.70	1.05	1.50	10	30	110	340	—
		brown	Unused OG	17	23.50	35	42.50	52.50	100	240	400
			Mint NH	32.50	55	87.50	130	200	700	2,400	4,500
335	5¢	blue	Used	1.05	1.55	2.25	9	27.50	110	325	—
			Unused OG	20	30	45	55	80	140	270	—
			Mint NH	42.50	70	110	200	300	1,150	2,750	—
336	6¢	red	Used	3	4.40	6	13.50	45	140	475	—
		orange	Unused OG	28	42.50	62.50	77.50	100	175	375	—
			Mint NH	55	92.50	145	200	350	1,400	3,600	7,750
337	8¢	olive	Used	1.25	2	2.75	9.25	32.50	120	375	—
		green	Unused OG	20.50	31.50	45	55	70	110	325	—
			Mint NH	42.50	70	110	175	275	1,100	3,000	—
338	10¢	yellow	Used	0.90	1.35	1.80	8	27.50	120	360	—
			Unused OG	32.50	47.50	70	82.50	100	160	400	775
			Mint NH	65	105	165	225	425	1,200	4,250	—
339	13¢	blue	Used	8	12	17.50	27.50	70	225	1,400	—
		green	Unused OG	15	25	37.50	45	60	110	250	425
			Mint NH	32.50	60	90	135	240	725	2,000	—
340	15¢	pale	Used	2.75	4.35	6	13.50	42.50	130	450	—
		ultramarine	Unused OG	27.50	42.50	67.50	77.50	95	170	370	600
			Mint NH	57.50	100	160	220	375	1,250	4,000	—
341	50¢	violet	Used	9.25	14	20	30	70	230	750	—
			Unused OG	130	180	275	350	450	725	1,550	2,750
			Mint NH	270	420	650	900	1,900	5,000	13,500	—
342	$1	violet	Used	42.50	65	95	125	220	700	2,150	—
		brown	Unused OG	210	300	450	550	725	1,275	2,500	4,500
			Mint NH	450	675	1,050	1,500	2,500	8,500	24,000	—
343	1¢	green	Used	2.40	3.50	5	6.50	10	32.50	75	200
			Unused OG	2.50	3.75	5.50	6.25	7.50	9	16	40
			Mint NH	3.60	5.75	9	11.50	17.50	30	60	120

SCT#	DENOM	COLOR	CONDITION	F 70	F-VF 75	VF 80	VF-XF 85	XF 90	XF-SUP 95	SUP 98	GEM 100
344	2¢	carmine	Used	1.25	1.80	2.75	4.25	6.50	32.50	75	200
			Unused OG	2.50	3.75	5.50	6.25	7.50	9	16	40
			Mint NH	3.60	5.75	9	11.50	17.50	30	60	120
345	3¢	deep violet type I	Used	9	14.25	20	23.50	27.50	55	125	400
			Unused OG	4.90	7.25	11	13	17	21	32.50	55
			Mint NH	8	12	19	22.50	27.50	45	95	190
346	4¢	orange brown	Used	8.75	13.25	20	24	30	60	145	400
			Unused OG	6.50	10.25	15	17	20	24	40	—
			Mint NH	8.75	15.50	25	30	37.50	65	140	275
347	5¢	blue	Used	13.75	21	32.50	37.50	50	95	210	575
			Unused OG	12.50	20	30	33.50	37.50	50	60	—
			Mint NH	17.50	30	50	55	62.50	115	230	480
348 Sgl.	1¢	green	Used	25	37.50	60	85	170	275	600	—
			Unused OG	16	28	45	50	60	90	175	275
			Mint NH	26.50	50	80	100	125	225	550	825
348 Pair	1¢	green	Used	87.50	120	170	200	400	625	—	—
			Unused OG	50	75	110	120	140	225	425	—
			Mint NH	87.50	150	225	260	325	600	1,250	2,500
348 LP	1¢	green	Used	450	575	800	1,000	1,300	2,750	—	—
			Unused OG	180	240	325	375	450	650	975	—
			Mint NH	300	450	650	750	1,200	2,700	3,750	—
349 Sgl.	2¢	carmine	Used	67.50	92.50	160	240	375	600	—	—
			Unused OG	49.50	71.50	110	130	160	260	500	750
			Mint NH	77.50	135	225	320	450	1,250	—	—
349 Pair	2¢	carmine	Used	200	265	425	675	1,150	1,750	—	—
			Unused OG	115	165	260	305	390	625	1,075	—
			Mint NH	215	360	600	775	1,150	3,250	4,500	—
349 LP	2¢	carmine	Used	700	975	1,300	1,750	2,750	—	—	—
			Unused OG	310	400	550	650	800	1,100	2,000	—
			Mint NH	650	925	1,350	1,825	2,250	4,650	10,000	—
350 Sgl.	4¢	orange brown	Used	110	165	250	390	775	1,500	—	—
			Unused OG	70	92.50	155	175	220	350	700	—
			Mint NH	120	185	325	475	750	2,000	3,250	—
350 Pair	4¢	orange brown	Used	425	575	800	1,200	1,950	—	—	—
			Unused OG	160	225	375	450	575	875	1,575	—
			Mint NH	335	550	900	1,250	2,000	6,000	8,500	—
350 LP	4¢	orange brown	Used	2,200	2,900	4,000	5,000	6,500	12,000	—	—
			Unused OG	625	850	1,175	1,450	2,500	3,250	5,000	6,500
			Mint NH	1,275	1,700	2,600	3,250	4,750	9,500	15,500	—
351 Sgl.	5¢	blue	Used	140	190	300	450	725	1,500	—	—
			Unused OG	70	92.50	155	175	220	350	700	1,100
			Mint NH	120	190	325	450	750	1,750	2,950	—
351 Pair	5¢	blue	Used	385	575	825	1,200	1,850	3,850	—	—
			Unused OG	175	250	400	450	525	875	1,400	1,650
			Mint NH	300	525	850	1,125	1,650	3,750	10,000	—
351 LP	5¢	blue	Used	1,600	2,000	3,000	4,000	5,750	12,750	—	—
			Unused OG	575	775	1,075	1,250	1,500	1,900	300	—
			Mint NH	1,100	1,525	2,350	3,000	4,250	7,500	12,500	—
352 Sgl.	1¢	green	Used	110	150	225	325	550	1,150	—	—
			Unused OG	45	67.50	110	125	175	300	550	900
			Mint NH	82.50	125	235	315	440	900	2,100	—
352 Pair	1¢	green	Used	300	425	650	950	1,500	3,750	—	—
			Unused OG	110	160	250	320	625	850	1,250	—
			Mint NH	185	310	550	825	2,250	3,500	6,000	—
352 LP	1¢	green	Used	875	1,150	1,650	2,250	3,250	6,500	—	—
			Unused OG	450	575	825	1,050	1,675	2,500	—	—
			Mint NH	875	1,200	1,800	2,750	3,850	8,000	—	—
353 Sgl.	2¢	carmine	Used	110	145	220	350	625	1,250	2,500	—
			Unused OG	42.50	57.50	100	125	145	250	425	—
			Mint NH	73.50	105	210	275	400	1,250	2,500	—
353 Pair	2¢	carmine	Used	275	375	575	850	1,400	2,750	—	—
			Unused OG	97.50	140	230	300	450	750	1,250	—
			Mint NH	170	275	500	900	1,750	3,500	—	—
353 LP	2¢	carmine	Used	2,100	2,700	4,000	5,250	6,500	—	—	—
			Unused OG	400	475	750	900	1,250	3,000	4,500	—
			Mint NH	850	1,100	1,750	2,750	5,000	8,500	—	—

SCT#	DENOM	COLOR	CONDITION	F 70	F-VF 75	VF 80	VF-XF 85	XF 90	XF-SUP 95	SUP 98	GEM 100
354 Sgl.	4¢	orange brown	Used	120	180	275	450	750	1,750	3,000	6,500
			Unused OG	96.50	130	220	260	330	450	1,100	1,900
			Mint NH	150	225	425	625	900	1,850	4,400	—
354 Pair	4¢	orange brown	Used	410	525	825	1,350	2,500	7,500	—	—
			Unused OG	210	325	500	575	775	1,200	1,900	2,500
			Mint NH	350	575	1,050	1,450	2,250	4,500	—	—
354 LP	4¢	orange brown	Used	1,100	1,500	2,000	2,750	4,250	7,250	12,500	—
			Unused OG	750	950	1,400	1,700	2,250	3,000	4,250	—
			Mint NH	1,375	1,850	3,000	4,250	6,000	12,500	—	—
355 Sgl.	5¢	blue	Used	110	175	300	450	725	1,550	3,850	—
			Unused OG	92.50	140	230	350	450	575	850	—
			Mint NH	150	260	450	650	1,000	2,150	5,000	—
355 Pair	5¢	blue	Used	465	625	875	1,250	2,000	3,750	—	—
			Unused OG	220	310	525	825	1,250	1,750	—	—
			Mint NH	375	575	1,100	1,650	3,250	7,750	—	—
355 LP	5¢	blue	Used	2,000	2,800	4,000	5,250	7,000	—	—	—
			Unused OG	800	1,025	1,500	1,750	2,250	2,750	—	—
			Mint NH	1,500	2,000	3,250	4,500	7,250	12,000	—	—
356 Sgl.	10¢	yellow	Used	3,000	4,250	6,250	7,500	9,250	—	—	—
			Unused OG	1,875	2,350	3,500	3,850	4,250	6,000	—	—
			Mint NH	3,000	5,250	8,000	9,250	11,750	—		
356 Pair	10¢	yellow	Used	6,500	9,000	15,000	18,500	22,500			
			Unused OG	4,000	5,250	8,000	9,000	11,000	14,750		
			Mint NH	—	—	17,500	23,500	27,500	32,500		
356 LP	10¢	yellow	Used			29,000		one known			
			Unused OG	9,000	12,000	16,000	21,500	28,500	—		
			Mint NH	22,500	27,500	45,000	67,500	95,000	—		

1909 BLUISH PAPERS

SCT#	DENOM	COLOR	CONDITION	F 70	F-VF 75	VF 80	VF-XF 85	XF 90	XF-SUP 95	SUP 98	GEM 100
357	1¢	green	Used	72.50	105	160	205	275	650	1,500	—
			Unused OG	40	62.50	90	105	130	225	425	—
			Mint NH	74	110	190	290	420	1,300	3,600	—
358	2¢	carmine	Used	67.50	97.50	150	190	260	600	1,500	—
			Unused OG	38	55	80	97.50	120	200	400	—
			Mint NH	62.50	100	170	260	500	1,650	4,250	7,500
359	3¢	deep violet type I	Used	5,500	7,250	12,500	14,250	17,250	—	—	—
			Unused OG	900	1,225	1,800	2,150	2,500	4,000	6,500	—
			Mint NH	1,600	2,500	4,000	6,000	8,500	18,500	—	—
360	4¢	orange brown	Unused OG	15,000	20,000	27,500	42,500	65,000	—		
			Mint NH	35,000	60,000	80,000	110,000	—	—		
361	5¢	blue	Used	—	—	20,000	—	—			
			Unused OG	3,250	4,750	6,500	7,750	9,750	14,000	25,000	—
			Mint NH	7,750	10,000	15,000	20,000	32,500	55,000	—	—
362	6¢	red orange	Used	6,500	9,500	12,500	16,000	22,500	—		
			Unused OG	625	850	1,250	1,500	1,900	3,750	5,500	—
			Mint NH	1,300	2,150	3,000	4,500	7,000	14,500	37,500	—
363	8¢	olive green	Unused OG	16,500	23,000	30,000	35,000	50,000	100,000	—	
			Mint NH	—	77,500	90,000	—	—			
364	10¢	yellow	Used	5,000	7,000	10,000	12,000	15,000	22,500	—	—
			Unused OG	800	1,125	1,600	2,000	3,250	4,500	6,500	—
			Mint NH	1,500	2,750	4,000	6,000	8,750	19,000	—	—
365	13¢	blue green	Used	1,850	2,650	3,750	4,250	5,500	10,000	—	—
			Unused OG	1,300	2,000	2,600	3,150	4,500	8,250	10,000	—
			Mint NH	2,300	4,000	6,000	9,000	13,500	30,000	—	—
366	15¢	pale ultramarine	Used	8,750	12,500	16,000	17,500	20,000	—	—	—
			Unused OG	675	875	1,300	1,500	2,000	3,000	5,000	—
			Mint NH	1,200	1,900	3,000	4,500	8,500	14,500	—	—

SCT#	DENOM	COLOR	CONDITION	F 70	F-VF 75	VF 80	VF-XF 85	XF 90	XF-SUP 95	SUP 98	GEM 100

1909 COMMEMORATIVES

SCT#	DENOM	COLOR	CONDITION	F 70	F-VF 75	VF 80	VF-XF 85	XF 90	XF-SUP 95	SUP 98	GEM 100
367	2¢	carmine	Used	0.70	1.30	1.75	8.75	22.50	105	280	—
			Unused OG	1.80	2.70	4.50	6.50	12.50	35	65	—
			Mint NH	3.60	6.25	9.50	16	32.50	115	350	950
368	2¢	carmine	Used	8.50	12.75	19	22.50	32.50	75	170	500
		imperforate	Unused OG	4	7.50	12.50	15	22.50	40	52.50	—
			Mint NH	8.75	14.50	24	29	37.50	65	125	325
369	2¢	carmine	Used	115	160	225	300	475	950	2,750	—
		bluish	Unused OG	70	100	150	170	200	275	450	700
		paper	Mint NH	125	200	300	400	550	1,100	3,500	7,000
370	2¢	carmine	Used	0.80	1.30	2	9	27.50	80	310	—
			Unused OG	3.60	4.50	6.75	8	12	25	50	—
			Mint NH	6.50	9.50	15	30	55	125	450	825
371	2¢	carmine	Used	8.75	11.75	21	25	35	70	155	260
		imperforate	Unused OG	4.50	8.25	14	16	19	27.50	40	—
			Mint NH	10.50	18.50	30	35	45	75	125	225
372	2¢	carmine	Used	2	3.25	4.75	12.50	47.50	160	650	—
			Unused OG	4	6	10	14	20	35	60	—
			Mint NH	8	12	21	45	85	210	600	1,200
373	2¢	carmine	Used	12.50	18	27.50	32.50	45	85	180	350
		imperforate	Unused OG	8	12	20	22	24.50	32.50	45	85
			Mint NH	14	26	40	42.50	47.50	75	145	275

1910-11 WASHINGTON-FRANKLIN ISSUE (SINGLE LINE WATERMARK)

SCT#	DENOM	COLOR	CONDITION	F 70	F-VF 75	VF 80	VF-XF 85	XF 90	XF-SUP 95	SUP 98	GEM 100
374	1¢	green	Used	0.25	0.25	0.25	10	20	50	150	325
			Unused OG	2.75	4.15	6	8	11	22.50	65	—
			Mint NH	6.50	9.25	14	25	47.50	140	500	—
374a Booklet Pane of 6	1¢	green	Used	240	315	400	500	650	1,150	—	—
			Unused OG	135	175	225	260	340	575	—	—
			Mint NH	190	270	375	450	650	1,250	—	—
375	2¢	carmine	Used	0.25	0.25	0.25	10	22.50	52.50	125	300
			Unused OG	2.75	4.60	6	8	11	22.50	60	—
			Mint NH	6.50	9.25	14	25	47.50	175	650	—
375a Booklet Pane of 6	2¢	carmine	Used	180	235	300	375	500	800	—	—
			Unused OG	75	97	125	155	200	375	—	—
			Mint NH	110	150	200	250	345	700	—	—
375b	2¢	lake	Unused OG	410	625	825	1,100	1,650	2,500	—	
			Mint NH	750	1,225	1,800	2,450	3,500	—	—	
376	3¢	deep	Used	0.90	1.40	2	12.50	35	100	375	—
		violet	Unused OG	8	12.50	18	22.50	27.50	57.50	125	—
		type I	Mint NH	16	26	40	62.50	100	275	1,100	—
377	4¢	brown	Used	0.45	0.65	1	11	27.50	90	300	800
			Unused OG	12.50	20	27.50	35	45	90	190	325
			Mint NH	24	42.50	65	90	160	400	1,150	—
378	5¢	blue	Used	0.40	0.60	0.75	4	22.50	85	290	800
			Unused OG	12.50	19	27.50	35	45	87.50	175	300
			Mint NH	24	42.50	65	95	160	575	1,500	4,000

SCT#	DENOM	COLOR	CONDITION	F 70	F-VF 75	VF 80	VF-XF 85	XF 90	XF-SUP 95	SUP 98	GEM 100
379	6¢	red	Used	0.55	0.80	1.25	12.50	35	90	300	725
		orange	Unused OG	17.50	23.50	37.50	45	57.50	95	210	—
			Mint NH	32.50	50	85	115	170	480	1,600	3,250
380	8¢	olive	Used	8	11	15	25	70	225	575	1,175
		green	Unused OG	42.50	60	90	110	160	310	525	—
			Mint NH	80	130	200	290	475	1,300	4,500	10,000
381	10¢	yellow	Used	3.20	4.40	6	15	60	150	450	950
			Unused OG	40	60	85	100	125	225	450	—
			Mint NH	85	140	200	325	500	1,225	3,750	7,500
382	15¢	pale	Used	9	13.25	20	30	75	260	750	—
		ultramarine	Unused OG	100	150	225	260	375	525	1,000	—
			Mint NH	190	310	500	725	1,300	2,650	6,750	—
383	1¢	green	Used	1.10	1.85	2.75	6	21.50	42.50	100	225
			Unused OG	1.10	1.65	2.50	5.75	18	26.50	35	70
			Mint NH	2.10	3.15	5	10	18.50	27.50	47.50	100
384	2¢	carmine	Used	1	1.80	2.75	5.50	18.50	37.50	90	175
			Unused OG	1.50	2.60	4	8	20	30	—	—
			Mint NH	3.45	5.25	8	11.50	18.50	28.50	55	110
385 Sgl.	1¢	green	Used	18.50	28	50	82.50	140	350	925	—
			Unused OG	22	32.50	50	60	75	105	175	—
			Mint NH	35	60	100	140	325	850	1,350	—
385 Pair	1¢	green	Used	125	175	250	325	500	950	—	—
			Unused OG	50	70	110	130	160	225	375	—
			Mint NH	95	150	240	325	750	1,900	3,000	—
385 LP	1¢	green	Used	450	650	850	1,000	1,500	2,900	—	—
			Unused OG	225	350	450	550	700	1,000	1,750	—
			Mint NH	425	750	1,000	1,300	1,800	4,000	8,500	—
386 Sgl.	2¢	carmine	Used	45	62.50	90	250	950	1,750	—	—
			Unused OG	62.50	92.50	130	150	200	325	650	—
			Mint NH	100	165	260	375	675	1,550	4,250	—
386 Pair	2¢	carmine	Used	12,500	18,750	25,000	—	—	—	—	—
			Unused OG	150	210	325	360	500	775	1,500	—
			Mint NH	275	450	700	1,050	2,000	4,000	9,000	—
386 LP	2¢	carmine	Used	2,400	3,250	4,000	5,750	—	—	—	—
			Unused OG	850	1,150	1,600	1,850	2,250	5,250	—	—
			Mint NH	1,500	2,400	3,500	4,500	8,000	12,500	—	—
387 Sgl.	1¢	green	Used	55	77.50	140	210	360	725	1,500	—
			Unused OG	95	135	200	250	400	575	950	—
			Mint NH	170	265	400	675	1,125	2,500	5,750	—
387 Pair	1¢	green	Used	275	375	500	900	2,500	4,000	—	—
			Unused OG	240	350	500	625	900	1,500	2,250	—
			Mint NH	475	700	1,100	1,850	3,775	8,250	12,500	—
387 LP	1¢	green	Used	1,350	2,000	2,500	3,250	4,500	7,500	—	—
			Unused OG	675	950	1,250	1,575	2,250	3,350	—	—
			Mint NH	1,250	1,675	2,500	3,750	6,250	13,500	—	—
388 Sgl.	2¢	carmine	Used	1,100	1,600	2,250	3,750	5,750	9,000	—	—
			Unused OG	700	1,050	1,600	1,850	2,250	3,000	6,000	—
			Mint NH	1,450	2,500	4,000	5,500	8,500	14,000	25,000	—
388 Pair	2¢	carmine	Used	3,250	5,250	7,500	10,250	14,000	18,500	—	—
			Unused OG	1,875	2,700	3,750	4,250	5,500	7,000	—	—
			Mint NH	3,600	5,250	8,250	12,500	18,000	—	—	—
388 LP	2¢	carmine	Used		30,000						
			Unused OG	5,250	6,800	9,000	11,000	13,500	—		
			Mint NH	—	14,500	24,000	—	—			
389 Sgl.	3¢	deep	Used	10,000	12,000	14,500	22,000	32,500	—		
		violet	Unused OG	90,000	110,000	—					
		type I	Mint NH	325,000							
389 Pair	3¢	deep violet	Used	42,500							
		type I	Unused OG	240,000	340,000						
390 Sgl.	1¢	green	Used	5.50	9	14	22.50	35	85	225	550
			Unused OG	2.15	3	4.50	9	20	37.50	55	—
			Mint NH	4.25	6.25	10	25	55	140	225	675

SCT#	DENOM	COLOR	CONDITION	F 70	F-VF 75	VF 80	VF-XF 85	XF 90	XF-SUP 95	SUP 98	GEM 100
390 Pair	1¢	green	Used	22.50	32.50	45	65	115	225	475	—
			Unused OG	5	7	10.50	20	45	85	125	—
			Mint NH	10	14.50	22	55	130	350	700	—
390 LP	1¢	green	Used	65	85	125	200	350	1,200	—	—
			Unused OG	17.50	25	35	45	65	150	325	—
			Mint NH	30	50	72.50	90	175	375	950	1,850
391 Sgl.	2¢	carmine	Used	16	32.50	50	85	150	310	600	—
			Unused OG	20	27.50	42.50	50	65	95	160	275
			Mint NH	37.50	55	90	135	225	525	1,000	—
391 Pair	2¢	carmine	Used	82.50	115	170	475	1,200	—	—	—
			Unused OG	50	75	110	130	170	210	350	—
			Mint NH	100	155	240	350	500	950	2,100	—
391 LP	2¢	carmine	Used	850	1,100	1,500	2,000	3,250	5,250	—	—
			Unused OG	140	180	260	300	375	500	800	—
			Mint NH	250	375	575	700	950	2,000	5,250	7,500
392 Sgl.	1¢	green	Used	16	30	50	72.50	125	300	600	—
			Unused OG	14.50	20	32.50	40	47.50	60	110	200
			Mint NH	25	42.50	65	90	140	425	850	—
392 Pair	1¢	green	Used	70	100	145	225	425	700	1,300	—
			Unused OG	32.50	50	75	85	110	150	250	—
			Mint NH	55	90	145	200	300	875	1,900	—
392 LP	1¢	green	Used	280	375	500	675	1,000	1,900	3,000	—
			Unused OG	95	135	190	225	260	355	600	850
			Mint NH	180	265	400	475	800	1,450	3,250	6,000
393 Sgl.	2¢	carmine	Used	15	37.50	55	85	130	260	425	1,200
			Unused OG	22.50	35	52.50	62.50	77.50	125	200	325
			Mint NH	42.50	67.50	105	140	215	450	1,000	1,000
393 Pair	2¢	carmine	Used	65	95	140	190	310	575	—	—
			Unused OG	62	87	135	160	185	275	425	700
			Mint NH	105	155	260	325	475	1,000	2,200	—
393 LP	2¢	carmine	Used	240	325	450	550	1,100	2,400	—	—
			Unused OG	150	210	300	350	425	575	975	—
			Mint NH	280	425	650	850	1,200	2,250	4,750	6,750
394 Sgl.	3¢ deep violet type I		Used	35	45	65	95	160	350	625	1,650
			Unused OG	35	47.50	67.50	82.50	110	150	250	375
			Mint NH	57.50	85	135	190	275	600	1,100	2,250
394 Pair	3¢ deep violet type I		Used	100	140	200	275	425	850	—	—
			Unused OG	72.50	105	150	175	240	375	600	—
			Mint NH	140	215	330	450	625	1,500	3,000	4,750
394 LP	3¢ deep violet type I		Used	350	450	650	900	1,400	2,750	—	—
			Unused OG	200	300	425	500	750	1,000	1,650	—
			Mint NH	410	625	925	1,150	1,500	3,500	6,750	12,000
395 Sgl.	4¢	brown	Used	30	42.50	65	95	175	400	925	—
			Unused OG	35	47.50	67.50	82.50	110	150	250	450
			Mint NH	52.50	87.50	135	185	250	600	1,250	2,650
395 Pair	4¢	brown	Used	95	140	190	275	430	850	2,150	—
			Unused OG	72.50	105	150	175	240	375	600	—
			Mint NH	140	215	330	450	675	1,500	3,000	—
395 LP	4¢	brown	Used	325	475	650	875	1,250	2,650	—	—
			Unused OG	225	320	475	550	650	875	1,500	—
			Mint NH	475	725	1,100	1,400	2,250	3,500	6,500	10,000
396 Sgl.	5¢	blue	Used	28	45	65	115	240	450	850	—
			Unused OG	35	47.50	67.50	82.50	110	150	250	400
			Mint NH	60	87.50	135	180	300	575	1,100	2,400
396 Pair	5¢	blue	Used	90	135	190	275	550	1,100	2,250	—
			Unused OG	70	105	160	175	225	350	550	850
			Mint NH	150	235	375	475	600	1,300	2,250	5,000
396 LP	5¢	blue	Used	400	575	825	1,150	1,700	3,500	—	—
			Unused OG	225	310	425	500	600	825	1,300	—
			Mint NH	450	650	975	1,350	2,250	3,750	6,500	—

SCT#	DENOM	COLOR	CONDITION	F 70	F-VF 75	VF 80	VF-XF 85	XF 90	XF-SUP 95	SUP 98	GEM 100

1913-15 PANAMA-PACIFIC EXPOSITION ISSUE

SCT#	DENOM	COLOR	CONDITION	F 70	F-VF 75	VF 80	VF-XF 85	XF 90	XF-SUP 95	SUP 98	GEM 100
397	1¢	green	Used	0.90	1.30	2	10	40	110	280	575
			Unused OG	6.75	9.75	15	20	30	50	100	175
			Mint NH	12.50	20	35	65	110	200	575	1,900
398	2¢	carmine	Used	0.35	0.55	1	8	25	90	250	575
			Unused OG	7	11	16	20	30	50	100	—
			Mint NH	12.50	20	35	50	90	210	700	1,250
398a	2¢	carmine	Unused OG	900	1,175	1,600	2,150	2,900	3,250	4,500	—
		lake	Mint NH	1,250	1,825	2,500	3,250	4,500	6,000		
398b	2¢	lake	Used			3,000					
			Unused OG	2,650	4,000	5,250	6,400	7,250	12,000	16,500	
			Mint NH	—	7,250	8,500	—				
399	5¢	blue	Used	5	7.50	10	22.50	60	180	600	—
			Unused OG	32.50	47.50	70	85	110	150	325	650
			Mint NH	62.50	100	160	220	325	675	1,750	2,750
400	10¢	orange	Used	10	14	20	35	90	225	775	—
		yellow	Unused OG	57.50	77.50	115	135	165	250	500	—
			Mint NH	100	170	250	375	500	850	2,600	—
400A	10¢	orange	Used	10	15	22.50	45	80	240	625	950
			Unused OG	72.50	110	175	220	300	450	825	—
			Mint NH	165	265	390	525	750	1,350	4,000	5,750
401	1¢	green	Used	3.50	4.75	7	15	45	175	400	675
			Unused OG	11.25	17	25	35	60	100	200	300
			Mint NH	21	40	60	80	125	375	1,000	1,500
402	2¢	carmine	Used	1.40	2	3	11	37.50	140	400	—
			Unused OG	35	47.50	70	82.50	110	150	300	1,100
			Mint NH	65	110	170	240	475	850	2,250	14,000
403	5¢	blue	Used	7	11	17.50	30	75	210	650	—
			Unused OG	82.50	110	160	180	215	325	600	1,200
			Mint NH	150	250	400	500	775	1,350	3,750	—
404	10¢	orange	Used	32.50	50	70	95	180	450	950	—
			Unused OG	350	475	675	750	850	1,250	2,100	2,750
			Mint NH	675	1,050	1,650	1,875	2,150	4,000	11,000	30,000
397-404 Set	9 stamps		Used	70.50	106.10	153	271.50	632.50	1,823	5,005	
			Unused OG	650	905.25	1,321	1,528	1,865	2,765	5,075	
			Mint NH	1,275	2,025	3,150	3,920	5,300	9,860	26,450	

1912-14 WASHINGTON-FRANKLIN ISSUE

SCT#	DENOM	COLOR	CONDITION	F 70	F-VF 75	VF 80	VF-XF 85	XF 90	XF-SUP 95	SUP 98	GEM 100
405	1¢	green	Used	0.25	0.25	0.25	4	30	65	150	400
			Unused OG	3	4.50	6.50	12	20	32.50	70	200
			Mint NH	6.25	9.50	15	25	50	160	425	—
405b Booklet Pane of 6	1¢	green	Used	40	55	75	90	110	300	—	—
			Unused OG	35	50	65	77.50	92.50	225	—	—
			Mint NH	60	85	110	140	180	500	—	—
406	2¢	carmine type I	Used	0.20	0.20	0.25	3.50	25	60	140	400
			Unused OG	3	4.50	6.50	9	12.50	25	70	200
			Mint NH	6.25	9.50	15	25	40	135	425	1,100
406a Booklet Pane of 6	2¢	dark carmine	Used	55	70	90	110	130	350	—	—
			Unused OG	35	50	65	77.50	92.50	225	—	—
			Mint NH	60	85	110	140	180	500	—	—

SCT#	DENOM	COLOR	CONDITION	F 70	F-VF 75	VF 80	VF-XF 85	XF 90	XF-SUP 95	SUP 98	GEM 100
406c	2¢	lake type I	Used	—	—	6,000	7,250	—	—		
			Unused OG	1,100	1,500	2,000	2,750	4,250	—	—	
			Mint NH	2,250	3,250	4,500	6,000	9,000	—		
407	7¢	black	Used	6.50	9	14	24	65	200	600	—
			Unused OG	32.50	47.50	70	85	115	200	475	—
			Mint NH	57.50	95	150	210	325	1,000	3,400	—
408	1¢	green	Used	0.45	0.70	1	2.50	5	10	35	110
			Unused OG	0.40	0.60	1	6	15	19	25	60
			Mint NH	0.75	1.10	2	10	22.50	27.50	42.50	100
409	2¢	carmine type I	Used	0.55	0.85	1.20	6	10	17.50	40	150
			Unused OG	0.50	0.75	1.20	5	10	17.50	25	—
			Mint NH	0.85	1.25	2.40	3	5	12	35	100
410 Sgl.	1¢	green	Used	5.75	9	12.50	25	65	250	450	—
			Unused OG	2.75	4.25	6	10	15	25	50	—
			Mint NH	5	8.50	13	22.50	40	80	250	650
410 Pair	1¢	green	Used	21.50	30	42.50	95	165	450	900	—
			Unused OG	7	10	15	22.50	35	57.50	110	—
			Mint NH	14	21	32.50	50	85	180	575	—
410 LP	1¢	green	Used	50	72	100	200	475	1,450	—	—
			Unused OG	16	22.50	30	37.50	50	90	175	—
			Mint NH	32.50	45	65	90	140	325	550	—
411 Sgl.	2¢	carmine type I	Used	7.50	10.50	17.50	27.50	65	160	375	—
			Unused OG	4.75	7	10	14	22.50	40	70	—
			Mint NH	10	14.50	22.50	30	45	100	230	550
411 Pair	2¢	carmine type I	Used	37.50	54.50	75	135	275	625	—	—
			Unused OG	12	16.50	25	32.50	50	90	160	—
			Mint NH	22.50	37.50	55	75	135	275	900	—
411 LP	2¢	carmine type I	Used	110	150	190	300	460	1,300	—	—
			Unused OG	27.50	40	55	65	85	150	250	—
			Mint NH	60	85	125	200	280	500	1,200	—
412 Sgl.	1¢	green	Used	13.50	26.50	40	80	135	260	525	1,100
			Unused OG	12	17	25	30	37.50	60	100	160
			Mint NH	22.50	35	55	70	100	200	475	1,050
412 Pair	1¢	green	Used	42.50	87.50	130	200	325	650	1,250	—
			Unused OG	27.50	40	60	75	95	150	225	—
			Mint NH	60	87.50	130	170	240	475	1,100	—
412 LP	1¢	green	Used	120	170	250	375	600	1,050	2,000	—
			Unused OG	65	85	120	140	170	250	425	—
			Mint NH	120	180	260	325	425	1,000	2,000	—
413 Sgl.	2¢	carmine	Used	16.50	32.50	50	85	140	260	500	1,150
			Unused OG	30	45	60	72.50	90	145	240	—
			Mint NH	60	85	130	165	230	500	800	—
413 Pair	2¢	carmine	Used	35	67.50	100	185	400	1,100	—	—
			Unused OG	62.50	92.50	125	155	190	315	500	—
			Mint NH	125	175	260	400	500	1,200	3,000	—
413 LP	2¢	carmine	Used	160	260	325	500	950	—	—	—
			Unused OG	145	200	275	340	500	625	1,000	—
			Mint NH	275	390	575	750	1,400	2,750	5,750	9,500
414	8¢	pale olive green	Used	1	1.40	2	12.50	35	130	425	1,250
			Unused OG	20	30	40	47.50	57.50	115	250	500
			Mint NH	40	65	100	135	190	550	1,800	4,250
415	9¢	salmon red	Used	6.50	9.50	14	25	57.50	200	750	—
			Unused OG	22.50	37.50	50	60	75	130	250	—
			Mint NH	47.50	77.50	120	170	240	650	2,750	5,000
416	10¢	orange yellow	Used	0.30	0.55	0.80	8	35	95	310	—
			Unused OG	20	30	40	50	65	125	325	—
			Mint NH	40	65	100	135	225	550	1,800	—
416a	10¢	brown yellow	Unused OG	700	850	1,250	1,450	1,750	2,250	4,500	—
			Mint NH	1,250	1,825	2,750	3,600	5,500	—	—	—
417	12¢	claret brown	Used	2.40	3.60	5	11.50	40	150	500	—
			Unused OG	20	30	40	47.50	70	170	300	—
			Mint NH	40	65	100	135	190	550	1,800	4,000
418	15¢	gray	Used	2	3	4	15	45	150	500	—
			Unused OG	37.50	55	80	92.50	110	210	435	—
			Mint NH	72.50	120	190	230	340	750	2,150	4,750

SCT#	DENOM	COLOR	CONDITION	F 70	F-VF 75	VF 80	VF-XF 85	XF 90	XF-SUP 95	SUP 98	GEM 100
419	20¢	ultramarine	Used	7.25	11.50	17.50	30	70	230	750	—
			Unused OG	90	125	190	225	290	475	825	1,250
			Mint NH	160	275	400	525	725	1,525	4,500	8,000
420	30¢	orange red	Used	7.25	11.50	17.50	30	110	300	850	—
			Unused OG	55	77.50	115	140	175	260	500	800
			Mint NH	95	160	250	350	550	1,250	3,000	6,250
421	50¢	violet	Used	10	18.50	27.50	45	110	325	925	—
			Unused OG	160	240	350	400	500	875	1,350	2,150
			Mint NH	325	525	775	950	1,500	4,000	10,000	—
422	50¢	violet	Used	9	15	25	40	105	300	900	—
			Unused OG	105	150	225	260	325	550	1,250	—
			Mint NH	220	340	500	700	1,000	2,750	10,000	—
423	$1	violet brown	Used	40	57.50	85	120	230	475	1,500	—
			Unused OG	210	325	475	525	600	975	1,800	2,750
			Mint NH	450	650	1,000	1,400	2,500	6,000	22,500	—

1914 COMPOUND PERFORATION ISSUES

SCT#	DENOM	COLOR	CONDITION	F 70	F-VF 75	VF 80	VF-XF 85	XF 90	XF-SUP 95	SUP 98	GEM 100
423A	1¢	green	Used	4,000	5,000	7,500	9,000	11,500			
			Unused OG	9,000	12,500	19,000	—				
			Mint NH			—					
423B	2¢	rose red type I	Used	8,000	10,000	17,500	20,000	23,500			
			Unused OG			175,000	only one known				
423C	5¢	blue	Used	10,000	15,000	20,000	22,000	25,000			
423D	1¢	green	Used	6,000	8,500	14,000					
423E	2¢	rose red type I	Used			—		only one known			

1913-15 WASHINGTON-FRANKLIN ISSUE (SINGLE LINE WATERMARK)

SCT#	DENOM	COLOR	CONDITION	F 70	F-VF 75	VF 80	VF-XF 85	XF 90	XF-SUP 95	SUP 98	GEM 100
424	1¢	green	Used	0.25	0.25	0.25	8	20	75	200	600
			Unused OG	1.10	1.55	2.25	3.40	7.50	20	40	—
			Mint NH	1.80	2.95	4.75	10.50	16.50	80	270	750
424d Booklet Pane of 6	1¢	green	Used	4.25	5.75	7.50	10	15	40	—	—
			Unused OG	2.50	3.80	5.25	6.50	8.50	20	—	—
			Mint NH	4	5.75	8.75	12.50	20	50	—	—
425	2¢	rose red type I	Used	0.25	0.25	0.25	8	20	75	200	600
			Unused OG	1	1.50	2.25	3.50	7.50	20	40	70
			Mint NH	2	3.25	5	11	17.50	80	260	750
425e Booklet Pane of 6	2¢	rose red type I	Used	14	19	25	35	50	130	—	—
			Unused OG	8.50	12.50	17.50	22.50	30	70	—	—
			Mint NH	13.50	20	30	47.50	70	145	—	—
426	3¢	deep violet type I	Used	0.60	0.90	1.25	8.25	20	100	325	900
			Unused OG	7	10	15	19	27.50	50	130	—
			Mint NH	14	22.50	35	52.50	80	325	950	2,900
427	4¢	brown	Used	0.35	0.60	0.90	8	17.50	100	300	900
			Unused OG	15	22.50	32.50	40	55	95	245	375
			Mint NH	30	52.50	75	110	225	750	2,000	—
428	5¢	blue	Used	0.35	0.60	0.90	8	17.50	100	300	800
			Unused OG	15	22.50	32.50	42.50	55	125	300	—
			Mint NH	30	52.50	75	115	170	550	1,950	—
429	6¢	red orange	Used	0.90	1.30	2	11.50	25	120	350	—
			Unused OG	22.50	32.50	45	57.50	75	120	300	—
			Mint NH	42.50	70	105	160	210	775	2,150	5,500
430	7¢	black	Used	2.50	3.60	4.75	12	37.50	160	450	—
			Unused OG	40	60	85	100	135	220	500	—
			Mint NH	77.50	120	190	275	450	1,300	4,500	—
431	8¢	pale olive green	Used	1.40	2	3	12.50	35	130	425	1,000
			Unused OG	20	27.50	40	50	62.50	100	225	—
			Mint NH	30	50	80	125	210	900	1,850	—

SCT#	DENOM	COLOR	CONDITION	F 70	F-VF 75	VF 80	VF-XF 85	XF 90	XF-SUP 95	SUP 98	GEM 100
432	9¢	salmon red	Used	4	5.75	8	15.50	50	175	550	—
			Unused OG	20	27.50	40	50	65	115	290	—
			Mint NH	30	50	80	125	210	900	1,850	5,000
433	10¢	orange yellow	Used	0.40	0.65	1	10	30	100	300	—
			Unused OG	20	27.50	40	52.50	72.50	115	290	—
			Mint NH	32.50	50	80	120	225	750	2,400	5,500
434	11¢	dark green	Used	3.75	5.75	8	15	50	165	575	1,600
			Unused OG	15	19.50	30	37.50	50	115	290	—
			Mint NH	30	47.50	75	100	175	650	1,500	2,750
435	12¢	claret brown	Used	2.65	3.75	5.50	11	37.50	140	475	—
			Unused OG	15	20	30	37.50	50	82.50	190	—
			Mint NH	30	47.50	75	100	175	650	1,500	3,250
435a	12¢	copper red	Used	3.25	4.65	6.50	13	42.50	150	500	—
			Unused OG	15	20	30	37.50	50	90	200	—
			Mint NH	30	45	75	110	190	850	2,000	—
437	15¢	gray	Used	3.75	5.75	8	17.50	47.50	150	450	—
			Unused OG	57.50	85	120	140	185	290	700	1,000
			Mint NH	110	170	275	400	600	2,250	4,250	—
438	20¢	ultramarine	Used	3.50	5.25	7	15	45	160	500	—
			Unused OG	100	140	200	240	310	525	1,125	2,000
			Mint NH	180	300	450	600	950	2,500	5,750	—
439	30¢	orange red	Used	9	13.50	20	32.50	70	225	725	1,900
			Unused OG	100	150	225	275	340	625	1,100	—
			Mint NH	200	325	500	700	1,250	3,250	9,000	—
440	50¢	violet	Used	9	13.50	20	32.50	70	250	900	—
			Unused OG	225	325	450	525	650	975	2,200	3,000
			Mint NH	440	700	1,100	1,350	2,150	4,500	10,000	25,000
441 Sgl.	1¢	green	Used	0.60	0.95	1.50	8.50	25	45	125	450
			Unused OG	0.45	0.70	1	7.50	22.50	40	65	120
			Mint NH	0.70	1.25	2	9	30	65	125	300
441 Pair	1¢	green	Used	3.70	5.25	7	22.50	100	225	375	—
			Unused OG	1.30	1.80	2.75	16	50	85	140	—
			Mint NH	2	3.50	5.75	20	65	140	275	700
441 LP	1¢	green	Used	22	29	40	60	150	500	750	—
			Unused OG	4	6	8	15	55	90	190	—
			Mint NH	7.75	12.50	17.50	30	70	375	650	1,400
442 Sgl.	2¢	carmine type I	Used	21	30	45	75	150	300	500	—
			Unused OG	5	7	10	15	25	50	80	—
			Mint NH	8.50	14	22.50	32.50	55	115	225	475
442 Pair	2¢	carmine type I	Used	50	85	130	210	375	875	—	—
			Unused OG	12	17	25	35	57.50	110	175	—
			Mint NH	20	35	55	75	125	250	475	1,000
442 LP	2¢	carmine type I	Used	140	215	300	500	900	1,750	—	—
			Unused OG	30	42.50	60	80	125	200	325	—
			Mint NH	60	85	130	180	350	700	1,500	3,000
443 Sgl.	1¢	green	Used	20	30	45	80	150	275	525	1,100
			Unused OG	15	21	30	40	60	90	140	250
			Mint NH	25	42.50	65	85	130	275	650	1,300
443 Pair	1¢	green	Used	57.50	90	135	225	375	850	1,150	—
			Unused OG	35	50	75	95	140	200	310	—
			Mint NH	65	100	160	210	300	750	1,500	—
443 LP	1¢	green	Used	140	200	250	450	850	1,500	—	—
			Unused OG	80	110	155	180	250	525	800	—
			Mint NH	150	210	325	425	575	1,100	1,900	3,500
444 Sgl.	2¢	carmine type I	Used	13.50	25	40	70	140	325	500	1,500
			Unused OG	25	35	50	62.50	80	140	240	—
			Mint NH	50	77.50	120	160	210	475	1,200	2,250
444 Pair	2¢	carmine type I	Used	55	85	125	200	375	750	1,150	—
			Unused OG	57.50	80	120	150	225	325	625	—
			Mint NH	105	165	250	340	500	1,050	2,600	—
444 LP	2¢	carmine type I	Used	100	135	210	400	1,000	2,000	—	—
			Unused OG	150	220	300	375	500	825	1,250	2,000
			Mint NH	280	425	650	850	1,500	2,750	4,500	—
444a Sgl.	2¢	lake	Used	1,100	1,500	2,000					

SCT#	DENOM	COLOR	CONDITION	F 70	F-VF 75	VF 80	VF-XF 85	XF 90	XF-SUP 95	SUP 98	GEM 100
445 Sgl.	3¢	violet	Used	115	165	250	350	525	1,000	3,500	—
			Unused OG	100	150	210	290	375	525	1,000	1,750
			Mint NH	200	325	500	650	900	1,750	3,000	—
445 Pair	3¢	violet	Used	380	525	750	1,000	1,250	2,000	7,000	—
			Unused OG	250	345	500	650	825	1,100	1,750	3,500
			Mint NH	455	700	1,100	1,375	1,925	3,850	—	—
445 LP	3¢	violet	Used	1,400	2,000	2,750	3,750	4,750	9,500	—	—
			Unused OG	600	825	1,200	1,400	1,650	2,250	3,750	6,500
			Mint NH	1,100	1,650	2,600	3,250	4,250	9,500	13,500	—
446 Sgl.	4¢	brown	Used	65	90	150	200	300	650	1,200	—
			Unused OG	65	90	130	160	200	280	500	—
			Mint NH	110	185	280	350	500	1,250	2,250	4,500
446 Pair	4¢	brown	Used	165	250	425	550	800	1,500	—	—
			Unused OG	150	200	300	350	425	600	1,050	—
			Mint NH	260	425	650	825	1,100	3,000	4,750	10,000
446 LP	4¢	brown	Used	650	900	1,250	1,550	2,000	4,000	—	—
			Unused OG	350	490	700	825	950	1,300	2,100	—
			Mint NH	675	1,000	1,550	1,900	2,600	4,500	8,000	—
447 Sgl.	5¢	blue	Used	50	75	110	160	250	575	—	—
			Unused OG	22.50	35	45	55	70	110	225	—
			Mint NH	40	62.50	100	125	175	350	750	1,500
447 Pair	5¢	blue	Used	160	250	375	525	900	1,750	3,500	—
			Unused OG	50	75	105	130	175	275	500	—
			Mint NH	95	140	220	300	425	800	1,650	3,000
447 LP	5¢	blue	Used	500	700	950	1,225	1,600	3,500	7,500	14,000
			Unused OG	120	165	240	275	315	440	700	—
			Mint NH	250	365	525	675	900	1,650	3,000	6,750
448 Sgl.	1¢	green	Used	5.75	11	17.50	47.50	100	210	425	1,150
			Unused OG	6	8.50	12.50	15	20	32.50	52.50	—
			Mint NH	9.50	15	25	37.50	62.50	175	425	950
448 Pair	1¢	green	Used	20	32.50	50	130	250	525	1,100	—
			Unused OG	15	20	30	37.50	55	80	130	—
			Mint NH	27.50	42.50	65	100	150	400	1,150	3,000
448 LP	1¢	green	Used	87.50	165	250	375	700	1,100	—	—
			Unused OG	40	60	80	105	145	200	325	—
			Mint NH	78	115	170	350	750	2,000	—	—
449 Sgl.	2¢	red type I	Used	325	475	650	825	1,050	1,850	3,750	—
			Unused OG	1,350	1,825	2,500	2,900	3,500	5,500	8,500	—
			Mint NH	2,750	3,750	5,500	6,500	8,250	13,000	—	—
449 Pair	2¢	red type I	Used	4,200	6,100	8,000	9,250	11,500	—	—	—
			Unused OG	3,400	4,500	6,000	6,750	8,250	—	—	—
			Mint NH	7,000	10,000	12,500	14,500	18,500	—	—	—
449 LP	2¢	red type I	Used	15,000	19,000	25,000	32,500	—	—	—	—
			Unused OG	7,250	10,000	13,500	15,000	17,750	—	—	—
			Mint NH	12,500	19,500	28,000	32,500	40,000	55,000	—	—
450 Sgl.	2¢	carmine type III	Used	7.50	15	25	57.50	100	210	375	1,050
			Unused OG	6	8.50	12.50	16	22	35	55	—
			Mint NH	10.50	16.50	27.50	45	125	400	1,100	—
450 Pair	2¢	carmine type III	Used	17.50	39	70	150	300	625	925	—
			Unused OG	15	21	30	40	52.50	80	125	—
			Mint NH	22.50	42.50	65	105	275	950	3,000	—
450 LP	2¢	carmine type III	Used	165	215	300	450	750	1,350	—	—
			Unused OG	115	160	240	360	550	1,050	—	—
			Mint NH	190	380	550	1,650	2,500	—	—	—
452 Sgl.	1¢	green	Used	5.25	11.50	17.50	45	90	240	500	—
			Unused OG	7.25	10	15	18	22.20	30	55	—
			Mint NH	11.50	19	30	40	65	140	290	550
452 Pair	1¢	green	Used	18.50	37.50	55	125	250	525	—	—
			Unused OG	17.50	23.50	35	42.50	52.50	67.50	125	—
			Mint NH	26	42.50	65	85	140	300	650	1,150
452 LP	1¢	green	Used	80	135	200	375	625	975	—	—
			Unused OG	40	60	90	110	135	175	225	—
			Mint NH	75	120	190	220	300	525	1,050	2,250
453 Sgl.	2¢	carmine rose type I	Used	22.50	30	45	90	190	400	700	—
			Unused OG	70	92.50	140	170	205	325	500	—
			Mint NH	130	195	300	390	600	1,100	2,250	—

SCT#	DENOM	COLOR	CONDITION	F 70	F-VF 75	VF 80	VF-XF 85	XF 90	XF-SUP 95	SUP 98	GEM 100
453 Pair	2¢	carmine rose type I	Used	50	90	140	225	425	900	1,600	—
			Unused OG	150	205	300	375	450	700	1,050	—
			Mint NH	270	410	625	825	1,700	2,600	4,750	—
453 LP	2¢	carmine rose type I	Used	250	400	600	850	1,250	2,500	—	—
			Unused OG	350	500	675	825	1,025	1,400	2,100	—
			Mint NH	625	975	1,450	2,000	4,000	5,500	—	—
454 Sgl.	2¢	red type II	Used	11.25	16	22.50	45	100	425	750	—
			Unused OG	35	47.50	70	80	92.50	130	225	—
			Mint NH	57.50	95	160	190	240	700	1,000	1,900
454 Pair	2¢	red type II	Used	27.50	45	70	120	225	525	—	—
			Unused OG	82.50	110	165	190	205	290	500	—
			Mint NH	140	230	360	425	550	1,500	2,100	—
454 LP	2¢	red type II	Used	300	400	600	800	1,150	2,250	—	—
			Unused OG	210	275	400	460	550	700	1,050	—
			Mint NH	425	575	850	1,050	1,500	2,500	—	—
455 Sgl.	2¢	carmine type III	Used	1.60	2.50	3.50	15	30	90	240	—
			Unused OG	4	5.50	8	12.50	25	40	60	—
			Mint NH	7	11.50	18	22.50	30	70	225	—
455 Pair	2¢	carmine type III	Used	13.50	19	27.50	75	250	500	—	—
			Unused OG	10	13	20	26.50	55	90	135	—
			Mint NH	17.50	26	42.50	50	70	150	450	—
455 LP	2¢	carmine type III	Used	92.50	135	200	325	700	1,050	—	—
			Unused OG	24	35	47.50	650	95	150	—	—
			Mint NH	47.50	72.50	105	150	230	500	1,650	—
456 Sgl.	3¢	violet type I	Used	80	120	170	240	360	900	1,500	—
			Unused OG	130	165	250	275	325	475	775	—
			Mint NH	220	360	550	600	750	1,650	3,250	7,000
456 Pair	3¢	violet type I	Used	325	440	650	775	1,100	2,650	4,000	—
			Unused OG	290	375	575	650	750	1,050	1,700	—
			Mint NH	500	750	1,200	1,400	1,800	3,500	6,750	—
456 LP	3¢	violet type I	Used	1,500	2,000	3,000	3,250	4,000	8,500	—	—
			Unused OG	675	900	1,300	1,400	1,550	2,000	3,250	—
			Mint NH	1,250	1,725	2,700	3,200	4,000	8,000	—	—
457 Sgl.	4¢	brown	Used	15	20	30	50	90	225	500	—
			Unused OG	14.50	21	30	35	42.50	60	90	—
			Mint NH	23	40	60	77.50	97.50	250	550	950
457 Pair	4¢	brown	Used	47.50	70	95	155	250	575	1,050	—
			Unused OG	35	49.50	70	80	95	125	190	—
			Mint NH	64.50	100	150	175	230	575	1,250	—
457 LP	4¢	brown	Used	130	180	275	400	750	1,100	2,000	—
			Unused OG	100	125	190	210	240	375	500	—
			Mint NH	190	250	390	475	600	1,200	3,250	—
458 Sgl.	5¢	blue	Used	14	20	30	55	95	240	400	—
			Unused OG	16	22	32.50	40	50	65	100	150
			Mint NH	25	42.50	65	85	130	260	525	900
458 Pair	5¢	blue	Used	45	65	95	170	300	600	1,250	—
			Unused OG	35	50	75	90	110	150	240	400
			Mint NH	67.50	100	160	190	425	675	1,200	—
458 LP	5¢	blue	Used	120	165	250	350	650	1,750	—	—
			Unused OG	90	120	180	200	225	310	475	—
			Mint NH	175	240	375	450	575	1,125	1,850	—
459 Sgl.	2¢	carmine type I	Used	750	1,000	1,300	1,500	1,750	2,250	—	—
			Unused OG	140	180	275	300	340	400	—	—
			Mint NH	220	260	400	425	460	500	600	850
459 Pair	2¢	carmine type I	Used	1,750	2,250	3,500	3,500	4,000	5,500	—	—
			Unused OG	300	400	600	650	725	825	—	—
			Mint NH	325	450	875	900	950	1,000	1,100	—
459 LP	2¢	carmine type I with crease	Unused OG	375	500	700	725	750	800	875	—
			Mint NH	550	825	1,200	1,250	1,325	1,400	1,550	—
		carmine type I type I without crease	Used	—	—	50,000					
			Unused OG	550	850	1,200	1,250	1,325	1,400	1,600	—
			Mint NH	725	1,375	2,000	2,100	2,250	2,500	4,250	—
460	$1	violet black	Used	70	90	140	185	280	800	2,000	—
			Unused OG	325	425	650	725	900	1,800	2,750	—
			Mint NH	650	925	1,450	1,750	2,250	5,250	12,500	—
461	2¢	pale carmine carmine red type I	Used	200	290	375	500	1,100	1,750	—	—
			Unused OG	80	105	160	190	230	350	925	—
			Mint NH	140	205	330	450	750	2,000	5,750	—

1916-22 WASHINGTON-FRANKLIN ISSUE (UNWATERMARKED)

SCT#	DENOM	COLOR	CONDITION	F 70	F-VF 75	VF 80	VF-XF 85	XF 90	XF-SUP 95	SUP 98	GEM 100
462	1¢	green	Used	0.25	0.25	0.35	8	22.50	85	325	950
			Unused OG	3.50	4.75	7	9	12.50	32.50	85	—
			Mint NH	6.50	10	16	27.50	45	200	850	1,800
462a Booklet Pane of 6	1¢	green	Used	7.50	10	12.50	16.50	22.50	60	—	—
			Unused OG	5	7	9.50	12	15	30	—	—
			Mint NH	8.50	11.75	16	20	27.50	60	—	—
463	2¢	carmine type I	Used	0.25	0.30	0.40	9	22.50	75	300	950
			Unused OG	2.20	3	4.50	11	17.50	35	72.50	—
			Mint NH	4	6.25	10	20	35	160	600	1,450
463a Booklet Pane of 6	2¢	carmine type I	Used	57.50	80	110	130	160	325	—	—
			Unused OG	57.50	80	110	125	150	240	—	—
			Mint NH	85	120	180	210	250	450	—	—
464	3¢	violet type I	Used	8.25	12	17.50	30	72.50	225	675	—
			Unused OG	32.50	50	65	80	100	180	425	—
			Mint NH	65	110	165	210	310	1,100	3,750	—
465	4¢	orange brown	Used	1.15	1.60	2.25	8	27.50	125	375	—
			Unused OG	30	40	60	75	90	150	325	550
			Mint NH	50	77.50	125	160	225	675	2,000	4,750
466	5¢	blue	Used	1.15	1.60	2.25	8	30	125	375	—
			Unused OG	32.50	45	65	80	100	145	410	725
			Mint NH	60	100	150	240	550	1,250	4,500	—
467	5¢	carmine	Used	1,500	2,150	3,250	3,600	4,250	8,500	—	—
			Unused OG	190	290	425	475	675	950	—	—
			Mint NH	290	525	800	1,025	1,400	4,250	10,500	25,000
467 Block of 9	5¢	carmine	Used	2,350	3,000	3,750	4,200	5,000	—	—	—
			Unused OG	325	600	900	1,000	1,125	1,600	—	—
			Mint NH	825	1,150	1,550	1,850	2,350	5,350	—	—
467 Block of 12	5¢	carmine	Used	3,000	3,900	5,250	5,750	8,500	—	—	—
			Unused OG	975	1,300	1,750	1,900	2,250	3,500	—	—
			Mint NH	1,500	2,000	2,900	3,250	4,250	12,000	—	—
468	6¢	red orange	Used	4	5.50	8	16	55	200	600	—
			Unused OG	50	70	100	120	150	240	525	—
			Mint NH	90	145	225	325	500	1,150	3,750	—
469	7¢	black	Used	6	9	13	22.50	65	225	675	—
			Unused OG	60	82.50	120	150	190	360	750	1,150
			Mint NH	105	165	270	375	525	1,450	4,000	—
470	8¢	olive green	Used	3.50	5	7	15	47.50	160	550	—
			Unused OG	40	55	80	100	130	250	500	850
			Mint NH	65	105	165	220	340	1,150	2,900	—
471	9¢	salmon red	Used	8.75	12.25	17.50	32.50	90	300	925	—
			Unused OG	45	60	90	115	140	185	400	—
			Mint NH	80	120	190	240	325	950	2,300	4,000
472	10¢	orange yellow	Used	1.50	2.10	3	15	40	145	450	—
			Unused OG	60	81	120	140	175	250	600	1,100
			Mint NH	100	160	250	325	450	1,250	4,750	10,000
473	11¢	dark green	Used	9.50	13.50	19	32.50	77.50	225	725	2,000
			Unused OG	25	35	50	57.50	72.50	125	260	—
			Mint NH	39.50	73.50	110	130	210	675	2,000	4,750
474	12¢	claret brown	Used	4	5.75	8	15	47.50	200	900	1,400
			Unused OG	27.50	37.50	55	67.50	95	160	350	—
			Mint NH	50	75	120	200	325	1,300	3,250	—
475	15¢	gray	Used	8	10.50	15	27.50	65	200	650	—
			Unused OG	85	115	170	220	325	475	875	1,500
			Mint NH	155	240	375	525	800	2,000	7,000	—
476	20¢	ultramarine	Used	8.75	12.25	17.50	30	65	190	625	—
			Unused OG	120	160	240	260	325	550	1,100	—
			Mint NH	200	325	500	625	1,250	2,900	7,000	—

SCT#	DENOM	COLOR	CONDITION	F 70	F-VF 75	VF 80	VF-XF 85	XF 90	XF-SUP 95	SUP 98	GEM 100
476A	30¢	orange red	Unused OG	2,000	3,250	5,750					
			Mint NH	4,250	6,750	8,500					
477	50¢	light violet	Used	40	55	80	125	210	550	1,650	
			Unused OG	425	600	850	975	1,125	1,500	3,000	—
			Mint NH	900	1,300	2,000	2,400	3,150	7,000	16,500	—
478	$1	violet black	Used	14	20	27.50	42.50	105	240	875	1,900
			Unused OG	300	415	600	675	775	1,075	2,150	—
			Mint NH	575	900	1,400	1,750	2,150	5,250	15,000	—
479	$2	dark blue	Used	21	28	40	57.50	95	325	850	—
			Unused OG	105	150	210	240	275	400	625	—
			Mint NH	180	310	475	600	800	1,400	2,750	6,750
480	$5	light green	Used	17.50	25	35	55	110	275	1,000	—
			Unused OG	85	115	170	190	215	265	475	—
			Mint NH	160	260	375	450	600	1,150	2,500	—
481	1¢	green	Used	0.45	0.75	0.95	1.75	5	9	35	75
			Unused OG	0.55	0.85	1.25	2.65	6.50	15	20	35
			Mint NH	0.75	1.25	1.90	6	12.50	25	35	65
482	2¢	carmine type I	Used	0.60	0.95	1.30	2.25	5.50	11	42.50	85
			Unused OG	0.75	1.05	1.50	7.50	11.50	15	20	35
			Mint NH	1.05	1.70	2.60	7	13.50	25	35	65
482A	2¢	deep rose type Ia	Used	40,000	47,500	55,000	80,000	110,000	—	—	
482A Pair	2¢	deep rose type Ia	Used	One known, VG grade, value $140,000.							
483	3¢	violet type I	Used	5	7.25	10	12.50	19	40	100	—
			Unused OG	5.75	8	12	14.50	18	27.50	37.50	—
			Mint NH	9	16	24	26	30	47.50	60	—
484	3¢	violet type II	Used	4	6	8	10	18	42.50	100	150
			Unused OG	5	7.25	10	12.50	16	25	35	—
			Mint NH	7.75	12.75	20	23	27.50	45	57.50	95
485	5¢	carmine	Unused OG	5,250	7,250	10,000	10,500	11,000	—	—	—
			Mint NH	5,750	9,500	14,000	14,750	15,750	17,500	22,500	30,000
485 Block of 9	5¢	carmine	Unused OG	10,500	13,500	17,500	18,500	20,000	21,500	24,000	—
			Mint NH	13,250	17,000	23,500	24,500	26,000	28,500	32,500	—
485 Block of 12	5¢	carmine	Unused OG	15,500	22,000	26,000	27,500	29,000	33,000	37,000	—
			Mint NH	20,000	27,500	33,500	35,000	37,000	40,000	47,500	—
486 Sgl.	1¢	green	Used	0.45	0.65	0.85	9	15	40	125	240
			Unused OG	0.45	0.55	0.85	2	5	20	40	—
			Mint NH	0.75	1.15	1.75	3.50	10	42.50	100	200
486 Pair	1¢	green	Used	1.40	1.85	2.50	27.50	45	125	350	—
			Unused OG	1	1.45	2	4.50	12.50	42.50	85	—
			Mint NH	1.80	2.90	4.25	8	30	120	240	450
486 LP	1¢	green	Used	7.50	10	15	32.50	85	200	350	—
			Unused OG	2.30	3.30	4.50	6.25	9	20	40	—
			Mint NH	4.50	6.50	9.50	17.50	45	130	300	—
487 Sgl.	2¢	carmine type II	Used	5.50	9.50	14	25	47.50	175	—	—
			Unused OG	6.25	8.25	12.50	15	22.50	35	70	—
			Mint NH	11	18	27.50	35	50	140	400	800
487 Pair	2¢	carmine type II	Used	17.50	25	37.50	70	130	425	—	—
			Unused OG	15	20	30	35	50	77.50	150	—
			Mint NH	26	42.50	65	85	120	290	850	1,650
487 LP	2¢	carmine type II	Used	50	95	140	260	650	1,150	—	—
			Unused OG	55	85	120	140	180	230	525	—
			Mint NH	125	175	275	385	525	1,500	2,100	—
488 Sgl.	2¢	carmine type III	Used	2.40	3.40	5	12.50	32.50	95	240	—
			Unused OG	1.50	2	3	6	12.50	30	65	—
			Mint NH	2.60	4.25	6.50	15	35	75	300	850
488 Pair	2¢	carmine type III	Used	8.50	11.50	17.50	35	95	240	600	—
			Unused OG	4	5.25	8	15	27.50	65	140	—
			Mint NH	7	11.50	17.50	35	75	175	750	—
488 LP	2¢	carmine type III	Used	62.50	87.50	110	225	450	900	—	—
			Unused OG	20	27.50	40	62.50	90	125	275	—
			Mint NH	30	60	90	150	240	550	950	—
489 Sgl.	3¢	violet type I	Used	1.10	1.50	2.25	5	19	65	150	—
			Unused OG	2.20	3	4.50	8	14	20	35	65
			Mint NH	4	6.50	10	15	25	60	160	350

SCT#	DENOM	COLOR	CONDITION	F 70	F-VF 75	VF 80	VF-XF 85	XF 90	XF-SUP 95	SUP 98	GEM 100
489 Pair	3¢	violet type I	Used	4.50	6	9	17.50	60	225	575	—
			Unused OG	5.25	7	10.50	17.50	32.50	45	75	—
			Mint NH	9	14	22.50	35	60	145	400	750
489 LP	3¢	violet type I	Used	19	30	40	70	300	850	—	—
			Unused OG	17	22	32.50	45	60	90	175	—
			Mint NH	32.50	45	70	120	250	950	—	—
490 Sgl.	1¢	green	Used	0.30	0.50	0.60	2.40	15	60	120	325
			Unused OG	0.25	0.35	0.50	3	12.50	25	40	80
			Mint NH	0.45	0.70	1.05	12.50	25	45	130	325
490 Pair	1¢	green	Used	1.35	1.50	2.25	6.75	35	130	260	—
			Unused OG	0.65	0.80	1.25	6.50	27.50	55	85	—
			Mint NH	1.05	1.75	2.60	27.50	30	125	425	—
490 LP	1¢	green	Used	4	8.25	12.50	50	140	325	—	—
			Unused OG	1.60	2.40	3.25	8	16	35	70	—
			Mint NH	3.25	5	7	12.50	35	175	500	—
491 Sgl.	2¢	carmine type II	Used	475	650	800	875	1,000	1,400	2,350	—
			Unused OG	1,250	1,925	2,500	3,000	3,500	4,250	6,000	—
			Mint NH	2,650	3,800	5,250	11,500	22,500	—	—	—
491 Pair	2¢	carmine type II	Used	2,000	2,750	3,750	4,500	6,000	9,500	—	—
			Unused OG	2,900	4,600	5,750	6,700	8,000	11,000	16,000	—
			Mint NH	7,200	9,500	12,500	18,500	45,000	—	—	—
491 LP	2¢	carmine type II	Used	9,250	14,000	17,500	27,500	—	—	—	—
			Unused OG	6,750	9,250	13,000	14,500	17,000	22,000	—	—
			Mint NH	13,000	19,000	26,000	35,000	—	—	—	—
492 Sgl.	2¢	carmine type III	Used	0.50	0.70	1	5	22.50	75	145	—
			Unused OG	4.50	6	9	11	14	25	47.50	—
			Mint NH	7.75	12	19	26	37.50	100	375	600
492 Pair	2¢	carmine type III	Used	2.25	3.50	5	20	70	175	300	—
			Unused OG	10.50	14.50	21.50	25	35	60	110	—
			Mint NH	18	30	45	55	85	225	800	1,250
492 LP	2¢	carmine type III	Used	17.50	25	35	80	180	400	—	—
			Unused OG	30	37.50	55	65	80	110	210	—
			Mint NH	57.50	75	115	140	350	950	—	—
493 Sgl.	3¢	violet type I	Used	2.25	3.20	4.50	12.50	42.50	120	325	—
			Unused OG	7	9.25	14	17	21	32.50	60	95
			Mint NH	12.50	19	30	40	55	140	300	—
493 Pair	3¢	violet type I	Used	6.25	8	12.50	32.50	115	275	700	—
			Unused OG	17.50	24	35	40	47.50	72.50	130	—
			Mint NH	32.50	45	75	100	120	310	625	1,200
493 LP	3¢	violet type I	Used	32.50	62.50	90	160	400	925	—	—
			Unused OG	55	80	110	125	140	200	350	—
			Mint NH	105	140	230	290	400	900	2,000	—
494 Sgl.	3¢	violet type II	Used	1.25	1.90	2.50	10	35	110	450	—
			Unused OG	5	6.50	10	12	16	27.50	55	—
			Mint NH	9	13.50	21.50	29	40	105	210	600
494 Pair	3¢	violet type II	Used	4.50	6.25	9	22.50	75	250	950	—
			Unused OG	12	16	24	32.50	42.50	70	135	—
			Mint NH	22.50	35	50	67.50	90	250	750	—
494 LP	3¢	violet type II	Used	22.50	35	50	100	275	—	—	—
			Unused OG	40	50	75	90	120	180	325	—
			Mint NH	75	105	160	240	450	1,200	—	—
495 Sgl.	4¢	orange brown	Used	3.50	4.90	7	25	80	160	450	—
			Unused OG	5	6.50	10	12	15	25	50	—
			Mint NH	9	13.50	21.50	29	42.50	100	350	700
495 Pair	4¢	orange brown	Used	10	15	20	60	200	425	975	—
			Unused OG	12	16	24	30	37.50	60	110	—
			Mint NH	22.50	32.50	50	70	100	225	750	1,500
495 LP	4¢	orange brown	Used	22.50	32.50	45	75	180	375	750	—
			Unused OG	37.50	55	75	90	110	170	325	—
			Mint NH	75	105	160	225	325	700	1,500	—
496 Sgl.	5¢	blue	Used	1.25	1.70	2.50	12.50	35	190	475	—
			Unused OG	1.60	2.20	3.25	7	14	26	50	—
			Mint NH	3	4.50	7	11	20	45	140	325
496 Pair	5¢	blue	Used	3.90	5.50	10	40	85	260	500	1,000
			Unused OG	4	5.25	8	17.50	32.50	60	110	—
			Mint NH	6	11	17.50	27.50	55	130	300	700

SCT#	DENOM	COLOR	CONDITION	F 70	F-VF 75	VF 80	VF-XF 85	XF 90	XF-SUP 95	SUP 98	GEM 100
496 LP	5¢	blue	Used	11	15	22.50	37.50	115	350	525	—
			Unused OG	17.50	21.50	30	37.50	47.50	60	115	180
			Mint NH	30	40	65	90	135	275	675	1,700
497 Sgl.	10¢	orange yellow	Used	8.25	11.50	17.50	35	95	225	525	—
			Unused OG	8.25	12	17.50	20	27.50	40	65	—
			Mint NH	13	23.50	35	42.50	60	115	300	675
497 Pair	10¢	orange yellow	Used	27.50	40	57.50	100	250	525	1,250	—
			Unused OG	20	27.50	40	45	62.50	90	150	—
			Mint NH	35	57.50	85	105	150	275	650	1,400
497 LP	10¢	orange yellow	Used	80	150	200	290	475	725	1,550	—
			Unused OG	5	92.50	120	130	145	160	260	—
			Mint NH	120	185	260	300	375	625	950	2,000

1917-19 WASHINGTON-FRANKLIN ISSUE (PERF. 11)

SCT#	DENOM	COLOR	CONDITION	F 70	F-VF 75	VF 80	VF-XF 85	XF 90	XF-SUP 95	SUP 98	GEM 100
498	1¢	green	Used	0.25	0.25	0.25	8	17.50	70	180	425
			Unused OG	0.25	0.35	0.50	1.75	8	17.50	30	—
			Mint NH	0.45	0.65	1	4	15	70	200	525
498e Booklet Pane of 6	1¢	green	Used	1.10	1.50	2	2.50	3.50	12.50	—	—
			Unused OG	1.40	1.90	2.50	4	6.50	11	—	—
			Mint NH	2.10	3	4.25	6.50	10.75	30	—	—
498f Booklet Pane of 30	1¢	green	Used			12,500					
			Unused OG	650	825	1,050	1,175	1,450	2,000	—	—
			Mint NH	850	1,225	1,700	2,000	2,500	3,750	12,500	—
499	2¢	rose type I	Used	0.25	0.25	0.25	8	17.50	70	190	—
			Unused OG	0.35	0.35	0.50	1.75	8	17.50	30	—
			Mint NH	0.45	0.65	1	4	15	70	200	525
499e Booklet Pane of 6	2¢	rose type I	Used	1.50	1.90	2.50	3.75	6	17.50	—	—
			Unused OG	2.20	3	4	5.75	8	17.50	—	—
			Mint NH	3.10	4.50	6.75	10	15	40	—	—
499f Booklet Pane of 30	2¢	rose type I	Unused OG	12,750	16,750	20,000	—	—	—		
			Mint NH	21,000	23,000	28,000	—	—			
499h	2¢	lake type I	Used	480	600	800	1,000	1,250	—	—	
			Unused OG	275	375	500	625	825	1,600	—	
			Mint NH	460	650	1,000	1,300	1,900	—	—	
500	2¢	deep rose type Ia	Used	140	180	240	275	425	1,100	2,650	—
			Unused OG	130	175	260	290	350	550	1,000	—
			Mint NH	260	380	575	725	1,100	2,350	5,250	10,000
501	3¢	light violet type I	Used	0.25	0.30	0.40	9	20	75	225	650
			Unused OG	4.50	6	9	11.50	16	32.50	70	—
			Mint NH	8.50	12.50	20	35	55	145	475	—
501b Booklet Pane of 6	3¢	light violet type I	Used	50	62.50	80	95	125	175	—	—
			Unused OG	40	55	75	85	110	220	—	—
			Mint NH	67.50	95	125	160	210	425	—	—
502	3¢	dark violet type II	Used	0.35	0.50	0.75	9	22.50	95	300	—
			Unused OG	6	8	12	15	20	42.50	90	—
			Mint NH	12	18.50	27.50	42.50	70	275	1,050	2,000
502b Booklet Pane of 6	3¢	dark violet type II	Used	45	57.50	75	85	100	190	—	—
			Unused OG	35	45	60	72.50	85	160	—	—
			Mint NH	52.50	72.50	100	120	150	300	—	—
503	4¢	brown	Used	0.25	0.30	0.40	8	20	80	270	775
			Unused OG	4.25	6	8.50	10.25	13.50	27.50	65	120
			Mint NH	8.50	12.50	19	30	47.50	190	650	1,200
504	5¢	blue	Used	0.25	0.25	0.35	8	20	80	250	700
			Unused OG	3.75	4.90	7.50	9.50	12.50	25	55	125
			Mint NH	7.50	11	17	27.50	50	180	525	1,300
505	5¢	rose	Used	350	475	600	900	1,250	2,250	5,750	—
			Unused OG	170	235	325	360	450	600	950	—
			Mint NH	300	440	625	775	1,000	1,900	4,000	8,500

SCT#	DENOM	COLOR	CONDITION	F 70	F-VF 75	VF 80	VF-XF 85	XF 90	XF-SUP 95	SUP 98	GEM 100
505 Block of 9	5¢	rose	Used	650	875	1,100	1,300	1,650	—	—	—
			Unused OG	350	490	650	700	825	1,550	—	—
			Mint NH	625	750	1,000	1,100	1,250	2,750	—	—
505 Block of 12	5¢	rose	Used	1,900	2,400	3,000	3,500	4,000	—	—	
			Unused OG	750	925	1,200	1,350	1,500	2,100	—	
			Mint NH	1,075	1,400	1,850	2,000	2,250	3,250	—	
506	6¢	red orange	Used	0.25	0.30	0.40	8	20	80	270	—
			Unused OG	5.50	7.25	11	13	17.50	30	70	—
			Mint NH	11	16.50	25	35	50	165	600	1,300
507	7¢	black	Used	0.60	0.90	1.25	11	25	90	325	—
			Unused OG	12.25	16.50	24	30	40	85	160	325
			Mint NH	21	37.50	55	80	125	350	1,250	3,000
508	8¢	olive bister	Used	0.30	0.45	0.65	9	22.50	90	300	850
			Unused OG	5.50	7.25	11	13	17.50	30	80	160
			Mint NH	11	16.50	25	35	50	175	600	1,400
509	9¢	salmon red	Used	0.80	1.15	1.60	10	25	90	325	850
			Unused OG	5.50	7.25	11	14	20	40	85	—
			Mint NH	11	16.50	25	37.50	57.50	175	550	1,450
510	10¢	orange yellow	Used	0.25	0.25	0.25	8	17.50	75	260	700
			Unused OG	7.50	10	15	18	22.50	42.50	95	190
			Mint NH	13.50	21.50	34	52.50	150	425	825	—
510a	10¢	brown yellow	Unused OG	800	1,075	1,400	1,600	1,900	—		
			Mint NH	1,450	2,150	3,250	4,000	5,250	—		
511	11¢	light green	Used	1.15	1.60	2.25	8	27.50	90	325	800
			Unused OG	3.75	5.25	7.50	9	11	25	55	120
			Mint NH	7.50	11.25	17	30	45	150	450	1,150
512	12¢	claret brown	Used	0.30	0.40	0.50	9	22.50	85	270	—
			Unused OG	4.25	6	8.50	10.50	13.50	27.50	60	—
			Mint NH	8.50	12.50	19	30	50	135	475	2,000
512a	12¢	brown carmine	Used	0.25	0.40	0.50	9	22.50	85	270	—
			Unused OG	4.25	6	8.50	11	15	30	100	—
			Mint NH	8.50	12.50	19	30	50	135	475	1,500
512c	12¢	claret red	Used	0.25	0.40	0.50	9	22.50	85	270	—
			Unused OG	4.25	6	8.50	11	15	30	100	—
			Mint NH	8.50	12.50	19	30	50	135	475	1,500
513	13¢	apple green	Used	2.75	4	5.50	12.50	40	130	500	—
			Unused OG	4.50	6.75	9.50	11.50	15	35	70	130
			Mint NH	9.50	13.25	21	32.50	65	200	575	1,400
514	15¢	gray	Used	0.70	0.95	1.40	9.50	30	110	375	1,100
			Unused OG	16.50	22.50	32.50	40	55	100	215	375
			Mint NH	30	50	75	105	150	500	1,000	3,250
515	20¢	light ultramarine	Used	0.25	0.30	0.45	9	22.50	100	280	800
			Unused OG	20	27.50	40	50	65	130	245	450
			Mint NH	35	55	85	120	190	500	1,350	3,500
516	30¢	orange red	Used	0.75	1.10	1.50	9	25	95	325	—
			Unused OG	15	20	30	37.50	52.50	110	225	450
			Mint NH	27.50	47.50	70	100	140	450	1,000	1,800
517	50¢	red violet	Used	0.35	0.50	0.75	9	22.50	100	325	—
			Unused OG	25	32.50	50	60	72.50	125	275	500
			Mint NH	52.50	77.50	120	145	180	475	1,150	3,250
518	$1	violet brown	Used	0.75	1.15	1.50	10	25	110	340	—
			Unused OG	19	25	37.50	45	55	110	190	350
			Mint NH	35	60	95	110	150	525	1,500	4,500
518b	$1	deep brown	Used	900	1,100	1,800	2,250	3,000	5,750	—	
			Unused OG	1,500	2,000	2,900	3,500	4,250	7,000	—	
			Mint NH	3,000	4,000	6,500	7,500	8,750	16,500	—	
519	2¢	carmine	Used	1,100	1,400	1,800	2,200	2,750	4,750	—	—
			Unused OG	215	285	425	525	650	850	1,550	—
			Mint NH	425	600	900	1,300	1,850	3,500	8,000	—
523	$2	orange red & black	Used	120	170	240	300	425	850	1,750	—
			Unused OG	260	350	525	600	675	775	1,250	—
			Mint NH	500	775	1,175	1,400	1,750	3,000	7,250	10,500
524	$5	deep green & black	Used	22.50	27.50	40	57.50	85	180	400	—
			Unused OG	80	110	160	185	230	320	525	750
			Mint NH	145	210	340	400	500	975	2,450	7,000

1918-20 OFFSET ISSUES

SCT#	DENOM	COLOR	CONDITION	F 70	F-VF 75	VF 80	VF-XF 85	XF 90	XF-SUP 95	SUP 98	GEM 100
525	1¢	gray	Used	0.45	0.65	0.90	9	22.50	100	325	—
		green	Unused OG	1.20	1.70	2.50	8	15	30	45	90
			Mint NH	2.45	3.95	6	10	19	85	375	900
525a	1¢	dark	Used	0.85	1.25	1.75	10	25	100	325	—
		green	Unused OG	5	6.75	10	12.50	20	37.50	52.50	—
			Mint NH	8.25	15	25	35	50	140	575	—
526	2¢	carmine	Used	2	2.75	4	11	35	125	400	—
			Unused OG	12.50	16	25	30	42.50	100	250	—
			Mint NH	22.50	35	57.50	95	160	525	1,500	4,000
527	2¢	carmine	Used	0.60	0.85	1.25	9	25	90	300	800
		type V	Unused OG	9	12.50	18	22.50	28	45	90	—
			Mint NH	18	26	40	62.50	110	350	1,100	3,000
528	2¢	carmine	Used	0.25	0.25	0.40	8	17.50	75	250	700
		type Va	Unused OG	5	7	10	14	25	32.50	45	—
			Mint NH	10	15	22.50	30	55	190	550	—
528A	2¢	carmine	Used	1	1.40	2	10	30	95	300	—
		type VI	Unused OG	23.50	31.50	47.50	55	62.50	95	200	—
			Mint NH	42.50	72.50	115	160	240	825	2,250	—
528B	2¢	carmine	Used	0.35	0.50	0.75	9	22.50	95	300	850
		type VII	Unused OG	9.75	13.25	20	25	30	50	100	—
			Mint NH	18	32.50	50	72.50	125	400	1,250	3,500
529	3¢	violet	Used	0.25	0.30	0.50	9	17.50	75	250	675
		type III	Unused OG	1.70	2.35	3.50	7	17.50	30	45	90
			Mint NH	3	5	7.75	12.50	40	175	525	—
530	3¢	purple	Used	0.25	0.25	0.30	8	16	70	240	725
			Unused OG	1	1.20	2	5	15	25	40	100
			Mint NH	1.60	3	4.50	7.50	16	80	330	850
531	1¢	green	Used	4	7.50	12	15	20	50	125	325
			Unused OG	4.75	8.50	14	16	19	22.50	30	45
			Mint NH	6.50	11.75	21	22.50	27.50	50	85	160
532	2¢	carmine	Used	15.50	25.50	42.50	47.50	55	105	230	450
		rose	Unused OG	20	30	50	55	62.50	72.50	90	130
		type IV	Mint NH	25	47.50	80	95	130	150	260	425
533	2¢	carmine	Used	60	92.50	150	165	190	260	600	1,050
		type V	Unused OG	50	82.50	120	130	145	160	175	—
			Mint NH	75	115	200	215	240	280	450	725
534	2¢	carmine	Used	5.50	8.25	15	20	30	65	125	275
		type Va	Unused OG	7.25	10.50	16.50	19	24	30	45	80
			Mint NH	9.75	15	26.50	31	40	65	135	240
534A	2¢	carmine	Used	16	24	40	45	55	100	210	700
		type VI	Unused OG	22.50	30	52.50	57.50	62.50	72.50	90	—
			Mint NH	30	57.50	90	100	110	140	280	525
534B	2¢	carmine	Used	750	1,075	1,500	1,600	1,750	1,900	2,500	4,000
		type VII	Unused OG	1,125	1,700	2,500	2,650	2,800	3,000	3,400	—
			Mint NH	1,600	2,500	3,750	3,900	4,250	4,600	5,500	7,250
535	3¢	violet	Used	3	4.25	6	9.50	15	40	90	190
		type IV	Unused OG	4.40	7.25	11	13.50	16.50	26	37.50	55
			Mint NH	6.75	10.75	18	20	22.50	35	72.50	120
536	1¢	gray	Used	16.50	22.50	35	50	82.50	180	—	—
		green	Unused OG	8.75	12.50	20	24	30	45	90	—
			Mint NH	16	26	45	67.50	120	375	1,175	3,000

SCT#	DENOM	COLOR	CONDITION	F 70	F-VF 75	VF 80	VF-XF 85	XF 90	XF-SUP 95	SUP 98	GEM 100
1919-21 ISSUES											
537	3¢	violet	Used	1.60	2.10	3.25	11	30	100	240	—
			Unused OG	5	7	10	12	15	20	40	80
			Mint NH	8	13.25	20	27.50	35	105	400	850
537a	3¢	deep	Used	1,800	2,250	3,000	3,300	3,650	—	—	—
		red	Unused OG	1,300	1,500	2,250	2,650	3,000	3,300	—	—
		violet	Mint NH	2,400	3,200	4,250	4,500	5,000	—	—	—
537b	3¢	light	Used	25	37.50	50	75	140	280	500	—
		reddish	Unused OG	75	90	150	180	225	310	440	—
		violet	Mint NH	145	180	300	400	525	1,275	—	—
537c	3¢	red	Used	30	42.50	60	85	150	290	550	—
		violet	Unused OG	100	130	200	225	275	375	525	—
			Mint NH	185	250	400	500	625	1,350	—	—
538	1¢	green	Used	4.50	6	9	17.50	50	185	500	—
			Unused OG	5	6.25	10	12	16	25	50	—
			Mint NH	9.25	14.75	23	32.50	60	190	675	1,650
539	2¢	carmine	Used	16,000	21,500	30,000	40,000	—			
		rose	Unused OG	2,700	3,500	5,650	7,500	9,500	—	—	
		type II	Mint NH	4,250	7,000	11,000	14,500	18,500	—	—	
540	2¢	carmine	Used	4.75	6.75	9.50	20	55	200	550	—
		rose	Unused OG	6	7.75	12	14	17.50	30	55	—
		type III	Mint NH	11	18.50	27.50	37.50	70	260	925	—
541	3¢	violet	Used	18.50	25	37.50	60	150	400	1,250	—
		type II	Unused OG	20	27.50	40	47.50	60	92.50	180	—
			Mint NH	37.50	65	100	145	220	750	2,350	—
542	1¢	green	Used	0.70	1	1.50	10	25	90	275	—
			Unused OG	6.75	8.50	12.50	16	22.50	32.50	62.50	—
			Mint NH	11	20	30	47.50	72.50	260	1,000	—
543	1¢	green	Used	0.25	0.25	0.40	8	19	72.50	200	550
			Unused OG	0.35	0.45	0.70	1.25	3	7.50	15	—
			Mint NH	0.60	1.20	1.75	10	30	90	325	750
544	1¢	green	Used	3,500	4,750	6,500	7,750	11,000	18,000	—	
			Unused OG	22,500	31,000	40,000	—	—	—	—	
			Mint NH	40,000	60,000	87,500	100,000	—	—	—	
545	1¢	green	Used	100	140	200	260	380	950	2,250	—
			Unused OG	115	150	225	275	325	450	800	—
			Mint NH	190	340	550	675	925	2,250	8,500	—
546	2¢	carmine	Used	95	125	190	230	350	900	2,150	—
		rose	Unused OG	45	70	105	125	155	300	500	—
		type III	Mint NH	82.50	150	230	310	525	1,500	5,250	—
547	$2	carmine	Used	20	27.50	40	57.50	97.50	190	375	875
		& black	Unused OG	62.50	85	125	140	170	310	475	—
			Mint NH	90	160	275	325	450	725	2,400	5,650
547a	$2	lake	Used	20	27.50	40	57.50	97.50	190	375	—
		& black	Unused OG	100	140	200	235	285	375	650	—
			Mint NH	150	285	425	525	725	1,750	3,750	—
548	1¢	green	Used	1	1.35	2	14	32.50	95	325	800
			Unused OG	1.90	2.75	4	8	15	27.50	47.50	—
			Mint NH	3.50	6.25	10	14	30	140	475	—
549	2¢	carmine	Used	0.80	1.10	1.60	13.50	27.50	95	375	—
		rose	Unused OG	2.75	3.75	5.50	9	17.50	30	55	—
			Mint NH	4.75	9	14	25	50	175	625	3,000
550	5¢	deep	Used	6.75	9	12.50	27.50	60	200	625	—
		blue	Unused OG	16.50	21.50	32.50	37.50	45	90	150	400
			Mint NH	25	45	70	105	170	450	1,500	4,500

SCT#	DENOM	COLOR	CONDITION	F 70	F-VF 75	VF 80	VF-XF 85	XF 90	XF-SUP 95	SUP 98	GEM 100
**1922-25 REGULAR ISSUE**										
551	½¢	olive	Used	0.25	0.25	0.25	8	20	95	200	425
		brown	Unused OG	0.25	0.25	0.25	2	8	15	25	—
			Mint NH	0.25	0.30	0.50	2	10	40	140	425
552	1¢	deep	Used	0.25	0.25	0.25	8	20	70	200	
		green	Unused OG	0.60	0.90	1.25	1.65	3.50	10	25	60
			Mint NH	1.10	1.85	2.75	6.50	14	55	230	700
552a Booklet Pane of 6	1¢	deep green	Used	2.30	3	4	5	6	15	—	—
			Unused OG	4.40	5.75	7.50	9.50	12.50	22.50	—	—
			Mint NH	6.50	9	12.50	16	22.50	675	—	—
553	1½¢	yellow	Used	0.25	0.25	0.25	8	17.50	70	200	
		brown	Unused OG	1	1.40	2	2.65	7	17.50	45	—
			Mint NH	1.80	2.90	4.10	8	20	80	325	650
554	2¢	carmine	Used	0.25	0.25	0.25	8	20	70	200	375
			Unused OG	0.50	0.75	1.10	1.75	3	12.50	25	—
			Mint NH	1	1.65	2.50	6	15	55	225	575
554c Booklet Pane of 6	2¢	carmine	Used	1.75	2.25	3	3.60	4.50	12	—	—
			Unused OG	4.15	5.50	7	9.25	12.50	25	—	—
			Mint NH	7	9.25	12	16	24	70	—	—
555	3¢	violet	Used	0.60	0.85	1.20	9	22.50	87.50	290	550
			Unused OG	6	8.75	13	16.50	21	35	80	—
			Mint NH	11	18.50	27.50	40	70	260	750	1,500
556	4¢	yellow	Used	0.25	0.35	0.50	9	17.50	67.50	215	—
		brown	Unused OG	8	11	16	20	25	45	105	—
			Mint NH	14	22.50	35	55	77.50	275	900	2,000
557	5¢	dark	Used	0.25	0.25	0.30	8	20	70	225	—
		blue	Unused OG	8	11	16	20	26.50	45	100	—
			Mint NH	14	22.50	35	55	85	275	11,500	—
558	6¢	red	Used	0.50	0.70	1	10	22.50	85	275	—
		orange	Unused OG	13	20	30	35	42.50	65	150	—
			Mint NH	22.50	42.50	65	85	125	300	1,400	2,500
559	7¢	black	Used	0.35	0.50	0.75	11	20	80	240	—
			Unused OG	3.75	5.25	7.25	9	11	20	45	—
			Mint NH	6.25	10.25	15.50	25	45	100	375	800
560	8¢	olive	Used	0.50	0.70	1	9	22.50	85	275	—
		green	Unused OG	19	25	37.50	45	57.50	75	200	—
			Mint NH	30	50	80	100	150	425	1,250	2,250
561	9¢	rose	Used	0.65	0.90	1.25	11	24	90	300	—
			Unused OG	5.50	7.25	11	13.50	16	27.50	55	100
			Mint NH	9.50	16	25	35	70	175	550	—
562	10¢	orange	Used	0.25	0.25	0.35	9	19	70	210	—
			Unused OG	6.75	9.50	13.50	16	20	37.50	90	—
			Mint NH	12	20	30	42.50	75	225	950	1,850
563	11¢	light	Used	0.25	0.40	0.60	10	17.50	70	225	500
		blue	Unused OG	0.65	0.85	1.25	1.95	4.15	10	17.50	—
			Mint NH	1	1.80	2.75	5.50	20	65	240	750
563a	11¢	light	Used	0.25	0.40	0.60	10	17.50	70	225	—
		bluish	Unused OG	0.65	0.85	1.25	1.95	4.15	10	17.50	—
		green	Mint NH	1	1.80	2.75	5.50	16	55	220	450
564	12¢	brown	Used	0.25	0.25	0.35	9	17.50	67.50	200	—
		violet	Unused OG	2.35	3.40	4.75	6.50	10	17.50	32.50	75
			Mint NH	4.40	6.75	10.50	16	27.50	80	275	575
565	14¢	blue	Used	0.45	0.65	0.90	10	20	85	275	—
			Unused OG	2.15	2.90	4.25	6	9	14	32.50	70
			Mint NH	3.85	6	9.50	15	30	85	350	575
566	15¢	gray	Used	0.25	0.25	0.30	9	17.50	65	210	425
			Unused OG	8	10.50	16	20	25	45	95	150
			Mint NH	14	22.50	35	47.50	72.50	180	650	1,350

SCT#	DENOM	COLOR	CONDITION	F 70	F-VF 75	VF 80	VF-XF 85	XF 90	XF-SUP 95	SUP 98	GEM 100
567	20¢	carmine	Used	0.25	0.25	0.30	9	17.50	70	220	—
		rose	Unused OG	8	10.50	16	19	24	47.50	97.50	170
			Mint NH	14	22.50	35	47.50	80	190	825	1,700
568	25¢	yellow	Used	0.35	0.50	0.75	10	20	90	250	—
		green	Unused OG	6.75	9	13.50	16.50	21.50	45	90	—
			Mint NH	12.50	18.50	30	40	80	225	1,000	1,700
569	30¢	olive	Used	0.25	0.35	0.60	9	18	75	230	—
		brown	Unused OG	11.25	15	22.50	27.50	35	50	135	180
			Mint NH	20	35	50	70	120	275	1,000	1,850
570	50¢	lilac	Used	0.25	0.30	0.40	9	20	65	260	—
			Unused OG	16.50	22.50	32.50	37.50	47.50	75	160	280
			Mint NH	27.50	47.50	70	85	125	300	1,000	2,100
571	$1	violet	Used	0.30	0.50	0.80	11.50	35	110	325	—
		brown	Unused OG	17.50	23.50	35	40	50	80	150	—
			Mint NH	27.50	47.50	75	85	130	225	950	1,800
572	$2	deep	Used	4.50	6.50	9	15	37.50	115	375	800
		blue	Unused OG	27.50	37.50	55	65	80	120	250	—
			Mint NH	50	70	120	140	180	300	700	1,500
573	$5	carmine	Used	7.50	10.50	15	20	42.50	150	450	—
		& blue	Unused OG	45	67.50	90	100	125	150	275	—
			Mint NH	67.50	110	180	200	250	425	1,250	10,000
573a	$5	carmine	Used	15	21	30	40	60	175	525	—
		lake &	Unused OG	85	125	180	205	240	285	375	—
		dark blue	Mint NH	175	270	375	525	700	1,100	1,900	—
551-573 Set		23 stamps	Used	19	25.95	36.35	229.50	508.50	1,903	5,850	
			Unused OG	220	304.20	439.60	523	672.15	1,059	2,280	
			Mint NH	365	597	940.60	1,212	1,862	4,510	15,610	
575	1¢	green	Used	2	3.25	5	7	9	27.50	75	190
			Unused OG	2.30	4	6	6.50	7.25	8.25	12	45
			Mint NH	3.15	6.75	11	12.50	16	25	57.50	140
576	1½¢	yellow	Used	0.70	1	1.50	2.50	5	12.50	50	120
		brown	Unused OG	0.70	1	1.50	2	2.60	3.75	6.50	—
			Mint NH	1	1.80	2.70	4	6	12.50	32.50	85
577	2¢	carmine	Used	0.60	0.85	1.25	2.25	4	11.50	45	115
			Unused OG	0.70	1	1.50	2	2.60	3.75	6.50	35
			Mint NH	1	1.80	2.70	4	6	12.50	32.50	85

1923 COIL WASTE ISSUES (PERF. 11X10)

SCT#	DENOM	COLOR	CONDITION	F 70	F-VF 75	VF 80	VF-XF 85	XF 90	XF-SUP 95	SUP 98	GEM 100
578	1¢	green	Used	85	120	160	200	275	800	—	—
			Unused OG	37.50	52.50	75	87.50	105	175	340	550
			Mint NH	57.50	100	150	200	300	900	3,250	—
579	2¢	carmine	Used	75	100	140	185	260	775	2,000	—
			Unused OG	35	47.50	70	85	100	165	315	—
			Mint NH	52.50	92.50	140	200	400	750	2,500	—

1923-25 REGULAR ISSUE (PERF. 10)

SCT#	DENOM	COLOR	CONDITION	F 70	F-VF 75	VF 80	VF-XF 85	XF 90	XF-SUP 95	SUP 98	GEM 100
581	1¢	green	Used	0.40	0.55	0.75	9	20	85	260	—
			Unused OG	5	6.75	10	13	20	40	95	—
			Mint NH	8.50	13.50	21	32.50	47.50	210	750	1,350
582	1½¢	brown	Used	0.30	0.50	0.65	9	20	80	250	—
			Unused OG	3	4.10	6	8.75	12	25	52.50	—
			Mint NH	5.25	8.50	13	21.50	32.50	150	525	—

SCT#	DENOM	COLOR	CONDITION	F 70	F-VF 75	VF 80	VF-XF 85	XF 90	XF-SUP 95	SUP 98	GEM 100
583	2¢	carmine	Used	0.25	0.25	0.30	8	17.50	50	200	425
			Unused OG	1.45	2	3	4.65	7	14	30	55
			Mint NH	2.50	4	6.25	10	20	85	360	625
583a	2¢	carmine	Used	95	120	150	185	240	350	—	—
Booklet			Unused OG	60	85	110	135	150	300	—	—
Pane of 6			Mint NH	105	145	200	275	450	675	—	—
584	3¢	violet	Used	1.50	2.20	3	12.50	30	115	380	750
			Unused OG	13.50	18.50	27.50	40	55	95	175	—
			Mint NH	22.50	38.50	60	87.50	135	450	1,075	2,000
585	4¢	yellow	Used	0.30	0.45	0.65	10	20	75	260	—
		brown	Unused OG	8.75	12.50	17.50	22.50	35	62.50	145	200
			Mint NH	15	23.50	37.50	55	77.50	250	875	1,500
586	5¢	blue	Used	0.25	0.25	0.40	10	20	65	200	—
			Unused OG	8.75	12.50	17.50	22.50	35	62.50	145	—
			Mint NH	15	23.50	37.50	55	90	350	1,100	—
587	6¢	red	Used	0.25	0.40	0.60	10	20	70	240	—
		orange	Unused OG	4.50	6.50	9.25	12.50	20	35	90	—
			Mint NH	7.50	12.50	20	35	55	250	850	1,500
588	7¢	black	Used	3.20	4.50	6.25	15	50	160	475	—
			Unused OG	6.25	8.25	12.50	17.50	25	45	100	—
			Mint NH	10	16.50	26	42.50	65	275	1,000	1,800
589	8¢	olive	Used	2.30	3.30	4.50	12.50	35	135	420	—
		green	Unused OG	13.50	17.50	27.50	37.50	50	90	180	—
			Mint NH	24	36	57.50	82.50	120	350	1,350	2,500
590	9¢	rose	Used	1.20	1.80	2.50	12.50	30	110	350	—
			Unused OG	3	4.25	6	9	12.50	30	75	150
			Mint NH	5	8	12.50	21	32.50	150	725	1,350
591	10¢	orange	Used	0.25	0.30	0.50	9	18	65	230	—
			Unused OG	20	27.50	40	55	75	130	250	—
			Mint NH	32.50	50	85	110	150	360	1,200	2,400
581-591	11 stamps		Used	10.25	14.50	20.10	117.50	279.50	1,010	3,265	
Set			Unused OG	87.50	120.35	176.75	242.90	346.50	629	1,338	
			Mint NH	150	234.50	376.25	552.50	825	2,870	9,810	

1923 COIL AND SHEET WASTE ISSUES (PERF. 11)

SCT#	DENOM	COLOR	CONDITION	F 70	F-VF 75	VF 80	VF-XF 85	XF 90	XF-SUP 95	SUP 98	GEM 100
594	1¢	green	Used	10,500	15,000	22,500	42,500	82,500			
			Unused NG	35,000	—	—					
			Unused OG	65,000							
595	2¢	carmine	Used	200	300	375	450	575	2,000	3,750	
			Unused OG	120	170	240	260	290	450	825	—
			Mint NH	190	300	450	625	875	2,000	7,000	—
596	1¢	green	Used, Machine cancel	250,000	300,000			five known			
			Used, Precancel	200,000	250,000			ten known			

1923-29 REGULAR ISSUE COILS

SCT#	DENOM	COLOR	CONDITION	F 70	F-VF 75	VF 80	VF-XF 85	XF 90	XF-SUP 95	SUP 98	GEM 100
597	1¢	green	Used	0.25	0.25	0.25	0.45	2	20	120	230
Sgl.			Unused OG	0.25	0.30	0.35	0.40	2.60	5.75	11.75	—
			Mint NH	0.25	0.40	0.60	3	27.50	75	190	475
597	1¢	green	Used	0.25	0.25	0.25	1	5	45	250	—
Pair			Unused OG	0.25	0.35	0.65	1.40	5.50	13	30	—
			Mint NH	0.60	0.95	1.40	7	60	160	375	—

SCT#	DENOM	COLOR	CONDITION	F 70	F-VF 75	VF 80	VF-XF 85	XF 90	XF-SUP 95	SUP 98	GEM 100
597 LP	1¢	green	Used	0.30	0.50	0.75	3	25	100	210	—
			Unused OG	1.25	1.60	2	4	10	20	45	—
			Mint NH	2.05	2.90	4	12.50	50	200	475	—
598 Sgl.	1½¢	brown	Used	0.25	0.25	0.25	1	10	35	100	—
			Unused OG	0.40	0.65	0.90	1.50	3	7.50	15	—
			Mint NH	0.75	1.25	1.80	10	20	55	160	—
598 Pair	1½¢	brown	Used	0.25	0.25	0.25	2	21	75	175	—
			Unused OG	0.85	1.30	1.90	3.10	7	16	32.50	—
			Mint NH	1.65	2.50	3.80	21	45	125	325	—
598 LP	1½¢	brown	Used	0.45	0.60	0.75	3	12	55	200	—
			Unused OG	2.10	3.20	4.50	7.50	11	16	25	—
			Mint NH	4.15	6.25	9	20	35	170	500	—
599 Sgl.	2¢	carmine type I	Used	0.25	0.25	0.25	4	25	60	140	325
			Unused OG	0.25	0.25	0.35	1.25	4.50	9	15	—
			Mint NH	0.30	0.45	0.70	3	25	45	125	—
599 Pair	2¢	carmine type I	Used	0.25	0.25	0.25	9	55	125	300	—
			Unused OG	0.35	0.55	0.75	2.60	9.50	20	35	—
			Mint NH	0.65	0.90	1.50	6.50	55	110	300	900
599 LP	2¢	carmine type I	Used	0.50	0.70	1	12.50	55	200	400	—
			Unused OG	1.20	1.60	2.25	10	20	60	100	—
			Mint NH	2.15	3.10	4.50	22.50	55	175	325	—
599b Sgl.	2¢	carmine lake type I	Mint NH	150	195	300	340	500	—	—	
599b Pair	2¢	carmine lake type I	Mint NH	270	430	650	725	1,100	2,000	—	
599b LP	2¢	carmine lake type I	Used	300	500	700	1,050	1,550			
			Unused OG	190	260	325	425	550			
			Mint NH	475	625	950	1,025	1,200	2,000	—	
599A Sgl.	2¢	carmine type II	Used	7.25	11	16	45	100	250	325	—
			Unused OG	60	87.50	120	135	160	200	325	—
			Mint NH	115	170	240	280	350	675	1,350	—
599A Pair	2¢	carmine type II	Used	25	45	60	95	225	525	900	—
			Unused OG	130	180	250	280	325	400	750	—
			Mint NH	255	355	500	600	750	1,600	2,850	—
599A LP	2¢	carmine type II	Used	160	275	400	550	750	1,250	—	—
			Unused OG	300	420	575	675	800	1,100	—	—
			Mint NH	550	800	1,150	1,450	2,400	3,750	—	—
599/ 599A LP	2¢	carmine type I & II	Used	425	800	1,100	1,300	—	—	—	
			Unused OG	370	500	700	775	900	1,300	—	
			Mint NH	650	950	1,350	1,700	2,500	4,100	—	
600 Sgl.	3¢	violet	Used	0.25	0.25	0.25	0.45	3	37.50	200	300
			Unused OG	2.50	3.50	5.25	5.75	6.75	11	25	—
			Mint NH	4.50	7.25	11	14	20	70	175	—
600 Pair	3¢	violet	Used	0.25	0.30	0.45	1.95	14.25	110	575	—
			Unused OG	6.50	8.50	13	15	17.50	25	55	—
			Mint NH	10.50	17.50	26	35	45	150	425	1,400
600 LP	3¢	violet	Used	2	2.75	4	20	65	220	500	—
			Unused OG	16	22	30	33.50	37.50	42.50	77.50	—
			Mint NH	27.50	42.50	60	72.50	87.50	175	550	—
601 Sgl.	4¢	yellow brown	Used	0.25	0.30	0.35	1	15	80	225	—
			Unused OG	1.80	2.50	3.75	4.50	5.50	9	20	—
			Mint NH	3	5	7.50	11	20	55	150	—
601 Pair	4¢	yellow brown	Used	0.50	0.60	0.95	3	35	150	—	—
			Unused OG	4	5.75	8.25	9.75	12.50	20	45	—
			Mint NH	6.25	11	16.50	22.50	45	120	350	850
601 LP	4¢	yellow brown	Used	5	7	10	29	115	315	1,550	—
			Unused OG	14	20	27.50	32.50	40	52.50	120	—
			Mint NH	27.50	40	55	80	150	400	625	—
602 Sgl.	5¢	dark blue	Used	0.25	0.25	0.25	2.50	10	95	250	—
			Unused OG	0.80	1.15	1.75	3	10	15	25	—
			Mint NH	1.40	2.35	3.50	7.50	19	45	135	—
602 Pair	5¢	dark blue	Used	0.25	0.25	0.35	7	25	200	525	—
			Unused OG	1.85	2.50	3.75	6.50	14	35	60	—
			Mint NH	3	5	7.50	16	40	100	290	—
602 LP	5¢	dark blue	Used	1.70	2.30	3	12	60	250	1,200	—
			Unused OG	5.75	8.50	11	15	22.50	35	75	—
			Mint NH	10.75	15.50	22.50	37.50	115	300	925	—

SCT#	DENOM	COLOR	CONDITION	F 70	F-VF 75	VF 80	VF-XF 85	XF 90	XF-SUP 95	SUP 98	GEM 100
603 Sgl.	10¢	orange	Used	0.25	0.25	0.25	0.50	5	40	200	—
			Unused OG	1.70	2.30	3.50	5	8	12	24	—
			Mint NH	2.70	4.50	7	13.50	27.50	120	260	725
603 Pair	10¢	orange	Used	0.25	0.25	0.25	2	11.50	90	425	
			Unused OG	4	5.25	8	11	17.50	27.50	50	—
			Mint NH	6.25	10.50	16	30	60	250	550	1,500
603 LP	10¢	orange	Used	2.25	3.25	4.50	12.50	80	300	1,250	—
			Unused OG	12.50	18	25	30	37.50	60	110	—
			Mint NH	22	35	50	65	95	300	900	—
604 Sgl.	1¢	green	Used	0.25	0.25	0.25	2	17.50	60	160	—
			Unused OG	0.25	0.25	0.40	1.25	6	12	40	150
			Mint NH	0.35	0.45	0.80	4	15	40	140	400
604 Pair	1¢	green	Used	0.25	0.25	0.25	4.25	37.50	125	350	—
			Unused OG	0.30	0.55	0.85	2.60	15	25	85	—
			Mint NH	0.65	0.95	1.70	8.50	32.50	100	300	700
604 LP	1¢	green	Used	0.55	0.80	1.25	5	35	125	525	—
			Unused OG	1.65	2.40	3.50	8.50	35	50	75	—
			Mint NH	2.90	4.70	7	25	65	175	750	1,200
605 Sgl.	1½¢	brown	Used	0.25	0.25	0.25	2	17.50	55	190	—
			Unused OG	0.25	0.25	0.40	1.40	6	12	40	—
			Mint NH	0.40	0.60	0.80	2.25	15	55	130	450
605 Pair	1½¢	brown	Used	0.25	0.25	0.35	4.50	40	130	425	—
			Unused OG	0.45	0.55	0.85	3	12.50	25	85	—
			Mint NH	0.80	1.25	1.70	4.75	32.50	150	280	700
605 LP	1½¢	brown	Used	1.60	2.65	4	12	30	110	525	—
			Unused OG	1.85	2.65	3.50	7	15	25	50	—
			Mint NH	3.45	5	7	25	70	200	850	—
606 Sgl.	2¢	carmine	Used	0.25	0.25	0.25	1.25	15	110	220	—
			Unused OG	0.25	0.25	0.40	2	6	15	30	—
			Mint NH	0.40	0.60	0.80	7.50	25	45	120	675
606 Pair	2¢	carmine	Used	0.25	0.30	0.45	3	35	200	450	—
			Unused OG	0.45	0.55	0.85	4.50	13	35	70	—
			Mint NH	0.80	1.25	1.70	16	55	100	260	850
606 LP	2¢	carmine	Used	1.75	2.45	3.50	10	85	300	600	—
			Unused OG	1.30	1.75	2.50	5	15	45	90	—
			Mint NH	2.30	3.50	5	15	55	150	350	1,100
606a Sgl.	2¢	carmine lake	Used	30	50	75	105	120	—		
			Unused OG	32.50	50	75	90	160	—		
			Mint NH	60	100	150	175	200	225	550	
606a Pair	2¢	carmine lake	Used	70	110	160	220	350			
			Unused OG	75	115	160	230	375	—	—	
			Mint NH	150	225	350	450	500	550	1,250	1,600
606a LP	2¢	carmine lake	Mint NH	360	525	775	875	1,500	2,250	—	—

1923-29 ISSUES

SCT#	DENOM	COLOR	CONDITION	F 70	F-VF 75	VF 80	VF-XF 85	XF 90	XF-SUP 95	SUP 98	GEM 100
610	2¢	black	Used	0.25	0.25	0.25	3	12.50	50	190	600
			Unused OG	0.25	0.30	0.50	1.25	3.50	20	40	110
			Mint NH	0.35	0.70	1	2.25	15	47.50	180	550
611	2¢	black	Used	1.75	2.75	4	6	10	27.50	90	125
			Unused OG	2	3	4.50	5	7.50	12.50	25	50
			Mint NH	3.75	6	9	13.25	19	35	52.50	90
612	2¢	black	Used	0.90	1.30	1.75	10	27.50	95	325	—
			Unused OG	7.50	10	15	19	24	35	75	—
			Mint NH	13.50	20	32.50	42.50	60	150	475	1,300
613	2¢	black	Used	35,000	55,000	77,500	90,000	120,000	—		
614	1¢	dark green	Used	1.40	2.10	3	11	30	105	325	—
			Unused OG	1.20	1.45	2.30	3.85	15	40	75	—
			Mint NH	1.90	2.85	4.25	10	35	125	400	1,250
615	2¢	carmine rose	Used	1	1.50	2.25	12	30	100	325	700
			Unused OG	1.90	2.65	3.75	5.50	12.50	35	55	—
			Mint NH	2.80	4.60	7	12.50	27.50	110	400	825

SCT#	DENOM	COLOR	CONDITION	F 70	F-VF 75	VF 80	VF-XF 85	XF 90	XF-SUP 95	SUP 98	GEM 100
616	5¢	dark	Used	6	9	13	20	42.50	140	450	—
		blue	Unused OG	7	9.50	15	17.50	20	40	105	—
			Mint NH	12	19	27.50	40	70	225	675	1,200
617	1¢	green	Used	1.10	1.75	2.50	12	27.50	95	280	575
			Unused OG	0.90	1.35	2	3	9	17.50	47.50	90
			Mint NH	1.50	2.45	3.75	7.50	13.50	35	135	300
618	2¢	carmine	Used	1.90	2.90	4	12.50	37.50	115	340	675
		rose	Unused OG	1.75	2.45	3.50	4.25	9	17.50	42.50	—
			Mint NH	2.50	4.25	6.50	9	17	42.50	145	375
619	5¢	dark	Used	6.50	9.50	13	20	42.50	145	450	—
		blue	Unused OG	7	9.75	14	17.50	22.50	37.50	65	—
			Mint NH	11.25	16.50	26	30	45	115	290	625
620	2¢	carmine	Used	1.30	1.90	2.75	9.50	27.50	95	300	—
		& black	Unused OG	1.50	2.10	3	5.50	12	20	40	—
			Mint NH	2.50	4.15	6	10.50	20	55	200	650
621	5¢	dark	Used	4.50	6.75	9	14	30	95	295	—
		blue	Unused OG	4.50	6.50	9	11	13.50	22.50	47.50	—
		& black	Mint NH	8	12	19	25	35	60	230	475
622	13¢	green	Used	0.25	0.35	0.75	9	22.50	85	275	450
			Unused OG	4.50	6	9	11	14	25	55	—
			Mint NH	7.50	12	19	25	32.50	90	275	525
623	17¢	black	Used	0.25	0.25	0.30	8	15	60	200	400
			Unused OG	4.50	6	9	11	12.50	22.50	47.50	105
			Mint NH	7.50	12	19	25	35	80	220	425
627	2¢	carmine	Used	0.25	0.25	0.50	8	17.50	65	200	375
		rose	Unused OG	1.10	1.60	2.25	3.25	6	12.50	30	75
			Mint NH	1.65	2.80	4	7.50	15	40	150	300
628	5¢	gray	Used	1.50	2.25	3.25	8.50	27.50	95	330	—
		lilac	Unused OG	2.50	3.60	5	6	7.50	12.50	30	—
			Mint NH	3.80	5.75	8.50	11	22.50	60	190	275
629	2¢	carmine	Used	0.80	1.25	1.70	10	20	90	250	—
		rose	Unused OG	0.80	1.10	1.60	3	6	10	25	—
			Mint NH	1.30	1.90	2.75	6.50	17.50	50	175	350
630	2¢	carmine	Used	260	350	450	475	525	700	—	
		rose	Unused OG	160	220	275	310	360	475	—	
		S/S	Mint NH	250	370	500	550	600	700	—	
631	1½¢	yellow	Used	0.85	1.25	1.70	3.25	8	17.50	55	100
		brown	Unused OG	1	1.45	2	2.20	3	8	15	40
		imperforate	Mint NH	1.30	1.95	3	5	10	20	40	75
632	1¢	green	Used	0.25	0.25	0.25	7	15	65	210	450
			Unused OG	0.25	0.25	0.25	1.25	7.50	12.50	30	—
			Mint NH	0.25	0.25	0.35	3.50	20	75	175	350
632a Booklet Pane of 6	1¢	green	Used	2.25	3	4	5	6.50	17.50	—	—
			Unused OG	2	3.50	5	6.25	8	14	—	—
			Mint NH	2.80	5	8	10	13.50	35	—	—
633	1½¢	yellow	Used	0.25	0.25	0.25	7	15	65	200	—
		brown	Unused OG	0.80	1.20	1.70	4	11	22.50	40	—
			Mint NH	1.15	1.70	2.60	6	22.50	62.50	200	500
634	2¢	carmine	Used	0.25	0.25	0.25	7	15	65	200	525
		type I	Unused OG	0.25	0.25	0.25	1.25	7.50	15	35	—
			Mint NH	0.25	0.25	0.30	3	20	70	175	375
634b	2¢	carmine	Used	—	—	500	—	—			
		lake	Unused OG	—	125	180	235	300	550		
		type I	Mint NH	—	300	425	525	700	900	1,450	2,500
634d Booklet Pane of 6	2¢	carmine type I	Used	0.85	1.15	1.50	1.90	2.50	9	—	—
			Unused OG	0.75	1.05	1.50	2	2.75	7	—	—
			Mint NH	1.10	1.70	2.50	3.25	5	12.50	—	—
634e Booklet Pane of 6	2¢	carmine lake type I	Used	—	1,000	—	—				
			Unused OG	—	400	—	—				
			Mint NH	—	750	—	—				
634A	2¢	carmine	Used	7	10	13.50	18.50	30	110	375	—
		type II	Unused OG	150	210	300	340	375	475	875	—
			Mint NH	225	375	600	700	825	2,000	4,500	8,250

SCT#	DENOM	COLOR	CONDITION	F 70	F-VF 75	VF 80	VF-XF 85	XF 90	XF-SUP 95	SUP 98	GEM 100
635	3¢	violet	Used	0.25	0.25	0.25	7	15	65	200	—
			Unused OG	0.25	0.45	0.75	2.20	6.25	15	37.50	—
			Mint NH	0.40	0.80	1.20	5.25	24	70	200	450
635a	3¢	bright	Used	0.25	0.25	0.25	5	12.50	55	175	—
		violet	Unused OG	0.25	0.30	0.35	1.75	5	12.50	35	—
			Mint NH	0.30	0.30	0.45	2.75	16	47.50	175	—
636	4¢	yellow	Used	0.25	0.25	0.25	7	15	60	200	—
		brown	Unused OG	0.95	1.30	1.90	3	7	15	35	—
			Mint NH	1.30	2	3	7.50	25	85	230	550
637	5¢	dark	Used	0.25	0.25	0.25	7	15	60	200	500
		blue	Unused OG	0.95	1.30	1.90	3	7	15	35	—
			Mint NH	1.30	2	3	7.50	20	85	220	550
638	6¢	red	Used	0.25	0.25	0.25	7	15	60	200	—
		orange	Unused OG	1	1.35	2	3	7	15	35	80
			Mint NH	1.40	2.15	3.20	8.25	22.50	95	225	550
639	7¢	black	Used	0.25	0.25	0.25	7	15	60	200	—
			Unused OG	1	1.35	2	3	7	15	35	—
			Mint NH	1.40	2.15	3.20	8.25	22.50	90	350	475
640	8¢	olive	Used	0.25	0.25	0.25	7	15	60	200	—
		green	Unused OG	1	1.35	2	3	7	15	35	—
			Mint NH	1.40	2.15	3.20	8.25	22.50	90	250	600
641	9¢	rose	Used	0.25	0.25	0.25	7	15	60	200	—
			Unused OG	0.95	1.30	1.90	3	7	15	35	—
			Mint NH	1.30	2	3	7.50	22.50	80	225	550
642	10¢	orange	Used	0.25	0.25	0.25	7	15	60	200	—
			Unused OG	1.55	2.20	3.25	4	8	1.50	37.50	90
			Mint NH	2.60	3.75	5.50	15	32.50	100	400	600
643	2¢	carmine	Used	0.40	0.55	0.80	10	22.50	80	290	—
		rose	Unused OG	0.60	0.90	1.20	2.50	6	12.50	30	—
			Mint NH	0.85	1.40	2	5	12	35	150	500
644	2¢	carmine	Used	1	1.50	2.10	11	25	100	325	—
		rose	Unused OG	1.45	2.10	3	4.50	7.50	12.50	35	—
			Mint NH	2.15	3.50	5.25	8	16.50	50	170	300
645	2¢	carmine	Used	0.25	0.25	0.50	8	17.50	65	230	475
		rose	Unused OG	0.55	0.75	1.15	2.50	5	11	27.50	—
			Mint NH	0.80	1.25	1.80	6.75	16.50	45	160	325
645a	2¢	lake	Unused OG	—	—	—	—	—	—	—	
			Mint NH	—	—	—	—	—	—	—	
646	2¢	carmine	Used	0.45	0.70	1	10	22.50	90	325	—
			Unused OG	0.50	0.70	1	2	4	12	25	60
			Mint NH	0.75	1.10	1.60	4.25	13	45	160	325
646b	2¢	carmine lake	Unused OG		—	2,500	—				
647	2¢	carmine	Used	1.80	2.75	4	11	30	115	325	—
			Unused OG	2	2.85	4	4.65	5.75	11	30	—
			Mint NH	3.50	4.90	7.25	10	25	80	275	525
648	5¢	dark	Used	6	8.75	12.50	17.50	35	140	500	—
		blue	Unused OG	4.50	7.75	11	12.50	14	22	52.50	90
			Mint NH	10	15	21.50	30	40	110	350	700
649	2¢	carmine	Used	0.40	0.60	0.80	12	24	95	325	600
		rose	Unused OG	0.55	0.75	1.10	2	4	9	22.50	55
			Mint NH	0.75	1.20	1.75	5	10	35	140	275
650	5¢	blue	Used	1.60	2.40	3.25	11	25	105	375	700
			Unused OG	2.25	3.10	4.50	5.25	6.50	11	30	70
			Mint NH	3.25	4.75	7	11	17.50	40	160	325
651	2¢	carmine	Used	0.25	0.25	0.50	8	17.50	67.50	250	450
		& black	Unused OG	0.35	0.50	0.70	1.40	3.75	10	25	—
			Mint NH	0.50	0.75	1.15	3.75	15	55	175	450
653	½¢	olive	Used	0.25	0.25	0.25	6	15	60	200	—
		brown	Unused OG	0.25	0.25	0.25	1.25	3.75	12.50	25	85
			Mint NH	0.30	0.30	0.35	3.50	10	30	120	250
654	2¢	carmine	Used	0.30	0.45	0.65	9	20	85	275	475
		rose	Unused OG	0.30	0.45	0.65	1.50	9	35	35	—
			Mint NH	0.55	0.80	1.20	4.50	12.50	40	160	325

SCT#	DENOM	COLOR	CONDITION	F 70	F-VF 75	VF 80	VF-XF 85	XF 90	XF-SUP 95	SUP 98	GEM 100
655	2¢	carmine	Used	0.25	0.25	0.25	8	15	60	175	—
		rose	Unused OG	0.35	0.45	0.65	1.75	4	10	22.50	—
			Mint NH	0.35	0.65	1.10	4.50	11	45	190	425
656	2¢	carmine	Used	0.85	1.25	1.75	8	27.50	85	250	—
Sgl.		rose	Unused OG	5	7	10	11	13	20	47.50	—
			Mint NH	9	14.25	20	26	35	75	200	750
656	2¢	carmine	Used	2	3	4	17.50	60	180	525	800
Pair		rose	Unused OG	11	16	22.50	27	32.50	45	100	—
			Mint NH	20	31	45	60	75	160	425	850
656	2¢	carmine	Used	15	21	27.50	40	125	350	750	—
LP		rose	Unused OG	27.50	40	55	62.50	72.50	100	200	—
			Mint NH	50	80	110	130	175	400	1,150	1,900
657	2¢	carmine	Used	0.30	0.40	0.55	7.50	18.50	50	150	375
		rose	Unused OG	0.30	0.35	0.55	1.40	3.25	10	25	—
			Mint NH	0.45	0.65	0.95	3.25	10	35	135	275
657a	2¢	lake	Used	—	—	250	—	—			
			Unused OG	200	275	375	425	500	600	1,000	—
			Mint NH	275	425	625	725	850	1,600	3,250	—

1929 KANSAS OVERPRINTS

SCT#	DENOM	COLOR	CONDITION	F 70	F-VF 75	VF 80	VF-XF 85	XF 90	XF-SUP 95	SUP 98	GEM 100
658	1¢	green	Used	1	1.45	2	10	27.50	110	350	—
			Unused OG	1.25	1.75	2.50	4	6.25	11	25	—
			Mint NH	2.20	3.50	5	9.50	27.50	90	320	675
659	1½¢	brown	Used	1.40	2.10	2.90	12.50	32.50	120	375	—
			Unused OG	1.50	2.10	3.25	5.25	7.50	11	30	—
			Mint NH	2.90	4.40	6.50	9.25	25	82.50	325	675
660	2¢	carmine	Used	0.55	0.75	1	10	25	125	325	—
			Unused OG	1.95	2.85	4	5.50	7.50	10	30	—
			Mint NH	3.20	4.80	7.50	11	32.50	85	360	—
661	3¢	violet	Used	7.50	11	15	25	50	160	500	—
			Unused OG	8.75	11.75	17.50	20	25	37.50	90	—
			Mint NH	14	22.50	35	45	65	275	675	1,500
662	4¢	yellow	Used	4.50	6.50	9	17.50	42.50	150	475	—
		brown	Unused OG	8.75	11.50	17.50	20	22.50	42.50	100	—
			Mint NH	14	22.50	35	47.50	70	225	625	—
663	5¢	deep	Used	4.75	7	9.75	20	45	150	325	—
		blue	Unused OG	6.25	8.75	12.50	15	18	27.50	65	—
			Mint NH	9.50	15	25	35	47.50	200	750	1,500
664	6¢	red	Used	9	13	18	25	50	160	550	—
		orange	Unused OG	12.50	17	25	27.50	32.50	65	160	—
			Mint NH	19	32.50	50	67.50	95	325	1,000	1,850
665	7¢	black	Used	13	19	27.50	37.50	60	175	675	—
			Unused OG	12.50	15	25	27.50	32.50	55	140	—
			Mint NH	17.50	30	50	67.50	90	325	1,000	2,000
666	8¢	olive	Used	40	50	65	92.50	145	475	—	—
		green	Unused OG	37.50	50	72.50	80	87.50	145	280	—
			Mint NH	60	100	145	170	200	450	1,400	2,750
667	9¢	light	Used	5	7.75	11.50	20	45	140	500	—
		rose	Unused OG	7	9.50	14	15	16.50	30	72.50	150
			Mint NH	11	17	27.50	40	55	160	650	—
668	10¢	orange	Used	6	8.25	12.50	22.50	45	150	525	—
		yellow	Unused OG	10.50	15	22.50	25	30	47.50	120	—
			Mint NH	18	27	45	62.50	115	300	1,050	2,100
658-668	11 stamps		Used	92.50	126.80	174.15	292.50	567.50	1,915	4,650	
Set			Unused OG	110	145.20	216.25	244.75	285.75	482	1,113	
			Mint NH	170	279.20	431.50	564.75	822.50	2,518	8,155	

SCT#	DENOM	COLOR	CONDITION	F 70	F-VF 75	VF 80	VF-XF 85	XF 90	XF-SUP 95	SUP 98	GEM 100

1929 NEBRASKA OVERPRINTS

SCT#	DENOM	COLOR	CONDITION	F 70	F-VF 75	VF 80	VF-XF 85	XF 90	XF-SUP 95	SUP 98	GEM 100
669	1¢	green	Used	1.10	1.60	2.25	12.50	30	110	400	—
			Unused OG	1.55	2.35	3.25	4.50	5.75	10	30	—
			Mint NH	2.60	4.15	6.50	10	27.50	90	300	600
670	1½¢	brown	Used	1.25	1.75	2.50	12.50	30	105	210	425
			Unused OG	1.50	2.05	3	4	6	12	25	—
			Mint NH	2.35	3.90	6	10	25	77.50	325	—
671	2¢	carmine	Used	0.60	0.90	1.30	12	25	100	225	450
			Unused OG	1.50	2.05	3	6	10	17.50	40	160
			Mint NH	2.35	3.90	6	10	25	75	300	650
672	3¢	violet	Used	5.75	8.25	12	22.50	50	155	525	—
			Unused OG	5.50	7.25	11	13.75	16.50	32	77.50	160
			Mint NH	9.25	13.75	22	32	47.50	170	600	1,400
673	4¢	yellow brown	Used	7.50	11	15	25	75	200	500	—
			Unused OG	8.75	11.50	17.50	22.50	30	60	125	—
			Mint NH	13.50	21	35	47.50	65	225	700	1,500
674	5¢	deep blue	Used	7.50	11	15	25	50	160	500	—
			Unused OG	7.50	9.50	15	19	30	40	90	—
			Mint NH	11.50	19	30	45	62.50	220	750	1,600
675	6¢	red orange	Used	12	17	24	32.50	62.50	175	625	—
			Unused OG	18.50	25	35	40	50	82.50	180	375
			Mint NH	27.50	45	70	90	115	400	1,150	2,500
676	7¢	black	Used	9	13	18	27.50	50	160	525	—
			Unused OG	10.50	15	22.50	27.50	32	50	120	—
			Mint NH	17.50	28.50	45	62.50	85	300	1,050	2,150
677	8¢	olive green	Used	12.50	17.50	25	35	57.50	170	650	1,400
			Unused OG	15	21	30	35	45	60	160	—
			Mint NH	23.50	36.50	60	80	125	450	1,400	3,000
678	9¢	light rose	Used	14	20	27.50	37.50	62.50	180	700	—
			Unused OG	16.50	25	35	40	47.50	80	200	400
			Mint NH	27.50	45	70	87.50	115	330	1,500	2,400
679	10¢	orange yellow	Used	11	16	22.50	32.50	55	160	600	—
			Unused OG	45	57.50	90	100	115	135	300	—
			Mint NH	72.50	115	180	220	280	350	1,000	2,000
669-679 Set	11 stamps		Used	82	118	165.05	273.50	522.50	1,635	5,685	
			Unused OG	130	178.20	265.25	310.25	381.25	558.50	1,303	
			Mint NH	210	335.70	530.50	694.50	972.50	2,688	8,525	

1929-56 ISSUES

SCT#	DENOM	COLOR	CONDITION	F 70	F-VF 75	VF 80	VF-XF 85	XF 90	XF-SUP 95	SUP 98	GEM 100
680	2¢	carmine rose	Used	0.30	0.40	0.65	8.50	19	85	290	700
			Unused OG	0.30	0.40	0.65	1.40	4	10	25	—
			Mint NH	0.45	0.70	1	3	10	37.50	130	325
681	2¢	carmine rose	Used	0.30	0.35	0.55	8.50	20	70	275	625
			Unused OG	0.30	0.35	0.55	1.25	3	9	22.50	—
			Mint NH	0.45	0.60	0.90	2.85	8.50	40	135	375
681a	2¢	lake	Used	—	—	—					
			Unused OG	—	425	—					
			Mint NH	—	650	—					
682	2¢	carmine rose	Used	0.25	0.35	0.50	8	17.50	70	250	—
			Unused OG	0.30	0.45	0.65	1.60	4	12	30	100
			Mint NH	0.40	0.60	0.95	3.25	10	30	145	350

SCT#	DENOM	COLOR	CONDITION	F 70	F-VF 75	VF 80	VF-XF 85	XF 90	XF-SUP 95	SUP 98	GEM 100
683	2¢	carmine	Used	0.50	0.70	1	9.50	21.50	95	325	—
		rose	Unused OG	0.50	0.70	1	2.10	3.75	9	24.50	—
			Mint NH	0.70	1	1.50	4	12	35	165	375
684	1½¢	brown	Used	0.25	0.25	0.25	7	15	60	210	—
			Unused OG	0.25	0.30	0.50	1.40	4.25	10	30	—
			Mint NH	0.30	0.50	0.70	3.75	17.50	40	170	425
685	4¢	brown	Used	0.25	0.25	0.25	7	15	60	210	—
			Unused OG	0.30	0.55	0.80	1.50	4	11	25	60
			Mint NH	0.45	0.75	1.25	5	15	52.50	225	550
686 Sgl.	1½¢	brown	Used	0.25	0.25	0.25	2.50	15	35	125	—
			Unused OG	0.80	1.20	1.75	2.50	4	10	30	75
			Mint NH	1.15	1.65	2.60	7.50	35	65	150	350
686 Pair	1½¢	brown	Used	0.20	0.25	0.30	6	35	75	275	—
			Unused OG	1.80	2.55	3.75	5.25	10	25	70	—
			Mint NH	2.60	4	5.75	16	60	135	350	1,000
686 LP	1½¢	brown	Used	0.20	0.30	0.75	7.50	45	150	375	—
			Unused OG	3.75	5.25	7.50	9	12.50	25	75	—
			Mint NH	5.25	7.75	11.50	25	60	150	400	1,050
687 Sgl.	4¢	brown	Used	0.20	0.25	0.45	2	10	190	400	—
			Unused OG	1.45	2.10	3	5	9	25	75	—
			Mint NH	2.10	3.10	4.50	9	18.50	42.50	110	—
687 Pair	4¢	brown	Used	0.50	0.70	1	4.50	24	325	—	—
			Unused OG	3	4.50	6.25	11	20	55	160	—
			Mint NH	4.25	6.25	9.50	20	40	90	225	500
687 LP	4¢	brown	Used	1.25	1.75	2.50	7.50	32.50	135	425	—
			Unused OG	5.50	7.50	11	14	20	35	75	—
			Mint NH	10	14	22	40	65	175	350	—
688	2¢	carmine	Used	0.40	0.60	0.85	8	22.50	90	300	—
		rose	Unused OG	0.45	0.55	0.85	1.30	6.25	10.50	23.50	—
			Mint NH	0.55	0.85	1.30	3	11	37.50	140	400
689	2¢	carmine	Used	0.25	0.25	0.50	8	17.50	70	250	—
		rose	Unused OG	0.25	0.30	0.50	1.25	4.50	9	20	—
			Mint NH	0.25	0.40	0.75	2.25	7.50	22.50	100	300
690	2¢	carmine	Used	0.25	0.25	0.25	6	13	62.50	200	—
		rose	Unused OG	0.25	0.25	0.30	0.75	3	9	17.50	—
			Mint NH	0.25	0.25	0.40	2.50	7	22.50	105	325
692	11¢	light	Used	0.25	0.25	0.25	7	13	62.50	200	—
		blue	Unused OG	1.25	1.75	2.50	4	9	20	40	—
			Mint NH	1.50	2.50	3.75	9	30	80	250	550
693	12¢	brown	Used	0.25	0.25	0.25	5	12.50	60	190	—
		violet	Unused OG	2.50	3.50	5	6.50	8.50	15	35	—
			Mint NH	3.50	5.50	8	12.50	30	75	300	600
694	13¢	yellow	Used	0.25	0.25	0.25	5	13	62.50	200	—
		green	Unused OG	1.15	1.65	2.25	3.75	7	15	35	—
			Mint NH	1.45	2.20	3.50	8	22.50	75	300	900
695	14¢	dark	Used	0.25	0.35	0.60	8	21	75	230	—
		blue	Unused OG	2	2.75	4	6	10	15	35	—
			Mint NH	2.50	4	6.25	12.50	35	110	325	650
696	15¢	gray	Used	0.25	0.25	0.25	5	13	62.50	200	—
			Unused OG	3.75	5.25	7.75	8.50	9.50	12.50	35	—
			Mint NH	4.75	7.50	12	17.50	30	85	300	625
697	17¢	black	Used	0.25	0.25	0.25	5	13	62.50	200	—
			Unused OG	2.35	3.35	4.75	6	7.50	12	30	—
			Mint NH	2.80	4.75	7.25	12.50	30	90	325	650
698	20¢	carmine	Used	0.25	0.25	0.25	5	13	62.50	200	—
		rose	Unused OG	3.75	5.50	7.75	8.50	9.50	12.50	35	—
			Mint NH	4.95	7.75	12.50	17.50	30	85	300	625
699	25¢	blue	Used	0.25	0.25	0.25	5	13	62.50	200	—
		green	Unused OG	4	5.75	8	8.75	10	14	37.50	120
			Mint NH	5.25	8.25	13	18	35	110	375	—
700	30¢	brown	Used	0.25	0.25	0.25	5	13	62.50	200	—
			Unused OG	6.25	8.25	12.50	14	17.50	35	75	—
			Mint NH	8.50	13	21	32.50	50	115	375	650
701	50¢	lilac	Used	0.25	0.25	0.25	5	13	62.50	200	—
			Unused OG	15	21	30	32.50	35	37.50	90	200
			Mint NH	20	32.50	50	60	85	165	525	1,000

SCT#	DENOM	COLOR	CONDITION	F 70	F-VF 75	VF 80	VF-XF 85	XF 90	XF-SUP 95	SUP 98	GEM 100
702	2¢	black	Used	0.25	0.25	0.25	5	14	60	190	—
		& red	Unused OG	0.25	0.25	0.25	0.75	3	11	22.50	—
			Mint NH	0.25	0.25	0.35	2	10	30	125	375
703	2¢	carmine	Used	0.25	0.25	0.25	5	13	65	200	475
		rose	Unused OG	0.25	0.25	0.35	0.60	0.75	6.50	16	—
		& black	Mint NH	0.25	0.30	0.50	2.50	9	32.50	190	475
703a	2¢	lake	Used	0.40	0.55	0.75	7	17.50	70	220	—
		& black	Unused OG	2.25	3.20	4.50	7.50	12.50	20	50	—
			Mint NH	2.50	4.10	6.25	10	20	65	240	—
703b	2¢	dark lake	Unused OG	250	370	500	575	675	800	1,750	—
		& black	Mint NH	425	675	950	1,150	1,400	1,750	5,000	—
704	½¢	olive	Used	0.25	0.25	0.25	1	3	17.50	60	—
		brown	Unused OG	0.25	0.25	0.25	0.50	1.90	8.75	20	—
			Mint NH	0.25	0.25	0.35	4	12.50	35	150	600
705	1¢	green	Used	0.25	0.25	0.25	1	3	17.50	60	—
			Unused OG	0.25	0.25	0.25	0.50	1.90	8.75	20	—
			Mint NH	0.25	0.25	0.35	4	12.50	35	140	—
706	1½¢	brown	Used	0.25	0.25	0.25	1	3	17.50	60	—
			Unused OG	0.25	0.35	0.45	0.90	2.50	10	25	—
			Mint NH	0.35	0.45	0.60	5	14	35	130	575
707	2¢	carmine	Used	0.25	0.25	0.25	1	3	17.50	60	—
		rose	Unused OG	0.25	0.25	0.30	0.60	2.25	9.50	24	—
			Mint NH	0.25	0.35	0.45	4.50	12.50	35	135	625
708	3¢	deep	Used	0.25	0.25	0.25	1	3	17.50	60	—
		violet	Unused OG	0.30	0.40	0.55	1.25	3	11	27.50	—
			Mint NH	0.40	0.55	0.80	4.50	12.50	35	150	—
709	4¢	light	Used	0.25	0.25	0.25	1	3	17.50	60	—
		brown	Unused OG	0.35	0.45	0.60	1.15	3.75	10	25	—
			Mint NH	0.45	0.65	0.85	6.75	15	40	150	650
710	5¢	blue	Used	0.25	0.25	0.25	1	3	17.50	60	—
			Unused OG	0.60	0.95	1.40	2.50	4.75	15	37.50	—
			Mint NH	1	1.50	2.25	5	15	40	150	650
711	6¢	red	Used	0.25	0.25	0.25	1	3	17.50	60	—
		orange	Unused OG	1.40	1.90	2.75	4.75	9.50	22.50	47.50	—
			Mint NH	2	3.10	4.50	9	16	40	150	600
712	7¢	black	Used	0.25	0.25	0.25	1	3	17.50	60	—
			Unused OG	0.30	0.40	0.60	1.25	3.25	11	30	—
			Mint NH	0.45	0.60	0.85	5	15	37.50	140	600
713	8¢	olive	Used	0.25	0.35	0.50	1.50	5	20	65	—
		bister	Unused OG	1.20	1.75	2.50	4.50	9	20	37.50	—
			Mint NH	1.75	2.50	4	7.50	16	37.50	140	600
714	9¢	pale	Used	0.25	0.25	0.25	1	3	16	55	—
		red	Unused OG	1	1.35	2	4.75	8	15	32.50	—
			Mint NH	1.40	2.25	3.25	6.50	15	35	165	—
715	10¢	orange	Used	0.25	0.25	0.25	1	3	17.50	60	—
		yellow	Unused OG	4.50	6.25	9	12	16	25	60	—
			Mint NH	6.25	10	15	20	30	45	150	600
720b Booklet Pane of 6	3¢	deep violet	Used	5	8.25	12.50	14	17.50	35	—	—
			Unused OG	18.50	25.50	35	38.50	45	80	—	—
			Mint NH	35	45	60	67.50	85	160	—	—
832	$1	purple	Used	0.25	0.25	0.25	0.90	1.50	6	25	—
		& black	Mint NH	2.70	4.60	7	15	40	65	225	1,200
832b	$1	watermarked	Used	30	45	65	75	90	125	250	—
			Mint NH	90	135	200	220	245	275	350	—
832c	$1	red violet	Used	0.25	0.25	0.25	0.80	1.40	5.75	22.50	—
		& black	Mint NH	2.60	4.50	6	12	25	45	200	1,500
832g	$1	bright magenta & black	Mint NH	30	50	70	100	125	200	400	2,500
833	$2	yellow green	Used	1.60	2.50	3.75	5	8	17.50	50	—
		& black	Mint NH	6.75	10.75	16	20	35	100	275	1,400
834	$5	carmine	Used	1.40	2.10	3	4	6.50	16	50	—
		& black	Mint NH	32.50	50	75	85	100	140	500	2,600
803-834 Set	32 stamps		Mint NH	52.50	87.50	140	275	500	975	3,450	

SCT#	DENOM	COLOR	CONDITION	F 70	F-VF 75	VF 80	VF-XF 85	XF 90	XF-SUP 95	SUP 98	GEM 100
834a	$5	red	Used			7,000					—
		brown	Unused OG	825	1,400	1,850	2,000	2,200	2,500	2,800	—
		& black	Mint NH	1,375	2,000	3,000	3,150	3,400	4,500	—	—
1053	$5	black	Used	3	5	6.75	7.50	15	30	75	100
			Mint NH	20	37.50	47.50	55	65	85	190	400

1918-23 FIRST AND SECOND AIRMAIL ISSUES

SCT#	DENOM	COLOR	CONDITION	F 70	F-VF 75	VF 80	VF-XF 85	XF 90	XF-SUP 95	SUP 98	GEM 100
C1	6¢	orange	Used	16	20	30	40	80	220	475	—
			Unused OG	30	42.50	55	67.50	85	125	200	525
			Mint NH	42.50	70	110	130	180	375	2,000	7,500
C2	16¢	green	Used	17.50	25	35	45	100	260	625	1,250
			Unused OG	32.50	45	60	72.50	90	140	260	600
			Mint NH	50	75	120	140	200	450	1,450	4,000
C3	24¢	carmine	Used	17.50	25	35	55	110	275	750	3,250
		rose	Unused OG	35	50	65	90	120	240	650	2,500
		& blue	Mint NH	52.50	82.50	130	160	225	550	2,250	6,000
C3a	24¢	invert	Unused OG	335,000	380,000	450,000	675,000	—	1,350,000		
			Mint NH	—	675,000	850,000	—	1,595,000			
C4	8¢	dark	Used	7.50	10	15	22.50	50	125	425	1,600
		green	Unused OG	8.25	11.50	17.50	20	25	40	67.50	140
			Mint NH	14	24	35	47.50	70	150	550	2,250
C5	16¢	dark	Used	14	20	30	37.50	80	220	475	—
		blue	Unused OG	32.50	45	60	70	85	130	225	450
			Mint NH	50	75	120	145	200	375	1,400	4,750
C6	24¢	carmine	Used	14	20	30	37.50	80	220	475	950
			Unused OG	35	50	65	75	92.50	140	250	—
			Mint NH	55	82.50	130	150	210	400	1,125	3,500
C1-C6 Set	6 stamps		Used	86.50	120	175	227.50	485	1,295	3,050	
			Unused OG	175	244	322.50	382.50	472.50	715	1,293	
			Mint NH	265	409	645	772.50	1,050	2,260	8,775	

1926-30 AIRMAILS

SCT#	DENOM	COLOR	CONDITION	F 70	F-VF 75	VF 80	VF-XF 85	XF 90	XF-SUP 95	SUP 98	GEM 100
C7	10¢	dark	Used	0.25	0.25	0.35	2	17.50	60	200	825
		blue	Unused OG	1.15	1.65	2.25	4	10	35	55	125
			Mint NH	1.60	2.65	4	8	25	90	450	1,600
C8	15¢	olive	Used	1.25	1.80	2.50	7.50	27.50	105	325	700
		brown	Unused OG	1.15	1.70	2.50	3.50	9	30	55	115
			Mint NH	1.90	3.25	4.75	10	25	85	275	1,100
C9	20¢	yellow	Used	1	1.45	2	6	27.50	105	325	700
		green	Unused OG	3.25	4.75	6.50	8	15	30	60	125
			Mint NH	5	8	12.50	18.50	32.50	90	275	1,350
C10	10¢	dark	Used	1.25	1.85	2.50	6	25	110	325	850
		blue	Unused OG	3.50	4.75	7	8.50	15	22.50	40	—
			Mint NH	5.25	7.50	12.50	20	35	120	360	1,650
C10a Booklet Pane of 3	10¢	dark blue	Used	39	50	65	80	110	225	—	—
			Unused OG	40	52.50	70	80	92.50	150	—	—
			Mint NH	47.50	72.50	115	145	180	310	—	—
C11	5¢	carmine	Used	0.40	0.55	0.75	5	30	85	275	1,200
		& blue	Unused OG	2.45	3.85	5.50	8	12	25	40	75
			Mint NH	3.50	6.25	10	17.50	35	120	550	2,100
C12	5¢	violet	Used	0.25	0.40	0.50	2.50	25	80	250	550
			Unused OG	4.75	6.50	9.50	11	13	20	40	80
			Mint NH	7	11	17.50	25	40	120	400	2,000

SCT#	DENOM	COLOR	CONDITION	F 70	F-VF 75	VF 80	VF-XF 85	XF 90	XF-SUP 95	SUP 98	GEM 100

1930 GRAF ZEPPELIN ISSUE

SCT#	DENOM	COLOR	CONDITION	F 70	F-VF 75	VF 80	VF-XF 85	XF 90	XF-SUP 95	SUP 98	GEM 100
C13	65¢	green	Used	95	120	150	200	250	550	1,100	—
			Unused OG	100	135	180	205	235	250	450	850
			Mint NH	120	175	250	300	425	600	1,550	4,250
C14	$1.30	brown	Used	225	280	350	425	550	750	1,900	3,750
			Unused OG	200	270	375	400	440	480	625	1,600
			Mint NH	265	400	575	625	750	1,100	3,000	8,500
C15	$2.60	blue	Used	330	400	525	650	850	1,175	2,700	6,000
			Unused OG	275	390	525	575	675	750	1,100	3,000
			Mint NH	425	650	850	975	1,200	1,650	4,000	10,500
C13-C15 Set	3 stamps		Used	650	800	1,025	1,275	1,650	2,450	5,500	
			Unused OG	575	795	1,080	1,180	1,350	1,480	1,975	
			Mint NH	800	1,225	1,675	1,875	2,350	3,300	8,550	

1931-44 AIRMAILS

SCT#	DENOM	COLOR	CONDITION	F 70	F-VF 75	VF 80	VF-XF 85	XF 90	XF-SUP 95	SUP 98	GEM 100
C16	5¢	violet	Used	0.35	0.45	0.60	3	25	85	275	—
			Unused OG	2.40	3.35	4.75	8	15	40	100	—
			Mint NH	3.90	5.75	8.50	17	82.50	200	675	2,000
C17	8¢	olive bister	Used	0.25	0.25	0.40	2	20	75	260	—
			Unused OG	1.05	1.50	2.25	3.25	9	22.50	65	—
			Mint NH	1.50	2.35	3.75	16.50	70	275	1,250	—
C18	50¢	green	Used	21.50	31	47.50	60	80	180	325	—
			Unused OG	22.50	34	45	52	61	76.50	110	225
			Mint NH	30	45	75	85	115	170	450	1,650
C19	6¢	dull orange	Used	0.25	0.25	0.25	1.50	20	75	300	625
			Mint NH	1.50	2.20	3.50	15	85	200	1,650	3,250
C20	25¢	blue	Used	0.50	0.70	1	5	12.50	35	75	—
			Mint NH	0.60	0.85	1.40	5	12.50	50	180	450
C21	20¢	green	Used	0.90	1.20	1.75	5.50	10	27.50	80	—
			Mint NH	4.25	6.75	10	15	25	65	500	1,900
C22	50¢	carmine	Used	2.60	3.70	5	10	16.50	40	125	—
			Mint NH	4.25	6.75	10	15	25	65	325	975
C23	6¢	dark blue & carmine	Used	0.25	0.25	0.25	10	25	60	125	425
			Mint NH	0.25	0.35	0.70	10	35	100	575	1,400
C24	30¢	blue	Used	0.70	1	1.50	6	14	35	115	—
			Mint NH	4.25	7	11	16	27.50	75	325	900
C25	6¢	carmine	Used	0.25	0.25	0.25	2	5	30	90	—
			Mint NH	0.25	0.25	0.25	2	12.50	40	175	475
C25a Booklet Pane of 3	6¢	carmine	Used	0.90	1.15	1.50	2	3	7.50	15	—
			Mint NH	1.85	2.65	3.50	4.75	7	12	25	—
C26	8¢	olive green	Used	0.25	0.25	0.25	2	5	27.50	90	—
			Mint NH	0.25	0.25	0.25	1.50	12.50	40	150	600
C27	10¢	violet	Used	0.25	0.25	0.25	2	5	27.50	90	—
			Mint NH	0.50	0.70	1.10	3.50	10	40	160	600
C28	15¢	brown carmine	Used	0.25	0.25	0.35	2.50	5.50	30	95	—
			Mint NH	0.95	1.40	2.10	6	12	37.50	160	525
C29	20¢	bright green	Used	0.25	0.25	0.30	2.25	5.25	27.50	90	—
			Mint NH	0.95	1.40	2.10	6	12	37.50	160	525
C30	30¢	blue	Used	0.25	0.25	0.35	2.50	5.50	30	95	—
			Mint NH	0.95	1.40	2.10	6	11	35	135	500
C31	50¢	orange	Used	1.75	2.40	3.25	6.50	12.50	45	125	—
			Mint NH	4.25	7.25	11	15	25	47.50	175	600

SCT#	DENOM	COLOR	CONDITION	F 70	F-VF 75	VF 80	VF-XF 85	XF 90	XF-SUP 95	SUP 98	GEM 100

1885-1925 SPECIAL DELIVERY ISSUES

SCT#	DENOM	COLOR	CONDITION	F 70	F-VF 75	VF 80	VF-XF 85	XF 90	XF-SUP 95	SUP 98	GEM 100
E1	10¢	blue	Used	40	50	80	120	190	325	825	—
			Unused OG	235	350	575	650	800	1,475	2,900	—
			Mint NH	475	850	1,300	2,100	3,250	7,500	30,000	—
E2	10¢	blue	Used	18	30	45	70	120	275	750	—
			Unused OG	220	300	500	600	750	1,350	2,600	4,500
			Mint NH	450	675	1,150	1,900	3,250	7,750	32,500	—
E3	10¢	orange	Used	25	32.50	50	80	135	250	900	—
			Unused OG	135	185	300	340	400	700	1,500	—
			Mint NH	250	425	650	875	1,250	3,850	—	—
E4	10¢	blue	Used	45	62.50	110	140	220	425	1,000	—
			Unused OG	400	600	875	1,000	1,350	2,250	4,400	—
			Mint NH	750	1,300	2,000	3,500	5,250	14,500	32,500	67,500
E5	10¢	blue	Used	4.50	7	12.50	30	85	175	500	—
			Unused OG	82.50	135	210	240	300	550	1,150	—
			Mint NH	175	285	475	625	1,000	2,750	7,250	—
E5a	10¢	blue	Used	25	32.50	50	67.50	95	250	600	—
		Dots	Unused OG	165	260	400	450	550	900	1,500	—
		in frame	Mint NH	285	500	800	950	1,300	4,500	8,500	—
E6	10¢	ultramarine	Used	5	7.25	10	25	60	160	375	—
			Unused OG	92.50	145	230	265	325	525	1,200	—
			Mint NH	180	320	500	775	1,400	3,750	7,500	17,000
E6a	10¢	blue	Used	6.25	9	12.50	30	60	175	450	—
			Unused OG	120	200	300	350	425	750	1,500	—
			Mint NH	255	475	750	900	1,500	4,000	8,500	—
E7	10¢	green	Used	22	32.50	50	85	130	260	650	—
			Unused OG	25	40	65	75	90	140	275	500
			Mint NH	47.50	75	140	175	240	525	1,150	2,750
E8	10¢	ultramarine	Used	5	7	10	17.50	30	100	300	—
			Unused OG	50	65	120	130	145	180	375	—
			Mint NH	95	160	250	310	550	1,050	2,100	4,250
E8b	10¢	violet	Used	7	10	14	27.50	50	140	350	—
		blue	Unused OG	70	95	160	180	220	350	600	—
			Mint NH	125	220	350	525	650	1,300	2,750	—
E9	10¢	ultramarine	Used	5	8	12	25	45	130	375	575
			Unused OG	80	110	190	210	240	375	700	1,150
			Mint NH	150	280	425	500	700	1,100	2,750	—
E9a	10¢	blue	Used	6	10	15	30	55	150	375	—
			Unused OG	95	145	260	285	310	475	800	—
			Mint NH	185	315	575	650	850	1,250	3,250	4,750
E10	10¢	pale	Used	22.50	35	50	85	150	280	650	—
		ultramarine	Unused OG	135	185	340	370	425	600	1,075	—
			Mint NH	300	430	750	850	1,100	1,800	3,750	7,000
E10a	10¢	blue	Used	27.50	35	55	100	165	300	675	—
			Unused OG	160	240	400	450	525	850	1,500	—
			Mint NH	300	475	800	950	1,250	2,250	4,750	—
E11	10¢	ultramarine	Used	0.25	0.40	0.75	5	20	75	225	—
			Unused OG	10	13	20	22.50	30	47.50	80	—
			Mint NH	17.50	27.50	45	90	150	275	750	1,650
E11b	10¢	gray	Used	1	1.60	3	10	35	150	1,000	—
		violet	Unused OG	22.50	30	35	52.50	75	125	200	400
			Mint NH	45	62.50	75	150	275	600	1,100	—
E11c	10¢	blue	Used	2.50	3.50	5	20	50	180	1,200	—
			Unused OG	35	60	100	110	135	175	300	—
			Mint NH	70	110	210	265	360	850	1,800	—
E12	10¢	gray	Used	1.20	1.75	3	10	20	75	325	—
		violet	Unused OG	16	25	45	50	57.50	95	180	—
			Mint NH	32.50	55	95	115	220	500	1,100	2,500

SCT#	DENOM	COLOR	CONDITION	F 70	F-VF 75	VF 80	VF-XF 85	XF 90	XF-SUP 95	SUP 98	GEM 100
E12a	10¢	deep ultramarine	Used	1.60	2.25	3.50	11.50	32.50	115	350	—
			Unused OG	22.50	35	55	60	67.50	115	210	—
			Mint NH	42.50	65	130	150	220	500	1,000	2,150
E13	15¢	deep orange	Used	1.50	2.25	3.75	12	32.50	135	—	—
			Unused OG	16	22.50	40	45	50	85	125	—
			Mint NH	27.50	45	75	90	115	170	375	—
E14	20¢	black	Used	0.50	0.70	1	4	20	70	190	—
			Unused OG	1	1.25	2	3.50	7.50	20	35	75
			Mint NH	1.30	2.25	4	6.50	15	45	150	300

1911 REGISTRATION STAMP

SCT#	DENOM	COLOR	CONDITION	F 70	F-VF 75	VF 80	VF-XF 85	XF 90	XF-SUP 95	SUP 98	GEM 100
F1	10¢	ultramarine	Used	4.75	7.50	14	25	40	125	375	—
			Unused OG	30	47.50	75	82.50	95	140	260	475
			Mint NH	50	87.50	160	210	275	450	825	—

1879-1956 POSTAGE DUES

SCT#	DENOM	COLOR	CONDITION	F 70	F-VF 75	VF 80	VF-XF 85	XF 90	XF-SUP 95	SUP 98	GEM 100
J1	1¢	brown	Used	6.75	9.75	14	20	35	85	200	—
			Unused OG	40	57.50	90	110	135	260	450	—
			Mint NH	90	150	260	325	525	975	2,200	—
J2	2¢	brown	Used	9	15	25	27.50	45	100	275	—
			Unused OG	185	275	450	500	625	1,000	1,600	—
			Mint NH	325	600	1,050	1,250	1,750	3,000	—	—
J3	3¢	brown	Used	2.90	4.25	6	9	17.50	40	125	—
			Unused OG	47.50	72.50	100	130	165	260	475	—
			Mint NH	95	165	280	350	575	1,050	—	—
J4	5¢	brown	Used	32.50	45	70	77.50	140	350	775	—
			Unused OG	300	450	800	900	1,150	1,600	—	—
			Mint NH	650	1,025	1,950	2,150	2,750	4,900	—	—
J5	10¢	brown	Used	32.50	45	70	77.50	140	350	700	—
			Unused OG	375	575	925	1,025	1,225	1,850	—	—
			Mint NH	825	1,375	2,500	2,750	3,500	5,000	—	—
J6	30¢	brown	Used	30	40	65	82.50	125	275	675	—
			Unused OG	160	230	400	450	525	725	1,250	—
			Mint NH	300	525	900	1,050	1,800	—	—	—
J7	50¢	brown	Used	42	60	90	125	225	450	1,100	—
			Unused OG	270	400	650	725	900	1,400	—	—
			Mint NH	525	900	1,600	1,850	2,500	4,250	—	—
J8	1¢	deep brown	Unused OG	10,750	12,500	16,000	22,000	27,500	—	—	—
J9	2¢	deep brown	Unused OG	9,750	11,750	15,000	21,000	27,000	—	—	—
J10	3¢	deep brown	Unused OG	12,000	16,500	20,000	27,000	37,500	—	—	—
J11	5¢	deep brown	Unused OG	8,750	10,500	13,000	17,250	24,000	—	—	—
J12	10¢	deep brown	Unused OG	4,000	5,250	6,750	8,750	11,500	—	—	—
J13	30¢	deep brown	Unused OG	4,250	5,500	7,000	9,250	12,500	—	—	—
J14	50¢	deep brown	Unused OG	4,250	5,500	7,000	9,250	12,500	—	—	—
J15	1¢	red brown	Used	3.20	4.50	7	12	20	650	125	—
			Unused OG	27.50	42.50	70	80	110	160	280	—
			Mint NH	70	90	190	260	360	650	1,400	—
J16	2¢	red brown	Used	2.70	4	6	10	25	55	160	—
			Unused OG	40	52.50	80	100	135	225	400	—
			Mint NH	80	140	225	325	450	850	1,900	3,500

SCT#	DENOM	COLOR	CONDITION	F 70	F-VF 75	VF 80	VF-XF 85	XF 90	XF-SUP 95	SUP 98	GEM 100
J17	3¢	red	Used	150	220	350	450	625	1,200	2,250	—
		brown	Unused OG	425	625	1,050	1,150	1,450	2,100	—	—
			Mint NH	900	1,375	2,500	2,750	3,750	—	—	—
J18	5¢	red	Used	22.50	30	50	62.50	85	190	525	1,050
		brown	Unused OG	220	330	550	625	750	1,200	—	—
			Mint NH	450	750	1,300	1,600	2,150	3,250	—	—
J19	10¢	red	Used	16.50	22.50	35	47.50	70	160	425	—
		brown	Unused OG	220	330	550	625	750	1,200	2,200	—
			Mint NH	450	750	1,300	1,600	2,500	3,500	6,500	—
J20	30¢	red	Used	32	45	70	81.50	115	290	750	—
		brown	Unused OG	95	150	225	260	310	525	850	—
			Mint NH	175	250	550	725	1,025	1,750	3,000	—
J21	50¢	red	Used	110	160	250	325	500	900	1,700	—
		brown	Unused OG	725	1,050	1,800	1,950	2,150	2,850	—	—
			Mint NH	1,225	2,000	3,750	4,250	5,000	7,500	—	—
J22	1¢	bright	Used	0.85	1.25	2	4	10	25	80	—
		claret	Unused OG	12.50	17.50	30	37.50	47.50	85	145	—
			Mint NH	27.50	45	85	110	170	350	750	—
J23	2¢	bright	Used	0.85	1.25	2	3.75	11	30	85	—
		claret	Unused OG	14	21	32.50	40	50	85	160	275
			Mint NH	30	50	90	120	200	425	825	—
J24	3¢	bright	Used	7.75	10.50	16	17.50	25	70	200	—
		claret	Unused OG	27.50	45	67.50	100	150	225	280	—
			Mint NH	57.50	100	180	250	360	725	2,500	—
J25	5¢	bright	Used	7.75	10.50	16	20	35	80	190	—
		claret	Unused OG	47.50	65	100	120	160	275	475	—
			Mint NH	90	160	290	375	650	1,100	2,700	5,250
J26	10¢	bright	Used	14.50	20	30	37.50	50	120	275	—
		claret	Unused OG	70	110	165	195	250	425	725	—
			Mint NH	150	260	500	575	750	1,300	3,000	—
J27	30¢	bright	Used	105	150	225	280	400	1,000	2,150	—
		claret	Unused OG	240	350	575	675	850	1,300	2,750	—
			Mint NH	525	850	1,700	1,900	2,500	4,500	—	—
J28	50¢	bright	Used	105	150	225	300	450	975	2,400	—
		claret	Unused OG	260	375	625	725	900	1,300	2,850	—
			Mint NH	525	900	1,750	1,850	2,000	3,750	—	—
J29	1¢	vermilion	Used	340	500	750	900	1,275	2,000	—	—
			Unused OG	950	1,400	2,350	2,700	3,350	5,000	—	—
			Mint NH	2,100	3,400	6,000	7,500	12,000	—	—	—
J30	2¢	vermilion	Used	160	235	350	450	625	1,300	2,900	—
			Unused OG	300	500	775	900	1,250	2,750	—	—
			Mint NH	600	900	1,900	2,200	2,650	4,500	—	—
J31	1¢	deep	Used	5.75	8.25	12	14.50	20	50	150	—
		claret	Unused OG	27.50	45	72.50	82.50	105	170	300	—
			Mint NH	65	130	260	300	450	750	1,800	—
J32	2¢	deep	Used	4.65	6.75	10	15	27.50	50	150	—
		claret	Unused OG	25	40	62.50	72.50	100	160	275	—
			Mint NH	60	120	240	300	375	800	1,650	—
J33	3¢	deep	Used	25	32.50	50	57.50	80	200	500	—
		claret	Unused OG	82.50	115	200	220	260	400	700	1,400
			Mint NH	150	260	575	650	800	1,450	3,000	—
J34	5¢	deep	Used	27.50	37.50	55	65	90	225	550	—
		claret	Unused OG	120	170	300	350	450	725	1,150	—
			Mint NH	250	425	850	1,000	1,500	2,250	—	—
J35	10¢	deep	Used	19	26	40	50	70	175	475	—
		claret	Unused OG	130	200	350	400	525	800	1,300	—
			Mint NH	275	500	1,000	1,200	1,650	2,400	5,000	—
J36	30¢	deep	Used	115	170	250	300	425	825	3,750	—
		claret	Unused OG	190	325	550	625	750	1,100	1,700	—
			Mint NH	350	675	1,250	1,450	2,000	3,000	—	—
J36a	30¢	carmine	Used	130	180	275	310	450	875	1,900	—
			Unused OG	205	340	675	725	775	1,000	2,350	—
			Mint NH	410	775	1,600	1,725	2,000	3,000	—	—
J36b	30¢	pale	Used	97.50	130	200	240	325	600	1,350	—
		rose	Unused OG	170	270	450	500	550	800	1,400	—
			Mint NH	310	550	1,100	1,225	1,375	2,200	4,400	—

SCT#	DENOM	COLOR	CONDITION	F 70	F-VF 75	VF 80	VF-XF 85	XF 90	XF-SUP 95	SUP 98	GEM 100
J37	50¢	deep	Used	375	525	800	975	1,400	2,500	5,000	—
		claret	Unused OG	750	1,075	1,800	2,100	2,750	4,000	—	—
			Mint NH	1,400	2,500	4,250	4,750	6,500	13,000	—	—
J37a	50¢	pale	Used	350	500	725	875	1,300	2,350	5,000	—
		rose	Unused OG	650	900	1,600	1,800	2,250	3,250	—	—
			Mint NH	1,600	2,500	3,750	4,500	6,000	12,000	—	—
J38	1¢	deep	Used	0.40	0.60	1	2	4	15	55	—
		claret	Unused OG	5.50	8	13.50	16	20	30	55	—
			Mint NH	15	27.50	40	60	130	275	600	—
J39	2¢	deep	Used	0.35	0.55	1	2	5	15	55	—
		claret	Unused OG	5.50	8	13.50	16	20	30	55	—
			Mint NH	15	27.50	40	60	90	275	600	—
J40	3¢	deep	Used	2.25	3.50	5	7	10.50	27.50	125	—
		claret	Unused OG	37.50	60	100	115	135	190	340	—
			Mint NH	60	120	225	290	425	825	1,600	—
J41	5¢	deep	Used	2.25	3.50	5	7	11	27.50	125	—
		claret	Unused OG	45	70	110	130	175	250	425	—
			Mint NH	92.50	175	280	360	625	975	1,850	—
J42	10¢	deep	Used	3.50	5	7.50	11	17.50	45	140	—
		claret	Unused OG	45	70	110	130	175	250	425	—
			Mint NH	92.50	175	280	360	500	950	1,750	—
J43	30¢	deep	Used	37.50	52.50	80	100	140	300	700	—
		claret	Unused OG	225	360	600	700	850	1,250	2,600	—
			Mint NH	440	825	1,500	1,750	2,250	3,500	—	—
J44	50¢	deep	Used	30	42.50	60	75	95	225	600	—
		claret	Unused OG	150	250	375	450	550	850	1,400	—
			Mint NH	27.50	500	925	1,150	1,650	2,500	—	—
J45	1¢	deep	Used	2.25	3.25	5	9	16	37.50	100	—
		claret	Unused OG	18	27.50	40	50	65	100	175	—
			Mint NH	40	75	115	160	240	425	850	—
J45a	1¢	rose	Used	2.25	3.25	5	9	16	37.50	100	—
		carmine	Unused OG	16	24	35	45	65	95	160	—
			Mint NH	35	67.50	105	140	225	375	750	—
J46	2¢	deep	Used	0.85	1.25	2	4	8	17.50	60	—
		claret	Unused OG	18	27.50	40	50	65	100	175	—
			Mint NH	40	75	115	160	240	400	850	—
J46a	2¢	rose	Used	0.85	1.25	2	4	8	17.50	60	—
		carmine	Unused OG	16	24	35	45	5	95	160	—
			Mint NH	35	67.50	105	140	225	375	750	—
J47	3¢	deep	Used	29	39	60	80	140	275	650	—
		claret	Unused OG	250	400	625	725	900	1,250	2,000	—
			Mint NH	500	925	1,600	1,850	2,650	5,000	—	—
J48	5¢	deep	Used	5.75	8.75	12	15	24	50	150	—
		claret	Unused OG	45	77.50	120	140	170	250	400	—
			Mint NH	92.50	185	275	350	475	750	1,500	—
J48a	5¢	rose	Used	5.75	8.75	12	15	24	50	150	—
		carmine	Unused OG	45	77.50	120	140	170	250	400	—
			Mint NH	92.50	185	275	350	475	750	1,500	—
J49	10¢	deep	Used	9.25	13	20	22.50	30	75	225	—
		claret	Unused OG	50	85	125	145	180	260	425	—
			Mint NH	92.50	185	280	360	475	750	1,500	—
J49a	10¢	rose	Used	9.25	13	20	22.50	30	72.50	225	—
		carmine	Unused OG	50	85	125	145	180	260	425	—
			Mint NH	92.50	185	280	360	475	750	1,500	—
J50	50¢	deep	Used	95	135	200	230	350	750	1,400	—
		claret	Unused OG	425	675	1,100	1,250	1,450	2,250	—	—
			Mint NH	875	1,600	2,900	3,250	4,250	7,500	—	—
J50a	10¢	rose	Used	87.50	130	190	225	350	775	1,375	—
		carmine	Unused OG	450	700	1,150	1,300	1,500	2,400	—	—
			Mint NH	900	1,650	3,000	3,350	4,500	7,750	—	—
J52	1¢	carmine	Used	7.25	10	15	17.50	25	70	200	—
		lake	Unused OG	35	55	80	95	125	175	300	—
			Mint NH	67.50	125	220	275	350	575	1,050	—
J52a	1¢	dull	Used	7.25	10	15	17.50	25	70	200	—
		rose	Unused OG	35	55	85	97.50	125	175	300	—
			Mint NH	72.50	130	230	290	375	600	1,100	—

SCT#	DENOM	COLOR	CONDITION	F 70	F-VF 75	VF 80	VF-XF 85	XF 90	XF-SUP 95	SUP 98	GEM 100
J53	2¢	carmine	Used	0.50	0.60	1	2	4	17.50	65	—
		lake	Unused OG	25	40	62.50	72.50	90	125	210	—
			Mint NH	42.50	80	170	200	260	500	900	—
J53a	2¢	dull	Used	0.70	1.20	2	4	8	22.50	75	—
		rose	Unused OG	30	45	67.50	80	100	140	225	—
			Mint NH	47.50	85	180	210	275	525	950	—
J53b	2¢	vermilion	Used	0.80	1.20	2	4	8	22.50	75	—
			Unused OG	30	45	67.50	80	100	140	225	—
			Mint NH	47.50	85	180	210	275	525	950	—
J54	3¢	carmine	Used	35	50	75	90	125	275	700	—
		lake	Unused OG	400	650	1,050	1,200	1,600	2,300	—	—
			Mint NH	900	1,700	3,000	3,600	4,250	6,750	—	—
J54a	3¢	dull	Used	35	47.50	75	90	125	275	700	—
		rose	Unused OG	385	625	1,000	1,150	1,525	2,200	—	—
			Mint NH	850	1,600	2,900	3,400	4,000	6,500	—	—
J55	5¢	carmine	Used	2.75	4	6	9	17.50	45	140	—
		lake	Unused OG	22.50	35	50	60	75	135	200	—
			Mint NH	50	87.50	140	180	270	475	1,100	—
J55a	5¢	dull	Used	1.85	2.50	4	7	12.50	30	110	—
		rose	Unused OG	20	30	45	55	70	125	190	—
			Mint NH	45	82.50	130	175	260	450	1,000	—
J56	10¢	carmine	Used	1.85	2.50	4	7	12.50	30	110	—
		lake	Unused OG	30	50	75	85	100	170	275	400
			Mint NH	55	110	200	250	325	500	1,100	—
J56a	10¢	dull	Used	2.25	3.50	5	8	12.50	35	125	—
		rose	Unused OG	32.50	55	80	92.50	110	185	300	—
			Mint NH	60	115	210	260	350	550	1,150	—
J57	30¢	carmine	Used	26	37.50	55	60	85	220	525	—
		lake	Unused OG	90	150	225	260	325	550	850	—
			Mint NH	175	330	525	675	950	1,375	2,750	—
J58	50¢	carmine	Used	850	1,200	1,700	2,400	3,250	—	—	—
		lake	Unused OG	7,750	11,500	16,000	—	—	—	—	—
			Mint NH	—	22,000	—	—	—	—	—	—
J59	1¢	rose	Used	300	475	750	900	1,200	2,600	—	—
			Unused OG	1,600	2,500	4,000	4,750	6,500	11,500	—	—
			Mint NH	3,250	5,250	9,000	12,000	17,500	30,000	—	—
J60	2¢	rose	Used	35	50	75	87.50	110	400	625	—
			Unused OG	92.50	145	250	340	425	650	1,050	—
			Mint NH	170	375	625	825	1,000	1,600	3,250	—
J61	1¢	carmine	Used	0.25	0.25	0.25	1.50	5	12.50	50	—
		rose	Unused OG	1.30	1.75	2.75	4	7.50	17.50	40	—
			Mint NH	3.75	5.50	9	16	35	110	300	—
J61a	1¢	rose	Used	0.25	0.25	0.25	1.50	5	12.50	50	—
		red	Unused OG	1.30	1.75	2.75	4	7.50	17.50	40	—
			Mint NH	3.75	5.50	9	16	35	110	300	—
J61b	1¢	deep	Used	0.25	0.25	0.25	1.50	5	12.50	50	—
		claret	Unused OG	1.30	1.75	2.75	4	7.50	17.50	40	—
			Mint NH	3.75	5.50	9	16	35	110	300	—
J62	2¢	carmine	Used	0.25	0.25	0.25	1.50	5	12.50	50	—
		rose	Unused OG	1.30	1.75	2.75	4	7.50	17.50	40	—
			Mint NH	3.75	5.50	9	16	35	110	300	—
J62a	2¢	rose	Used	0.25	0.25	0.25	1.50	5	12.50	50	—
		red	Unused OG	1.30	1.75	2.75	4	7.50	17.50	40	—
			Mint NH	3.75	5.50	9	16	35	110	300	—
J62b	2¢	deep	Used	0.25	0.25	0.25	1.50	5	12.50	50	—
		claret	Unused OG	1.30	1.75	2.75	4	7.50	17.50	40	—
			Mint NH	3.75	5.50	9	16	35	110	300	—
J63	3¢	carmine	Used	0.40	0.55	0.80	1.60	3.75	13.50	60	—
		rose	Unused OG	5.50	8	13.50	16	19	27.50	55	—
			Mint NH	11	20	35	47.50	85	225	550	—
J63a	3¢	rose	Used	0.40	0.55	0.80	1.60	3.75	13.50	60	—
		red	Unused OG	5.50	8	13.50	16	19	27.50	55	—
			Mint NH	11	20	35	47.50	85	200	550	—

SCT#	DENOM	COLOR	CONDITION	F 70	F-VF 75	VF 80	VF-XF 85	XF 90	XF-SUP 95	SUP 98	GEM 100
J63b	3¢	deep claret	Used	0.40	0.55	0.80	1.60	3.75	13.50	60	—
			Unused OG	5.50	8	13.50	16	19	27.50	55	—
			Mint NH	11	20	35	47.50	85	200	550	—
J64	5¢	carmine rose	Used	0.40	0.55	0.80	2	5	15	60	—
			Unused OG	5	7.50	11	14	17.50	25	50	—
			Mint NH	10	19	32.50	45	80	190	550	—
J64a	5¢	rose red	Used	0.40	0.55	0.80	2	5	15	60	—
			Unused OG	5	7.50	11	14	17.50	25	50	—
			Mint NH	10	19	32.50	45	80	190	525	—
J64b	5¢	deep claret	Used	0.40	0.55	0.80	1.60	3.75	13.50	60	—
			Unused OG	5	7.50	11	14	17.50	25	50	—
			Mint NH	10	19	32.50	45	80	190	525	900
J65	10¢	carmine rose	Used	0.50	0.75	1	1.75	4.25	17.50	70	—
			Unused OG	10	15	22.50	27.50	35	47.50	85	—
			Mint NH	19	37.50	65	82.50	115	325	675	—
J65a	10¢	rose red	Used	0.50	0.75	1	1.75	4.25	17.50	70	—
			Unused OG	10	15	22.50	27.50	35	47.50	85	—
			Mint NH	19	37.50	65	82.50	115	325	675	—
J65b	10¢	deep claret	Used	0.50	0.75	1	1.75	4.25	17.50	70	—
			Unused OG	10	15	22.50	27.50	32.50	42.50	85	—
			Mint NH	19	37.50	65	82.50	115	325	675	—
J66	30¢	carmine rose	Used	0.80	1.20	2	4	12.50	30	100	—
			Unused OG	35	50	80	92.50	120	175	300	—
			Mint NH	60	120	220	260	350	575	1,200	—
J66a	30¢	deep claret	Used	0.80	1.20	2	4	9.50	27.50	100	—
			Unused OG	35	50	80	92.50	120	175	300	—
			Mint NH	60	120	220	260	350	575	1,200	—
J67	50¢	carmine rose	Used	0.50	0.75	1	2	6	22.50	70	—
			Unused OG	47.50	75	140	155	175	275	450	—
			Mint NH	97.50	175	325	400	500	800	1,650	—
J67a	50¢	rose red	Used	0.50	0.75	1	2	6	22.50	70	—
			Unused OG	47.50	75	140	155	175	275	450	—
			Mint NH	97.50	175	325	400	500	800	1,650	—
J67b	50¢	deep claret	Used	0.50	0.75	1	2	6	22.50	70	—
			Unused OG	47.50	75	140	155	175	275	450	—
			Mint NH	97.50	175	325	400	500	800	1,650	—
J68	½¢	dull red	Used	0.25	0.25	0.25	1.50	3.50	14	50	—
			Unused OG	0.45	0.65	1	1.40	2.10	5.50	12.50	—
			Mint NH	0.70	1.10	1.75	3.50	7	22.50	92.50	—
J69	½¢	carmine	Used	0.90	1.20	1.90	2.50	9.50	30	110	—
			Unused OG	2	2.75	4.25	5	6	9.75	22.50	—
			Mint NH	4	6.25	9.50	15	24	100	250	—
J70	1¢	carmine	Used	0.30	0.30	0.35	1.10	3.75	13	50	—
			Unused OG	1.30	1.85	2.75	3.50	4.50	8	15	—
			Mint NH	2.75	4.50	6.25	11.50	18	90	210	400
J71	2¢	carmine	Used	0.25	0.25	0.35	1.10	3.75	13	50	—
			Unused OG	1.70	2.50	3.75	4.50	5.75	9	17.50	—
			Mint NH	3.75	5.50	8.50	13.50	22.50	105	250	—
J72	3¢	carmine	Used	1.30	1.75	2.75	5	12.50	35	125	—
			Unused OG	8.50	11.50	20	24	30	42.50	67.50	—
			Mint NH	16.50	26	47.50	62.50	95	225	450	—
J73	5¢	carmine	Used	2.35	3.25	5	9	19	72.50	200	—
			Unused OG	7.50	10.50	18	20	24	37.50	55	—
			Mint NH	14.50	24	42.50	55	85	190	380	—
J74	10¢	carmine	Used	0.85	1.25	2	4	11	32.50	115	—
			Unused OG	15	23.50	42.50	47.50	55	85	130	—
			Mint NH	37.50	70	95	115	150	300	850	—
J75	30¢	carmine	Used	1.75	2.50	4	10	37.50	125	250	—
			Unused OG	50	82.50	125	140	175	250	375	—
			Mint NH	85	150	275	325	400	625	1,250	2,250
J76	50¢	carmine	Used	0.90	1.25	2	4	11	32.50	115	—
			Unused OG	65	110	175	200	260	550	—	—
			Mint NH	120	220	375	450	600	950	1,750	—

SCT#	DENOM	COLOR	CONDITION	F 70	F-VF 75	VF 80	VF-XF 85	XF 90	XF-SUP 95	SUP 98	GEM 100
J77	$1	carmine	Used	0.25	0.25	0.35	1.50	3.50	15	50	—
			Unused OG	11.50	18.50	32.50	37.50	42.50	55	85	—
			Mint NH	20	37.50	65	80	110	240	500	—
J77a	$1	scarlet	Used	0.25	0.25	0.35	1.50	3.50	15	50	—
			Unused OG	9.50	16.50	27.50	32.50	37.50	45	72.50	—
			Mint NH	17.50	30	55	70	100	220	475	—
J78	$5	carmine	Used	0.25	0.25	0.35	1.50	3.50	15	50	—
			Unused OG	14	22.50	37.50	42.50	55	80	115	—
			Mint NH	26	47.50	85	100	140	290	625	—
J78a	$5	scarlet	Used	0.25	0.25	0.35	1.10	3.50	15	50	—
			Unused OG	12	18.50	32.50	37.50	45	62.50	90	—
			Mint NH	22.50	40	70	85	125	240	550	—
J79	½¢	dull	Used	0.25	0.25	0.25	0.80	2	9	40	—
		carmine	Unused OG	0.55	0.85	1.25	1.90	2.75	6.25	12.50	—
			Mint NH	0.75	1.10	1.80	4	12.50	27.50	45	—
J79a	½¢	scarlet	Used	0.25	0.25	0.25	0.80	2	9	40	—
			Unused OG	0.40	0.60	0.90	1.40	2	4.50	10	—
			Mint NH	0.55	0.80	1.30	3	10	25	45	—
J80	1¢	dull	Used	0.25	0.25	0.25	0.80	2	8.50	40	—
		carmine	Unused OG	0.25	0.25	0.40	0.70	1.50	4.25	9	—
			Mint NH	0.25	0.35	0.50	2.50	8	20	35	—
J80a	1¢	scarlet	Used	0.25	0.25	0.25	0.80	2	9	40	—
			Unused OG	0.25	0.25	0.25	0.45	0.90	2.75	7.75	—
			Mint NH	0.25	0.25	0.30	1.50	6	15	35	—
J81	2¢	dull	Used	0.25	0.25	0.25	0.80	2	9	40	—
		carmine	Unused OG	0.25	0.25	0.40	0.70	1.50	4.25	9	—
			Mint NH	0.25	0.35	0.50	2.50	8	20	35	—
J81a	2¢	scarlet	Used	0.25	0.25	0.25	0.80	2	8.50	40	—
			Unused OG	0.25	0.25	0.25	0.45	0.90	2.75	7.75	—
			Mint NH	0.25	0.25	0.30	1.50	5	12.50	35	—
J82	3¢	dull	Used	0.25	0.25	0.25	0.80	2	9	40	—
		carmine	Unused OG	0.25	0.25	0.40	0.70	1.50	4.25	9	—
			Mint NH	0.25	0.35	0.50	2.50	8	20	35	—
J82a	3¢	scarlet	Used	0.25	0.25	0.25	0.80	2	9	40	—
			Unused OG	0.25	0.25	0.25	0.55	1.10	3	8.50	—
			Mint NH	0.25	0.30	0.45	2	6	15	35	—
J83	5¢	dull	Used	0.25	0.25	0.25	0.80	2	9	40	—
		carmine	Unused OG	0.35	0.45	0.75	1.25	2.25	6	12.50	—
			Mint NH	0.50	0.65	1.15	2.50	10	25	50	—
J83a	5¢	scarlet	Used	0.25	0.25	0.25	0.80	2	9	40	—
			Unused OG	0.25	0.25	0.40	0.80	1.60	4.50	9.50	—
			Mint NH	0.25	0.35	0.60	3	8	20	40	—
J84	10¢	dull	Used	0.25	0.25	0.25	0.80	2	9	40	—
		carmine	Unused OG	0.75	1	1.60	2	3	7.50	15	—
			Mint NH	1.05	1.50	2.50	6	12.50	30	60	—
J84a	10¢	scarlet	Used	0.25	0.25	0.25	0.80	2	9	40	—
			Unused OG	0.55	0.80	1.25	1.60	2.40	5.25	11	—
			Mint NH	0.80	1.10	1.90	5.25	10	27.50	47.50	—
J85	30¢	dull	Used	0.25	0.25	0.25	0.90	2.50	9.50	45	—
		carmine	Unused OG	6	8	12.50	16.50	22.50	35	90	—
			Mint NH	7.50	12.50	20	30	50	75	175	325
J85a	30¢	scarlet	Used	0.25	0.25	0.25	0.90	2.50	9.50	45	—
			Unused OG	3.50	4.60	7.50	9.75	16	30	70	—
			Mint NH	4.25	7.25	11.50	16	30	75	160	—
J86	50¢	dull	Used	0.25	0.25	0.25	0.90	2.50	9.50	45	—
		carmine	Unused OG	6	8	12.50	16.50	22.50	35	90	—
			Mint NH	7.50	12.50	20	30	50	75	175	—
J86a	50¢	scarlet	Used	0.25	0.25	0.25	0.90	2.50	9.50	45	—
			Unused OG	4.25	6	9	11.50	20	37.50	85	—
			Mint NH	5.75	8.50	15	20	32.50	75	160	—
J87	50¢	scarlet	Used	0.25	0.25	0.25	0.90	2.50	9.50	45	—
			Unused OG	14	20	30	37.50	50	85	145	—
			Mint NH	19.50	32.50	52.50	62.50	90	150	325	575

SCT#	DENOM	COLOR	CONDITION	F 70	F-VF 75	VF 80	VF-XF 85	XF 90	XF-SUP 95	SUP 98	GEM 100
align											

1919-22 U.S. POSTAL AGENCY IN CHINA

SCT#	DENOM	COLOR	CONDITION	F 70	F-VF 75	VF 80	VF-XF 85	XF 90	XF-SUP 95	SUP 98	GEM 100
K1	2¢/1¢	green	Used	32.50	50	70	100	160	425	1,100	—
			Unused OG	11.25	15	22.50	27.50	37.50	70	125	—
			Mint NH	30	45	67.50	87.50	140	475	1,050	—
K2	4¢/2¢	rose	Used	32.50	50	70	100	160	425	1,100	—
		type I	Unused OG	11.25	15	22.50	27.50	37.50	70	125	—
			Mint NH	30	45	67.50	90	175	700	1,250	—
K3	6¢/3¢	violet	Used	70	97.50	140	210	325	900	2,250	—
		type II	Unused OG	22.50	40	55	67.50	75	150	275	—
			Mint NH	52.50	88.50	140	190	320	1,300	2,750	—
K4	8¢/4¢	brown	Used	70	97.50	140	210	325	975	2,100	—
			Unused OG	22.50	40	55	67.50	75	150	275	—
			Mint NH	52.50	88.50	140	190	320	1,300	2,400	—
K5	10¢/5¢	blue	Used	70	97.50	140	210	400	1,150	—	—
			Unused OG	25	42.50	60	70	80	155	280	—
			Mint NH	57.50	95	160	240	375	1,250	2,500	—
K6	12¢/6¢	red	Used	100	145	210	290	500	1,200	2,750	—
		orange	Unused OG	37.50	52.50	80	90	110	210	375	—
			Mint NH	77.50	145	210	250	375	1,350	3,250	—
K7	14¢/7¢	black	Used	110	150	210	310	450	1,250	2,750	—
			Unused OG	40	55	82.50	92.50	120	260	425	—
			Mint NH	80	150	215	260	400	1,400	3,750	—
K8	16¢/8¢	olive	Used	77.50	110	160	225	400	1,000	2,750	—
		bister	Unused OG	30	45	65	77.50	100	175	300	—
			Mint NH	65	105	170	240	400	1,350	2,650	—
K8a	16¢/8¢	olive	Used	72.50	100	140	210	375	975	—	—
		green	Unused OG	22.50	40	55	67.50	75	150	275	—
			Mint NH	65	95	150	200	320	1,075	2,500	4,000
K9	18¢/9¢	salmon	Used	87.50	135	175	260	425	—	—	—
		red	Unused OG	27.50	42.50	60	67.50	100	180	—	—
			Mint NH	65	95	150	200	300	1,300	2,850	—
K10	20¢/10¢	orange	Used	70	100	140	215	325	850	2,100	—
		yellow	Unused OG	27.50	40	55	67.50	90	160	325	—
			Mint NH	57.50	87.50	140	225	375	1,450	2,750	—
K11	24¢/12¢	brown	Used	75	105	160	240	360	1,250	2,600	—
		carmine	Unused OG	37.50	52.50	75	87.50	110	210	375	—
			Mint NH	75	120	190	260	475	1,500	3,500	—
K11a	24¢/12¢	claret	Used	125	150	240	325	500	1,750	3,250	—
		brown	Unused OG	50	75	110	130	170	290	500	—
			Mint NH	95	180	275	350	600	2,250	5,750	—
K12	30¢/15¢	gray	Used	110	150	230	320	525	1,400	3,150	—
			Unused OG	40	57.50	82.50	95	120	225	450	900
			Mint NH	80	135	200	290	425	1,300	3,500	8,500
K13	40¢/20¢	deep	Used	150	210	325	450	700	1,900	4,250	—
		ultramarine	Unused OG	60	82.50	120	145	175	350	650	—
			Mint NH	120	200	300	450	750	1,850	3,750	—
K14	60¢/30¢	orange	Used	130	185	275	400	750	1,650	3,750	—
		red	Unused OG	50	75	110	130	165	340	550	—
			Mint NH	100	170	260	400	800	2,250	3,650	—
K15	$1/50¢	light	Used	485	675	1,000	1,750	2,250	5,750	—	—
		violet	Unused OG	240	385	550	650	800	1,425	2,350	—
			Mint NH	450	825	1,200	1,600	2,500	6,500	14,500	—
K16	$2/$1	violet	Used	425	575	750	1,150	1,800	4,250	10,500	—
		brown	Unused OG	190	285	425	500	600	1,000	1,750	—
			Mint NH	340	600	925	1,250	2,250	7,500	12,500	—
K17	2¢/1¢	green	Used	105	160	225	340	500	1,250	3,250	—
			Unused OG	45	67.50	100	125	155	275	480	—
			Mint NH	90	150	225	300	425	1,850	3,250	—

SCT#	DENOM	COLOR	CONDITION	F 70	F-VF 75	VF 80	VF-XF 85	XF 90	XF-SUP 95	SUP 98	GEM 100
K18	4¢/2¢	carmine	Used	105	160	225	340	500	1,250	3,250	—
			Unused OG	45	67.50	100	125	155	275	480	—
			Mint NH	90	150	225	300	425	1,850	3,250	—

OFFICIAL STAMPS

1873 Agriculture Department

SCT#	DENOM	COLOR	CONDITION	F 70	F-VF 75	VF 80	VF-XF 85	XF 90	XF-SUP 95	SUP 98	GEM 100
O1	1¢	yellow	Used	110	145	200	250	375	850	—	—
			Unused NG	90	115	170	190	215	265	—	—
			Unused OG	155	205	300	430	625	1,350	—	—
			Mint NH	300	550	1,000	1,350	1,750	3,500	—	—
O2	2¢	yellow	Used	52.50	67.50	100	130	175	500	—	—
			Unused NG	70	85	130	145	165	250	—	—
			Unused OG	130	170	275	400	550	1,100	—	—
			Mint NH	175	315	575	800	1,200	2,700	—	—
O3	3¢	yellow	Used	9	12	17.50	22.50	37.50	125	—	—
			Unused NG	57.50	75	105	115	135	190	—	—
			Unused OG	100	155	225	320	435	875	—	—
			Mint NH	130	235	425	600	900	1,975	—	—
O4	6¢	yellow	Used	35	42.50	60	85	125	375	—	—
			Unused NG	70	85	130	145	165	250	525	—
			Unused OG	125	185	275	400	575	1,175	—	—
			Mint NH	180	315	575	800	1,200	2,650	—	—
O5	10¢	yellow	Used	110	140	200	260	350	700	—	—
			Unused NG	120	170	240	275	300	475	—	—
			Unused OG	250	370	525	700	1,050	2,000	—	—
			Mint NH	400	650	1,150	1,650	2,500	5,250	—	—
O6	12¢	yellow	Used	135	180	260	350	475	1,100	—	—
			Unused NG	110	175	250	260	325	450	—	—
			Unused OG	245	300	450	625	950	1,850	—	—
			Mint NH	400	550	1,000	1,400	2,100	4,500	—	—
O7	15¢	yellow	Used	120	160	230	320	450	1,000	1,900	—
			Unused NG	85	160	225	250	300	425	700	—
			Unused OG	225	285	425	600	925	1,750	—	—
			Mint NH	350	525	950	1,350	2,000	4,500	—	—
O8	24¢	yellow	Used	130	170	250	310	425	950	—	—
			Unused NG	85	160	225	255	300	425	—	—
			Unused OG	225	285	425	600	950	1,800	—	—
			Mint NH	350	550	950	1,350	2,100	4,500	—	—
O9	30¢	yellow	Used	145	190	280	375	550	1,100	—	—
			Unused NG	110	175	275	300	375	600	—	—
			Unused OG	300	400	550	850	1,200	2,250	—	—
			Mint NH	450	675	1,200	1,700	2,650	5,500	—	—

1873 Executive

SCT#	DENOM	COLOR	CONDITION	F 70	F-VF 75	VF 80	VF-XF 85	XF 90	XF-SUP 95	SUP 98	GEM 100
O10	1¢	carmine	Used	280	390	550	800	1,150	2,600	—	—
			Unused NG	175	300	450	475	575	825	—	—
			Unused OG	425	625	900	1,175	1,750	3,250	—	—
			Mint NH	1,200	2,000	3,500	4,750	7,500	11,500	—	—
O11	2¢	carmine	Used	135	185	260	370	550	1,250	—	—
			Unused NG	110	185	260	290	350	525	—	—
			Unused OG	210	390	575	725	1,150	2,200	3,500	—
			Mint NH	450	775	1,400	1,950	2,750	6,000	—	—

SCT#	DENOM	COLOR	CONDITION	F 70	F-VF 75	VF 80	VF-XF 85	XF 90	XF-SUP 95	SUP 98	GEM 100
O12	3¢	carmine	Used	115	160	225	310	455	1,025	—	—
			Unused NG	150	230	325	360	450	750	—	—
			Unused OG	350	475	700	950	1,450	2,750	—	—
			Mint NH	550	900	1,600	2,200	3,450	7,500	—	—
O12a	3¢	violet	Used	140	200	275	360	500	1,100	—	—
		rose	Unused NG	210	310	450	500	575	700	—	—
			Unused OG	500	775	1,100	1,375	2,250	3,500	—	—
			Mint NH	775	1,425	2,500	3,500	4,750	—	—	—
O13	6¢	carmine	Used	300	435	600	875	1,300	2,850	—	—
			Unused NG	200	360	425	460	550	825	—	—
			Unused OG	400	600	900	1,150	1,750	3,000	—	—
			Mint NH		—	—	3,250	4,500		—	—
O14	10¢	carmine	Used	500	725–	1,000	1,375	1,825	4,000	—	
			Unused NG	275	450	600	650	850	1,400	—	
			Unused OG	575	825	1,200	1,600	2,500	4,000	—	
			Mint NH	800	1,450	2,500	3,750	5,500	—		

						1873 Interior					
O15	1¢	vermilion	Used	5	7	10	14	25	75	175	—
			Unused NG	17.50	22.50	35	40	52.50	80	—	—
			Unused OG	40	55	75	110	170	300	—	—
			Mint NH	70	110	170	245	390	800	1,600	—
O16	2¢	vermilion	Used	6	8.75	12	20	35	80	—	—
			Unused NG	15	20	30	35	45	90	—	—
			Unused OG	40	50	70	105	175	325	—	—
			Mint NH	70	100	160	225	390	800	—	—
O17	3¢	vermilion	Used	3	4.25	6	8.50	17.50	50	—	—
			Unused NG	20	27.50	40	45	57.50	85	—	—
			Unused OG	45	60	80	140	200	375	—	—
			Mint NH	75	110	175	275	425	850	—	—
O18	6¢	vermilion	Used	5	7.25	10	13.50	25	70	—	—
			Unused NG	15	22.50	30	37.50	47.50	70	—	—
			Unused OG	40	50	70	105	165	300	—	—
			Mint NH	75	110	160	275	425	800	—	—
O19	10¢	vermilion	Used	10	15	20	28	50	125	—	—
			Unused NG	15	22.50	30	37.50	47.50	70	—	—
			Unused OG	40	50	70	105	170	300	—	—
			Mint NH	75	90	160	275	425	800	—	—
O20	12¢	vermilion	Used	6	8.75	12	20	40	90	190	—
			Unused NG	22.50	32.50	45	55	70	110	—	—
			Unused OG	50	65	90	130	225	400	—	—
			Mint NH	80	110	200	275	425	950	—	—
O21	15¢	vermilion	Used	12.50	18	25	35	60	145	—	—
			Unused NG	45	65	90	105	125	185	—	—
			Unused OG	110	135	200	280	425	825	—	—
			Mint NH	175	250	450	625	975	2,200	—	—
O22	24¢	vermilion	Used	11	14	20	28	50	125	—	—
			Unused NG	42.50	62.50	85	100	120	175	—	—
			Unused OG	100	125	180	260	400	750	—	—
			Mint NH	170	225	400	550	950	1,950	—	—
O23	30¢	vermilion	Used	10	14	20	28	50	125	—	—
			Unused NG	70	95	130	150	175	270	—	—
			Unused OG	150	200	290	400	600	1,225	—	—
			Mint NH	225	375	625	850	1,350	3,050	—	—
O24	90¢	vermilion	Used	25	37.50	50	72.50	125	400	—	—
			Unused NG	70	100	140	160	210	300	—	—
			Unused OG	160	225	325	450	625	1,250	—	—
			Mint NH	240	400	700	925	1,550	3,400	—	—

SCT#	DENOM	COLOR	CONDITION	F 70	F-VF 75	VF 80	VF-XF 85	XF 90	XF-SUP 95	SUP 98	GEM 100
			1873 Justice								
O25	1¢	purple	Used	50	72	100	140	250	525	—	—
			Unused NG	60	87.50	120	140	175	275	—	—
			Unused OG	130	175	250	350	500	1,000	—	—
			Mint NH	200	325	550	775	1,200	2,650	—	—
O26	2¢	purple	Used	55	80	110	150	225	550	—	—
			Unused NG	72.50	100	135	150	195	300	—	—
			Unused OG	160	225	310	450	625	1,225	—	—
			Mint NH	240	400	700	975	1,450	3,300	—	—
O27	3¢	purple	Used	17.50	25	35	50	85	200	—	—
			Unused NG	72.50	110	135	160	200	300	—	—
			Unused OG	150	215	300	425	650	1,300	—	—
			Mint NH	240	410	700	925	1,550	3,450	—	—
O28	6¢	purple	Used	22.50	32.50	45	60	95	250	—	—
			Unused NG	72.50	110	135	150	195	290	—	—
			Unused OG	160	225	310	440	650	1,250	—	—
			Mint NH	240	400	700	975	1,450	3,300	—	—
O29	10¢	purple	Used	50	70	100	140	210	475	—	—
			Unused NG	72.50	110	135	150	195	300	—	—
			Unused OG	160	225	310	460	650	1,250	—	—
			Mint NH	425	725	1,250	1,750	2,600	3,500	—	—
O30	12¢	purple	Used	37.50	52.50	75	105	650	—	—	—
			Unused NG	62.50	92.50	125	145	175	260	—	—
			Unused OG	120	175	260	350	525	1,050	—	—
			Mint NH	525	850	1,500	2,150	3,000	5,500	—	—
O31	15¢	purple	Used	110	140	200	280	425	1,000	—	—
			Unused NG	110	170	240	260	325	525	—	—
			Unused OG	265	340	500	700	1,050	2,000	—	—
			Mint NH	525	850	1,500	2,150	3,000	5,500	—	—
O32	24¢	purple	Used	215	300	425	600	900	2,250	—	—
			Unused NG	240	400	600	650	775	1,200	—	—
			Unused OG	600	900	1,250	1,650	2,250	4,250	—	—
			Mint NH		—	4,250	—	6,500			
O33	30¢	purple	Used	175	250	350	500	750	1,800	—	—
			Unused NG	250	425	625	675	800	1,250	—	—
			Unused OG	525	900	1,300	1,800	2,500	4,450	—	—
			Mint NH		—	—	—	6,500			
O34	90¢	purple	Used	450	600	900	1,350	2,000	4,500	—	—
			Unused NG	340	650	900	1,000	1,175	1,700	—	—
			Unused OG	725	1,200	1,900	2,300	3,750	5,500	—	—
			Mint NH		—	4,000	6,250	9,000			

SCT#	DENOM	COLOR	CONDITION	F 70	F-VF 75	VF 80	VF-XF 85	XF 90	XF-SUP 95	SUP 98	GEM 100
			1873 Navy								
O35	1¢	ultramarine	Used	25	37.50	50	70	105	250	—	—
			Unused NG	35	55	75	82.50	100	145	—	—
			Unused OG	75	110	160	225	325	600	—	—
			Mint NH	125	200	350	475	850	1,800	—	—
O35a	1¢	dull blue	Used	25	35	50	70	105	250	—	—
			Unused NG	40	62.50	87.50	97.50	115	160	—	—
			Unused OG	95	135	200	250	350	—	—	—
			Mint NH	145	230	400	525	900	—	—	—

SCT#	DENOM	COLOR	CONDITION	F 70	F-VF 75	VF 80	VF-XF 85	XF 90	XF-SUP 95	SUP 98	GEM 100
O36	2¢	ultramarine	Used	12.50	17.50	25	35	55	150	325	—
			Unused NG	35	55	75	82.50	100	145	—	—
			Unused OG	75	110	160	225	325	600	—	—
			Mint NH	125	200	350	475	850	1,800	—	—
O36a	2¢	dull	Used	12.50	18	25	35	55	150	—	—
		blue	Unused NG	40	62.50	87.50	97.50	115	160	—	—
			Unused OG	95	135	200	250	350	650	—	—
			Mint NH	145	230	400	525	925	2,000	—	—
O37	3¢	ultramarine	Used	7.50	10.50	15	22.50	35	90	—	—
			Unused NG	37.50	57.50	80	90	105	155	—	—
			Unused OG	85	110	170	250	350	675	—	—
			Mint NH	650	975	1,750	2,250	3,000	4,000	—	—
O37a	3¢	dull	Used	7.50	10.50	15	22.50	35	90	180	—
		blue	Unused NG	45	72.50	100	120	145	190	—	—
			Unused OG	110	150	225	280	400	800	—	—
			Mint NH	165	260	450	600	900	2,250	—	—
O38	6¢	ultramarine	Used	12.50	18	25	35	60	125	—	—
			Unused NG	35	50	70	85	110	150	—	—
			Unused OG	70	105	150	215	325	650	1,300	—
			Mint NH	165	250	450	625	1,050	2,250	—	—
O38a	6¢	dull	Used	12.50	18	25	35	60	140	—	—
		blue	Unused NG	42.50	60	82.50	100	130	195	—	—
			Unused OG	92.50	115	175	260	400	700	—	—
			Mint NH	160	235	385	525	900	1,950	—	—
O39	7¢	ultramarine	Used	120	165	230	340	950	—	—	—
			Unused NG	155	235	325	365	450	700	—	—
			Unused OG	325	485	700	950	1,350	2,600	—	—
			Mint NH		—	—	—				
O39a	7¢	dull	Used	120	165	230	340	750	1,250	—	—
		blue	Unused NG	155	235	325	365	450	700	—	—
			Unused OG	350	525	750	1,025	1,450	2,750	—	—
			Mint NH	575	900	1,600	2,400	—			
O40	10¢	ultramarine	Used	24	32.50	45	62.50	200	260	400	—
			Unused NG	47.50	70	95	110	125	200	—	—
			Unused OG	110	`150	210	260	425	825	—	—
			Mint NH	425	625	1,000	1,200	1,500	2,500	—	—
O40a	10¢	dull	Used	24	32.50	45	62.50	100	240	—	—
		blue	Unused NG	55	80	110	125	145	235	—	—
			Unused OG	120	160	225	300	450	875	—	—
			Mint NH	425	625	1,000	1,250	1,600	2,600	—	—
O41	12¢	ultramarine	Used	24	32.50	45	62.50	100	240	—	—
			Unused NG	57.50	82.50	115	130	160	250	—	—
			Unused OG	120	160	240	325	525	950	—	—
			Mint NH	350	500	900	1,150	1,500	2,500	—	—
O42	15¢	ultramarine	Used	40	57.50	80	105	160	375	—	—
			Unused NG	97.50	145	200	225	270	425	—	—
			Unused OG	200	285	425	575	875	1,650	3,500	—
			Mint NH		—	—	—				
O43	24¢	ultramarine	Used	42.50	60	85	120	180	425	—	—
			Unused NG	97.50	145	200	225	270	425	—	—
			Unused OG	225	280	425	575	875	1,650	3,500	—
			Mint NH		—	1,750	—				
O43a	24¢	dull	Used	40	55	80	110	170	400	—	—
		blue	Unused NG	97.50	145	200	225	270	425	—	—
			Unused OG	225	280	425	575	875	1,650	—	—
			Mint NH	—	—	1,350	1,750	—			
O44	30¢	ultramarine	Used	25	37.50	50	70	110	250	1,000	—
			Unused NG	77.50	115	160	175	210	325	—	—
			Unused OG	170	235	350	475	750	1,350	2,950	—
			Mint NH		—	3,000	—				
O45	90¢	ultramarine	Used	190	265	375	525	725	1,700	—	—
			Unused NG	200	330	500	575	700	950	—	—
			Unused OG	500	725	1,050	1,400	2,100	3,550	—	—
			Mint NH		—	6,000	—				

SCT#	DENOM	COLOR	CONDITION	F 70	F-VF 75	VF 80	VF-XF 85	XF 90	XF-SUP 95	SUP 98	GEM 100
			1873 Post Office								
O47	1¢	black	Used	6.50	8.75	12	17	27.50	50	95	—
			Unused NG	6	8.50	12	13.50	17.50	25	40	—
			Unused OG	12	17.50	25	37.50	55	—	—	—
			Mint NH	20	35	60	85	160	500	—	—
O48	2¢	black	Used	5.50	7	10	14	20	40	85	—
			Unused NG	7	10	14	16	20	27.50	46	—
			Unused OG	14	20	30	47.50	70	120	260	—
			Mint NH	25	42.50	75	110	170	390	—	—
O49	3¢	black	Used	1	1.25	2	3.50	10	17.50	32.50	—
			Unused NG	2.25	3.25	4.50	6	9.75	22.50	32.50	—
			Unused OG	4.25	7	10	15	22.50	42.50	75	—
			Mint NH	7.50	14	25	36	55	160	325	—
O50	6¢	black	Used	4	5.75	8	11	17.50	35	70	—
			Unused NG	7	10.50	14	17	21	30	45	—
			Unused OG	14	20	30	45	70	120	260	—
			Mint NH	25	42.50	75	110	170	400	—	—
O51	10¢	black	Used	27.50	37.50	55	80	115	180	350	—
			Unused NG	27.50	45	65	72.50	92.50	135	230	—
			Unused OG	70	100	140	200	275	525	—	—
			Mint NH	120	200	325	460	700	1,550	—	—
O52	12¢	black	Used	6	8.75	12	17	24	45	95	—
			Unused NG	27.50	37.50	55	65	80	115	175	—
			Unused OG	57.50	80	120	170	260	450	925	—
			Mint NH	90	150	275	390	625	1,375	—	—
O53	15¢	black	Used	10	14	20	30	43.50	85	175	—
			Unused NG	27.50	45	65	72.50	92.50	135	230	—
			Unused OG	70	100	140	200	280	525	1,150	—
			Mint NH	125	200	325	460	700	1,550	—	—
O54	24¢	black	Used	12.50	17.50	25	35	47.50	80	160	—
			Unused NG	52.50	75	105	125	150	215	360	—
			Unused OG	105	165	225	310	450	850	1,500	—
			Mint NH	160	300	500	675	1,000	2,250	—	—
O55	30¢	black	Used	12.50	17.50	25	35	47.50	90	175	—
			Unused NG	45	65	90	105	130	200	300	—
			Unused OG	95	145	200	275	425	850	1,750	—
			Mint NH	145	275	450	650	1,000	2,150	—	—
O56	90¢	black	Used	12.50	17.50	25	35	47.50	80	160	—
			Unused NG	52.50	72.50	105	125	150	225	360	—
			Unused OG	115	145	220	300	440	875	1,900	—
			Mint NH	170	290	500	700	1,100	2,450	—	—

SCT#	DENOM	COLOR	CONDITION	F 70	F-VF 75	VF 80	VF-XF 85	XF 90	XF-SUP 95	SUP 98	GEM 100
			1873 State								
O57	1¢	dark	Used	37.50	52.50	75	120	165	250	475	—
		green	Unused NG	47.50	85	125	140	175	250	425	—
			Unused OG	105	175	260	330	525	900	1,750	—
			Mint NH	175	320	575	800	1,250	2,900	—	—

SCT#	DENOM	COLOR	CONDITION	F 70	F-VF 75	VF 80	VF-XF 85	XF 90	XF-SUP 95	SUP 98	GEM 100
058	2¢	dark	Used	50	70	100	140	200	325	600	—
		green	Unused NG	75	105	150	170	210	315	525	—
			Unused OG	125	200	310	420	625	1,250	2,500	—
			Mint NH	—	—	—	1,000	1,500	—		
059	3¢	dark	Used	12.50	17.50	25	35	47.50	85	160	—
		green	Unused NG	47.50	75	105	125	150	210	375	—
		bright	Unused OG	87.50	145	220	300	475	875	1,750	—
		green	Mint NH	150	275	500	675	1,000	2,400	—	—
060	6¢	bright	Used	15	21	30	42.50	62.50	100	200	—
		green	Unused NG	55	85	120	140	170	240	400	—
			Unused OG	100	165	250	350	550	950	1,850	—
			Mint NH	165	315	550	750	1,100	2,500	—	—
061	7¢	dark	Used	32.50	45	65	95	175	750		
		green	Unused NG	70	100	140	160	200	300	475	—
			Unused OG	115	200	290	400	600	1,150	2,250	—
			Mint NH	200	350	650	900	1,350	3,100	—	—
062	10¢	dark	Used	27.50	40	55	75	105	175	360	—
		green	Unused NG	50	82.50	120	140	175	275	500	—
			Unused OG	105	165	250	325	500	950	1,750	—
			Mint NH	175	300	575	775	1,200	2,750	—	—
063	12¢	dark	Used	62.50	90	125	180	260	400	750	—
		green	Unused NG	75	105	150	170	210	315	525	—
			Unused OG	125	200	310	400	625	1,200	—	—
			Mint NH	210	375	700	950	1,400	3,200	—	—
064	15¢	dark	Used	45	62.50	90	130	185	275	450	—
		green	Unused NG	85	120	170	190	240	350	650	—
			Unused OG	135	230	350	465	675	1,325	2,650	—
			Mint NH	235	430	775	1,075	1,650	3,650	—	—
065	24¢	dark	Used	115	165	230	340	485	725	1,250	—
		green	Unused NG	90	200	275	325	400	650	975	—
			Unused OG	220	375	550	675	1,000	1,800	3,000	—
			Mint NH		—	1,200	1,750	2,500	—		
066	30¢	dark	Used	90	125	180	260	375	575	1,000	—
		green	Unused NG	87.50	175	260	300	350	435	700	—
			Unused OG	210	350	525	625	850	1,600	2,750	—
			Mint NH		—	1,150	1,700	2,500	4,000	6,000	—
067	90¢	dark	Used	165	225	325	475	675	1,050	1,750	—
		green	Unused NG	175	350	525	575	700	1,125	—	—
			Unused OG	400	675	1,100	1,300	1,700	2,900	—	—
			Mint NH		—	2,400	3,150	4,250	—		
068	$2	green	Used	1,500	2,100	3,000	3,500	4,500			
		& black	Unused NG	350	575	850	975	1,275	—	—	
			Unused OG	850	1,225	1,800	2,500	3,850	7,000	15,000	
			Mint NH	1,125	2,100	3,750	5,500	8,000	—	—	
069	$5	green	Used	6,500	9,000	13,000	17,000	22,500	—	—	
		& black	Unused NG	1,600	2,800	3,750	4,300	5,250	—	—	
			Unused OG	3,750	5,250	8,000	10,500	15,500	20,000	—	
			Mint NH		—	—	—				
070	$10	green	Used	6,250	8,250	12,500	15,000	20,000	—	—	
		& black	Unused NG	1,350	1,850	2,500	3,000	3,750	—	—	
			Unused OG	2,000	3,000	4,500	6,500	10,000	—	—	
			Mint NH	3,250	6,000	10,500	15,000	24,000	—	—	
071	$20	green	Used	2,750	4,000	5,500	7,000	10,000	—	—	
		& black	Unused NG	1,300	1,750	2,500	3,000	3,600	—	—	
			Unused OG	2,350	3,500	5,000	6,500	11,000	—	—	
			Mint NH	3,500	6,500	11,500	16,500	26,000	—	—	

SCT#	DENOM	COLOR	CONDITION	F 70	F-VF 75	VF 80	VF-XF 85	XF 90	XF-SUP 95	SUP 98	GEM 100
						1873 Treasury					
072	1¢	brown	Used	5	7.25	10	15	22.50	45	95	—
			Unused NG	30	40	55	67.50	85	130	180	—
			Unused OG	60	75	120	190	275	525	950	—
			Mint NH	100	140	250	360	575	1,250	—	—
073	2¢	brown	Used	4	5.75	8	12	17.50	40	85	—
			Unused NG	32.50	37.50	57.50	72.50	95	145	230	—
			Unused OG	70	80	125	215	300	575	1,050	—
			Mint NH	125	155	275	440	650	1,450	—	—
074	3¢	brown	Used	1	1.40	2	4	12.50	27.50	65	—
			Unused NG	25	35	50	65	85	120	180	—
			Unused OG	55	70	110	160	250	475	950	—
			Mint NH	100	130	230	340	625	1,350	—	—
075	6¢	brown	Used	2	2.80	4	8	17.50	37.50	75	—
			Unused NG	27.50	37.50	55	67.50	87.50	125	190	—
			Unused OG	65	80	120	180	275	500	1,000	—
			Mint NH	110	140	250	425	650	1,400	—	—
076	7¢	brown	Used	17.50	24	35	50	75	130	275	—
			Unused NG	60	85	120	140	170	250	375	—
			Unused OG	105	165	250	360	500	1,000	2,050	—
			Mint NH	190	300	550	825	1,200	2,450	—	—
077	10¢	brown	Used	6	8.75	12	17.50	27.50	50	110	—
			Unused NG	52.50	80	110	130	160	230	350	—
			Unused OG	95	155	240	350	500	950	1,900	—
			Mint NH	225	300	525	800	1,175	2,450	—	—
078	12¢	brown	Used	5	7.25	10	15	22.50	47.50	90	—
			Unused NG	80	110	160	185	225	360	550	—
			Unused OG	170	235	350	500	675	1,275	2,450	—
			Mint NH	260	460	750	1,075	1,625	3,500	—	—
079	15¢	brown	Used	6	8.75	12	18.50	25	50	100	—
			Unused NG	70	100	140	160	195	310	450	—
			Unused OG	140	200	300	400	600	1,100	2,100	—
			Mint NH	220	400	650	925	1,400	3,100	—	—
080	24¢	brown	Used	50	70	100	140	210	325	575	—
			Unused NG	165	235	325	350	450	775	1,200	—
			Unused OG	365	525	725	950	1,400	2,700	—	—
			Mint NH	—	—	—	4,000	—			
081	30¢	brown	Used	6	8.75	12	17.50	25	55	110	—
			Unused NG	90	130	180	200	245	375	550	—
			Unused OG	190	285	400	550	825	1,600	—	—
			Mint NH	—	700	—	—	1,850	—		
082	90¢	brown	Used	8.75	12.50	17.50	22.50	35	70	210	—
			Unused NG	115	160	225	250	300	485	750	—
			Unused OG	225	340	475	650	975	1,900	—	—
			Mint NH	—	950	1,400	1,900	—			

SCT#	DENOM	COLOR	CONDITION	F 70	F-VF 75	VF 80	VF-XF 85	XF 90	XF-SUP 95	SUP 98	GEM 100
						1873 War					
083	1¢	rose	Used	7.50	10.50	15	22.50	35	60	130	—
			Unused NG	57.50	82.50	115	135	165	245	400	—
			Unused OG	125	160	240	350	500	950	1,600	—
			Mint NH	360	525	850	1,175	1,800	3,500	—	—

SCT#	DENOM	COLOR	CONDITION	F 70	F-VF 75	VF 80	VF-XF 85	XF 90	XF-SUP 95	SUP 98	GEM 100
O84	2¢	rose	Used	7.50	10.50	15	21	32.50	60	120	—
			Unused NG	62.50	90	125	150	180	250	425	—
			Unused OG	135	175	260	375	550	1,025	2,000	—
			Mint NH	525	725	1,200	1,650	2,500	4,500	—	—
O85	3¢	rose	Used	2.50	3.50	5	7	15	27.50	55	—
			Unused NG	67.50	100	135	160	195	280	475	—
			Unused OG	145	185	275	400	600	1,150	2,000	—
			Mint NH	220	400	650	925	1,400	3,100	—	—
O86	6¢	rose	Used	6.25	8.75	12.50	17.50	25	45	95	—
			Unused NG	165	235	325	360	450	700	1,000	—
			Unused OG	340	460	675	950	1,400	2,750	4,500	—
			Mint NH	600	800	1,450	2,000	3,100	7,000	—	—
O87	7¢	rose	Used	47.50	65	90	130	190	300	550	—
			Unused NG	40	65	90	100	120	170	310	—
			Unused OG	82.50	120	175	250	350	650	1,200	—
			Mint NH	215	335	600	850	1,250	2,750	—	—
O88	10¢	rose	Used	12.50	18	25	35	50	100	190	—
			Unused NG	32.50	42.50	65	82.50	110	160	300	—
			Unused OG	70	95	140	190	300	550	1,000	—
			Mint NH	150	230	375	525	875	1,750	—	—
O89	12¢	rose	Used	6	8.75	12	17.50	26	50	150	—
			Unused NG	65	95	130	150	180	240	425	—
			Unused OG	135	180	275	375	525	1,100	1,850	—
			Mint NH	250	410	700	975	1,450	3,500	—	—
O90	15¢	rose	Used	7.50	10.50	15	22.50	32.50	60	120	—
			Unused NG	20	30	40	50	65	100	175	—
			Unused OG	40	55	85	120	180	350	625	—
			Mint NH	105	150	260	360	625	1,200	1,750	—
O91	24¢	rose	Used	6	8.75	12	17.50	27.50	50	100	—
			Unused NG	20	30	40	50	65	100	175	—
			Unused OG	40	55	85	120	190	350	650	—
			Mint NH	75	110	190	260	450	1,050	—	—
O92	30¢	rose	Used	6	8.75	12	17.50	27.50	50	100	—
			Unused NG	32.50	42.50	65	82.50	110	160	275	—
			Unused OG	60	85	130	180	275	500	900	—
			Mint NH	110	160	275	400	675	1,350	—	—
O93	90¢	rose	Used	30	42.50	60	80	110	180	325	—
			Unused NG	55	80	110	125	160	240	360	—
			Unused OG	110	150	225	310	475	850	1,600	—
			Mint NH	325	475	800	1,100	1,900	3,750	—	—

			1879 American Bank Note Issues (Soft Paper)								
O94	1¢	yellow	Unused NGAI	3,650	4,500	5,750	6,250	7,650	14,000	19,000	—
O95	3¢	yellow	Used	62.50	91	125	170	250	400	750	—
			Unused NG	97.50	165	260	290	350	525	875	—
			Unused OG	250	365	550	725	1,150	2,000	3,500	—
			Mint NH	400	700	1,250	1,775	2,750	5,650	—	—
O96	1¢	vermilion	Used	205	275	400	675	1,150	—	—	—
			Unused NG	52.50	110	150	165	200	290	500	—
			Unused OG	120	200	300	375	575	1,050	—	—
			Mint NH	200	350	550	775	1,200	2,700	—	—
O97	2¢	vermilion	Used	1.50	2.10	3	7	15	25	55	—
			Unused NG	2.25	3.15	4.50	7.50	12.50	22.50	30	—
			Unused OG	4	6.75	10	15	22.50	42.50	80	—
			Mint NH	5.25	9.75	17.50	27.50	45	100	—	—
O98	3¢	vermilion	Used	1.50	2.10	3	7	15	25	55	—
			Unused NG	2.25	3.15	4.50	7.50	12.50	22.50	30	—
			Unused OG	4	6.75	10	15	22.50	42.50	80	—
			Mint NH	6.75	12.50	22.50	32.50	52.50	115	—	—

SCT#	DENOM	COLOR	CONDITION	F 70	F-VF 75	VF 80	VF-XF 85	XF 90	XF-SUP 95	SUP 98	GEM 100
O99	6¢	vermilion	Used	6	8.50	12.50	18.50	27.50	47.50	100	—
			Unused NG	2.25	3.15	4.50	7.50	12.50	22.50	30	—
			Unused OG	4	6.75	10	15	35	60	120	—
			Mint NH	5.25	9.25	17.50	27.50	50	100	—	—
O100	10¢	vermilion	Used	40	55	75	110	155	230	400	—
			Unused NG	30	42.50	55	65	85	130	225	—
			Unused OG	47.50	75	110	165	240	450	875	—
			Mint NH	75	140	250	360	550	1,100	—	—
O101	12¢	vermilion	Used	62.50	87.50	115	165	250	375	650	—
			Unused NG	47.50	80	115	130	160	220	450	—
			Unused OG	95	155	230	300	400	825	1,600	—
			Mint NH	160	290	525	700	1,100	2,600	—	—
O102	15¢	vermilion	Used	270	365	500	625	775	—	—	—
			Unused NG	100	140	200	225	300	475	825	—
			Unused OG	195	270	400	550	825	1,500	2,500	—
			Mint NH	270	500	900	1,275	1,900	4,250	—	—
O103	24¢	vermilion	Used	—	—	6,250	—	—	—	—	—
			Unused NG	1,150	1,650	2,200	2,450	3,250	—	—	—
			Unused OG	2,250	3,400	4,500	5,750	8,250	—	—	—
			Mint NH	3,000	5,500	10,000	14,000	21,000	—	—	—
O106	3¢	bluish purple	Used	62.50	87.50	125	175	225	375	700	—
			Unused NG	60	87.50	120	135	160	200	375	—
			Unused OG	100	165	250	300	475	850	1,400	—
			Mint NH	175	330	575	800	1,100	2,400	—	—
O107	6¢	bluish purple	Used	150	225	300	425	575	850	1,500	—
			Unused NG	125	180	250	275	350	525	825	—
			Unused OG	190	315	475	625	825	1,600	3,200	—
			Mint NH	315	575	1,050	1,500	2,400	5,250	—	—
O108	3¢	black	Used	4.50	7	10	15	25	40	100	—
			Unused NG	7	10	14	17.50	22.50	31.50	42.50	—
			Unused OG	12	20	30	42.50	67.50	120	230	—
			Mint NH	21	40	70	100	155	325	—	—
O109	3¢	brown	Used	4.50	7	10	15	25	50	100	—
			Unused NG	17.50	25	35	40	47.50	65	110	—
			Unused OG	32.50	52.50	80	115	175	300	600	—
			Mint NH	52.50	97.50	175	250	400	850	—	—
O110	6¢	brown	Used	25	36.50	50	70	100	150	275	—
			Unused NG	45	62.50	90	110	140	200	300	—
			Unused OG	82.50	130	200	275	425	800	1,450	—
			Mint NH	135	250	450	650	975	2,200	—	—
O111	10¢	brown	Used	40	55	80	115	160	300	475	—
			Unused NG	65	95	130	155	190	280	390	—
			Unused OG	110	185	275	370	575	1,000	2,000	—
			Mint NH	200	360	650	875	1,300	3,000	—	—
O112	30¢	brown	Used	280	390	550	700	1,500	—	—	—
			Unused NG	600	850	1,200	1,350	1,750	2,600	5,000	—
			Unused OG	1,200	1,650	2,400	3,250	4,750	8,500	15,500	—
			Mint NH		—	—	—				
O113	90¢	brown	Used	375	475	750	900	1,250	1,850	3,000	—
			Unused NG	2,500	3,750	5,000	5,500	6,250	—	—	—
			Unused OG	4,750	7,000	10,000	12,250	15,000	—	—	—
			Mint NH		—	—	—				
O114	1¢	rose red	Used	2	2.90	4	7.50	15	25	45	—
			Unused NG	1.80	2.35	3.50	6	12.50	22.50	32.50	—
			Unused OG	3	5	7.50	12.50	22.50	40	75	—
			Mint NH	4.50	8.25	15	26	47.50	115	200	—
O115	2¢	rose red	Used	2	2.75	4	7.50	15	25	45	—
			Unused NG	3.50	4.75	7	12.50	22.50	37.50	60	—
			Unused OG	6	10.25	15	22.50	32.50	57.50	110	—
			Mint NH	9	17.50	30	47.50	80	160	—	—
O116	3¢	rose red	Used	1	1.40	2	4	9	17.50	35	—
			Unused NG	1.65	2.25	3.25	6.25	11.50	18	32.50	—
			Unused OG	4	6.75	10	15	22.50	37.50	80	—
			Mint NH	6	12.50	20	32.50	60	160	—	—
O117	6¢	rose red	Used	1.50	2.10	3	5.50	12	20	37.50	—
			Unused NG	3	4	6	11	20	35	55	—
			Unused OG	5	8.50	12.50	19	27.50	50	100	—
			Mint NH	7.50	13.75	25	40	75	160	250	—

SCT#	DENOM	COLOR	CONDITION	F 70	F-VF 75	VF 80	VF-XF 85	XF 90	XF-SUP 95	SUP 98	GEM 100
O118	10¢	rose	Used	25	37.50	50	70	100	170	325	—
		red	Unused NG	17.50	22.50	35	45	57.50	72.50	125	—
			Unused OG	30	50	75	105	160	290	525	—
			Mint NH	45	82.50	150	220	375	700	—	—
O119	12¢	rose	Used	7	9.75	14	20	27.50	45	110	—
		red	Unused NG	17.50	25	35	47.50	65	90	125	—
			Unused OG	28	45	70	100	150	290	450	—
			Mint NH	42.50	77.50	140	195	350	700	—	—
O120	30¢	rose	Used	50	70	100	130	180	325	600	—
		red	Unused NG	55	80	110	125	150	225	350	—
			Unused OG	95	150	225	375	525	950	1,800	—
			Mint NH	150	280	500	700	1,150	2,750	—	—

		1875 Special Printings (Overprinted "SPECIMEN")									
O1S	1¢	yellow	Unused NGAI	12.50	22.50	32.50	45	70	130	235	—
O2S	2¢	yellow	Unused NGAI	22.50	37.50	55	82.50	120	200	325	—
O3S	3¢	yellow	Unused NGAI	180	265	400	550	800	1,400	—	—
O4S	6¢	yellow	Unused NGAI	180	265	400	550	800	1,400	—	—
O5S	10¢	yellow	Unused NGAI	180	265	400	550	800	1,400	—	—
O6S	12¢	yellow	Unused NGAI	180	265	400	550	800	1,400	—	—
O7S	15¢	yellow	Unused NGAI	180	265	400	550	800	1,400	—	—
O8S	24¢	yellow	Unused NGAI	180	265	400	550	800	1,400	—	—
O9S	30¢	yellow	Unused NGAI	180	265	400	550	800	1,400	—	—
O10S	1¢	carmine	Unused NGAI	12.50	22.50	32.50	45	70	130	235	—
O11S	2¢	carmine	Unused NGAI	22.50	38.50	55	80	120	200	330	—
O12S	3¢	carmine	Unused NGAI	27.50	47.50	67.50	95	150	240	400	—
O13S	6¢	carmine	Unused NGAI	27.50	47.50	67.50	95	150	240	400	—
O14S	10¢	carmine	Unused NGAI	27.50	47.50	67.50	95	150	240	400	—
O15S	1¢	vermilion	Unused NGAI	25	42.50	60	87.50	130	220	350	—
O16S	2¢	vermilion	Unused NGAI	62.50	95	140	200	300	450	850	—
O17S	3¢	vermilion	Unused NGAI	1,175	1,750	2,500	3,200	5,000	7,500	—	—
O18S	6¢	vermilion	Unused NGAI	1,175	1,750	2,500	3,200	5,000	7,500	—	—
O19S	10¢	vermilion	Unused NGAI	1,175	1,750	2,500	3,200	5,000	7,500	—	—
O20S	12¢	vermilion	Unused NGAI	1,175	1,750	2,500	3,200	5,000	7,500	—	—
O21S	15¢	vermilion	Unused NGAI	1,175	1,750	2,500	3,200	5,000	7,500	—	—
O22S	24¢	vermilion	Unused NGAI	1,175	1,750	2,500	3,200	5,000	7,500	—	—
O23S	30¢	vermilion	Unused NGAI	1,175	1,750	2,500	3,200	5,000	7,500	—	—
O24S	90¢	vermilion	Unused NGAI	1,175	1,750	2,500	3,200	5,000	7,500	—	—
O25S	1¢	purple	Unused NGAI	12.50	22.50	32.50	45	70	130	235	—
O26S	2¢	purple	Unused NGAI	22.50	38.50	55	80	120	200	325	—
O27S	3¢	purple	Unused NGAI	550	875	1,250	1,800	2,650	4,150	—	—
O28S	6¢	purple	Unused NGAI	550	875	1,250	1,800	2,650	4,150	—	—
O29S	10¢	purple	Unused NGAI	550	875	1,250	1,800	2,650	4,150	—	—
O30S	12¢	purple	Unused NGAI	550	875	1,250	1,800	2,650	4,150	—	—
O31S	15¢	purple	Unused NGAI	550	875	1,250	1,800	2,650	4,150	—	—
O32S	24¢	purple	Unused NGAI	550	875	1,250	1,800	2,650	4,150	—	—
O33S	30¢	purple	Unused NGAI	550	875	1,250	1,800	2,650	4,150	—	—
O34S	90¢	purple	Unused NGAI	550	875	1,250	1,800	2,650	4,150	—	—
O35S	1¢	ultramarine	Unused NGAI	15	25	35	50	77.50	140	250	—
O36S	2¢	ultramarine	Unused NGAI	31.50	53	75	105	160	275	500	—
O37S	3¢	ultramarine	Unused NGAI	775	1,200	1,750	2,250	3,500	5,500	—	—
O38S	6¢	ultramarine	Unused NGAI	775	1,200	1,750	2,250	3,500	5,500	—	—
O39S	7¢	ultramarine	Unused NGAI	255	400	550	800	1,150	2,150	—	—

SCT#	DENOM	COLOR	CONDITION	F 70	F-VF 75	VF 80	VF-XF 85	XF 90	XF-SUP 95	SUP 98	GEM 100
040S	10¢	ultramarine	Unused NGAI	775	1,200	1,750	2,250	3,500	5,500	—	—
041S	12¢	ultramarine	Unused NGAI	775	1,200	1,750	2,250	3,500	5,500	—	—
042S	15¢	ultramarine	Unused NGAI	775	1,200	1,750	2,250	3,500	5,500	—	—
043S	24¢	ultramarine	Unused NGAI	775	1,200	1,750	2,250	3,500	5,500	—	—
044S	30¢	ultramarine	Unused NGAI	775	1,200	1,750	2,250	3,500	5,500	—	—
045S	90¢	ultramarine	Unused NGAI	775	1,200	1,750	2,250	3,500	5,500	—	—
047S	1¢	black	Unused NGAI	20	32.50	45	62.50	95	180	325	—
048S	2¢	black	Unused NGAI	150	220	325	450	700	1,100	1,750	—
049S	3¢	black	Unused NGAI	725	1,050	1,600	2,050	3,250	5,000	—	—
050S	6¢	black	Unused NGAI	725	1,050	1,600	2,050	3,250	5,000	—	—
051S	10¢	black	Unused NGAI	450	725	1,000	1,325	2,200	3,400	—	—
052S	12¢	black	Unused NGAI	725	1,050	1,600	2,050	3,250	5,000	—	—
053S	15¢	black	Unused NGAI	725	1,050	1,600	2,050	3,250	5,000	—	—
054S	24¢	black	Unused NGAI	725	1,050	1,600	2,050	3,250	5,000	—	—
055S	30¢	black	Unused NGAI	725	1,050	1,600	2,050	3,250	5,000	—	—
056S	90¢	black	Unused NGAI	725	1,050	1,600	2,050	3,250	5,000	—	—
057S	1¢	bluish green	Unused NGAI	12.50	22.50	32.50	45	70	130	235	—
058S	2¢	bluish green	Unused NGAI	40	65	90	135	190	340	550	—
059S	3¢	bluish green	Unused NGAI	65	100	140	205	300	475	850	—
060S	6¢	bluish green	Unused NGAI	160	240	350	500	750	1,150	2,100	—
061S	7¢	bluish green	Unused NGAI	64	100	140	205	300	475	850	—
062S	10¢	bluish green	Unused NGAI	260	375	550	725	1,150	1,750	—	—
063S	12¢	bluish green	Unused NGAI	255	375	550	725	1,150	1,750	—	—
064S	15¢	bluish green	Unused NGAI	280	425	600	800	1,250	1,900	—	—
065S	24¢	bluish green	Unused NGAI	280	425	600	800	1,250	1,900	—	—
066S	30¢	bluish green	Unused NGAI	280	425	600	800	1,250	1,900	—	—
067S	90¢	bluish green	Unused NGAI	280	425	600	800	1,250	1,900	—	—
068S	$2	green & black	Unused NGAI	8,000	12,000	15,000	21,500	27,500	—	—	—
069S	$5	green & black	Unused NGAI	36,500	47,500	67,500	—	—	—	—	—
070S	$10	green & black	Unused NGAI	50,000	70,000	100,000	—	—	—	—	—
071S	$20	green & black	Unused NGAI	72,500	102,500	145,000	—	—	—	—	—
072S	1¢	dark brown	Unused NGAI	37.50	57.50	80	125	175	275	500	—
073S	2¢	dark brown	Unused NGAI	205	300	450	600	950	1,450	2,650	—
074S	3¢	dark brown	Unused NGAI	725	1,050	1,600	2,050	3,250	5,000	—	—
075S	6¢	dark brown	Unused NGAI	725	1,050	1,600	2,050	3,250	5,000	—	—
076S	7¢	dark brown	Unused NGAI	445	650	950	1,250	1,900	3,000	—	—
077S	10¢	dark brown	Unused NGAI	725	1,050	1,600	2,050	3,250	5,000	—	—
078S	12¢	dark brown	Unused NGAI	725	1,050	1,600	2,050	3,250	5,000	—	—
079S	15¢	dark brown	Unused NGAI	725	1,050	1,600	2,050	3,250	5,000	—	—

SCT#	DENOM	COLOR	CONDITION	F 70	F-VF 75	VF 80	VF-XF 85	XF 90	XF-SUP 95	SUP 98	GEM 100
O80S	24¢	dark brown	Unused NGAI	725	1,050	1,600	2,050	3,250	5,000	—	—
O81S	30¢	dark brown	Unused NGAI	725	1,050	1,600	2,050	3,250	5,000	—	—
O82S	90¢	dark brown	Unused NGAI	750	1,075	1,650	2,150	3,350	5,250	—	—
O83S	1¢	deep rose	Unused NGAI	15	25	35	50	75	130	225	—
O84S	2¢	deep rose	Unused NGAI	57.50	90	125	165	260	425	750	—
O85S	3¢	deep rose	Unused NGAI	675	950	1,400	1,875	2,850	4,000	—	—
O86S	6¢	deep rose	Unused NGAI	675	950	1,400	1,875	2,850	4,000	—	—
O87S	7¢	deep rose	Unused NGAI	200	290	425	625	900	1,400	—	—
O88S	10¢	deep rose	Unused NGAI	625	950	1,400	1,800	2,800	4,500	—	—
O89S	12¢	deep rose	Unused NGAI	675	950	1,400	1,800	2,800	4,500	—	—
O90S	15¢	deep rose	Unused NGAI	675	950	1,400	1,800	2,800	4,500	—	—
O91S	24¢	deep rose	Unused NGAI	675	950	1,400	1,800	2,800	4,500	—	—
O92S	30¢	deep rose	Unused NGAI	675	950	1,400	1,800	2,800	4,500	—	—
O93S	90¢	deep rose	Unused NGAI	675	950	1,400	1,800	2,800	4,500	—	—
O10xS	1¢	violet rose	Unused NGAI	42.50	65	95	140	200	350	575	—
O35xS	1¢	gray blue	Unused NGAI	45	70	100	140	220	360	600	—
O57xS	1¢	yellow green	Unused NGAI	82.50	125	180	240	390	675	1,150	—

1910-11 POSTAL SAVINGS MAIL STAMPS

SCT#	DENOM	COLOR	CONDITION	F 70	F-VF 75	VF 80	VF-XF 85	XF 90	XF-SUP 95	SUP 98	GEM 100
O121	2¢	black	Used	1	1.40	2	5.50	12	20	45	—
			Unused OG	9	12	17.50	22.50	37.50	62.50	100	—
			Mint NH	15	25	40	55	75	180	375	—
O122	50¢	dark green	Used	32.50	45	60	90	130	200	350	—
			Unused OG	87.50	115	175	220	355	600	975	—
			Mint NH	170	260	425	600	875	1,850	3,400	—
O123	$1	ultramarine	Used	8	11	15	22.50	32.50	60	120	—
			Unused OG	100	125	200	275	400	675	1,050	—
			Mint NH	180	270	450	650	950	2,250	4,000	9,000
O124	1¢	dark violet	Used	1	1.40	2	5.50	15	35	75	150
			Unused OG	6.25	8.50	12.50	15	18.50	30	50	—
			Mint NH	10.50	16.50	27.50	37.50	55	110	250	—
O125	2¢	black	Used	3.75	5	7	12.50	20	40	85	—
			Unused OG	32.50	45	65	82.50	130	215	350	—
			Mint NH	52.50	85	150	210	310	650	1,325	—
O126	10¢	carmine	Used	1	1.60	2	5.50	12	20	45	—
			Unused OG	10	13.50	20	27.50	42.50	75	125	—
			Mint NH	20	32.50	50	65	105	220	475	—

NEWSPAPER AND PERIODICAL STAMPS

SCT#	DENOM	COLOR	CONDITION	F 70	F-VF 75	VF 80	VF-XF 85	XF 90	XF-SUP 95	SUP 98	GEM 100
1865 Issues											
PR1	5¢	dark blue	Used	1,200	1,600	2,000	2,300	2,750	—		
			Unused NGAI	380	550	750	1,100	1,650	2,250	—	
PR1a	5¢	light blue	Used	—	—	4,250	—	—			
			Unused NGAI	675	950	1,350	1,900	2,850	3,500	—	
PR2	10¢	blue green	Used	1,450	1,950	2,250	2,650	3,150	—		
			Unused NGAI	150	215	300	425	575	900	—	
PR2a	10¢	green	Used	1,000	1,225	2,000	2,350	2,800	—		
			Unused NGAI	150	215	300	400	575	900	—	
PR3	25¢	orange red	Used	1,650	2,100	2,500	2,850	3,400	—		
			Unused NGAI	210	265	400	525	700	1,150	—	
PR3a	25¢	carmine red	Used	1,650	2,100	2,500	2,850	3,400	—		
			Unused NGAI	245	315	475	600	800	1,300	—	
PR4	5¢	light blue	Used	2,500	3,250	5,000	5,750	6,750	—		
			Unused NGAI	425	600	900	1,050	1,350	2,000	—	
PR4a	5¢	dark blue	Unused NGAI	425	600	900	1,050	1,350	2,000	—	
1875 Reprints of the 1865 Issues											
PR5	5¢	dull blue	Unused NGAI	150	175	225	350	650	1,250	1,850	2,750
PR6	10¢	dk bluish green	Unused NGAI	175	200	250	375	675	900	1,700	3,000
PR7	25¢	dark carmine	Unused NGAI	150	215	300	400	750	1,100	1,800	3,000
PR8	5¢	dark blue	Unused NGAI	375	500	750	1,350	2,250	3,500	—	—

				F 70	F-VF 75	VF 80	VF-XF 85	XF 90	XF-SUP 95	SUP 98	GEM 100
1875 Issue											
PR9	2¢	black	Used	32.50	45	70	95	140	750	—	—
			Unused NG	75	100	140	165	200	—	—	—
			Unused OG	175	250	350	450	650	—	—	—

SCT#	DENOM	COLOR	CONDITION	F 70	F-VF 75	VF 80	VF-XF 85	XF 90	XF-SUP 95	SUP 98	GEM 100
PR10	3¢	black	Used	35	50	77.50	100	145	—	—	—
			Unused NG	75	100	140	165	200	—	—	—
			Unused OG	175	250	350	500	750	—	—	—
PR11	4¢	black	Used	32.50	45	70	95	140	—	—	—
			Unused NG	75	110	140	165	200	—	—	—
			Unused OG	175	250	350	450	650	—	—	—
PR12	6¢	black	Used	35	50	77.50	100	145	—	—	—
			Unused NG	75	110	140	165	200	—	—	—
			Unused OG	175	250	350	450	650	—	—	—
PR13	8¢	black	Used	55	75	115	150	210	—	—	—
			Unused NG	75	110	140	165	200	—	—	—
			Unused OG	175	250	350	450	650	—	—	—
PR14	9¢	black	Used	82.50	140	210	275	360	—	—	—
			Unused NG	120	165	225	260	350	—	—	—
			Unused OG	300	400	600	750	1,000	—	—	—
PR15	10¢	black	Used	50	67.50	110	150	225	—	—	—
			Unused NG	67.50	97.50	135	150	185	—	—	—
			Unused OG	195	255	375	450	625	—	—	—
PR16	12¢	rose	Used	72.50	110	165	220	320	—	—	—
			Unused NG	160	225	325	375	475	850	—	—
			Unused OG	400	550	800	1,250	2,000	2,750	—	—
PR17	24¢	rose	Used	95	175	210	280	400	750	—	—
			Unused NG	150	260	400	450	550	—	—	—
			Unused OG	525	700	1,000	1,300	2,000	—	—	—
PR18	36¢	rose	Used	150	200	240	310	450	—	—	—
			Unused NG	150	260	400	450	550	—	—	—
			Unused OG	525	700	1,000	1,300	1,700	—	—	—
PR19	48¢	rose	Used	350	500	750	900	1,125	—	—	—
			Unused NG	225	300	450	525	675	—	—	—
			Unused OG	625	850	1,250	1,600	2,250	—	—	—
PR20	60¢	rose	Used	75	125	190	240	375	—	—	—
			Unused NG	275	360	550	600	775	—	—	—
			Unused OG	750	1,025	1,500	1,900	2,650	—	—	—
PR21	72¢	rose	Used	290	450	650	825	1,050	—	—	—
			Unused NG	275	365	550	675	825	—	—	—
			Unused OG	750	1,000	1,500	1,950	2,500	—	—	—
PR22	84¢	rose	Used	290	450	650	825	1,050	—	—	—
			Unused NG	325	450	650	750	1,050	—	—	—
			Unused OG	925	1,300	1,850	2,300	3,250	—	—	—
PR23	96¢	rose	Used	200	300	425	625	825	—	—	—
			Unused NG	375	625	875	1,050	1,250	—	—	—
			Unused OG	1,125	1,575	2,250	2,750	3,650	—	—	—
PR24	$1.92	dark brown	Used	180	300	425	550	700	—	—	—
			Unused NG	375	575	825	950	1,150	—	—	—
			Unused OG	1,125	1,550	2,250	2,800	3,750	—	—	—
PR25	$3	vermilion	Used	400	600	750	925	1,100	—	—	—
			Unused NG	490	675	975	1,150	1,400	—	—	—
			Unused OG	1,175	1,675	2,500	3,100	4,000	—	—	—
PR26	$6	ultramarine	Used	650	825	1,250	1,500	2,000	—	—	—
			Unused NG	850	1,150	1,700	1,950	2,500	—	—	—
			Unused OG	2,150	2,800	4,250	5,250	7,000	—	—	—
PR27	$9	yellow orange	Used	2,400	3,100	4,500	5,250	6,750	—	—	—
			Unused NG	875	1,225	1,750	2,150	2,850	—	—	—
			Unused OG	2,250	3,100	4,500	5,500	8,000	—	—	—
PR28	$12	blue green	Used	1,250	1,700	2,500	2,700	3,500	—	—	—
			Unused NG	950	1,275	1,850	2,100	2,500	—	—	—
			Unused OG	2,250	3,250	4,750	5,500	7,500	—	—	—
PR29	$24	dark gray violet	Used	1,400	1,900	2,800	3,500	4,250	—	—	—
			Unused NG	950	1,275	1,850	2,100	2,500	—	—	—
			Unused OG	2,250	3,250	4,750	5,500	7,500	—	—	—
PR30	$36	brown rose	Used	1,600	2,200	3,150	3,850	4,750	—	—	—
			Unused NG	1,175	1,550	2,250	2,500	3,150	—	—	—
			Unused OG	2,600	3,750	5,500	7,500	9,750	—	—	—
PR31	$48	red brown	Used	1,800	2,500	3,600	4,150	5,200	—	—	—
			Unused NG	1,400	1,900	2,750	3,250	4,000	—	—	—
			Unused OG	4,000	5,250	7,500	9,500	12,000	—	—	—

SCT#	DENOM	COLOR	CONDITION	F 70	F-VF 75	VF 80	VF-XF 85	XF 90	XF-SUP 95	SUP 98	GEM 100
PR32	$60	violet	Used	2,000	2,600	3,750	4,250	5,400	—	—	—
			Unused NG	1,350	1,800	2,600	3,000	3,750	—	—	—
			Unused OG	3,750	5,000	7,000	8,750	11,500	—	—	—
1875 Special Printings of the 1875 Issue											
PR33	2¢	gray black	Unused NGAI	325	480	700	900	1,300	—	—	—
PR33a	2¢	gray black	Unused NGAI	290	435	525	800	1,175	1,750	—	—
PR34	3¢	gray black	Unused NGAI	325	480	700	900	1,300	—	—	—
PR34a	3¢	gray black	Unused NGAI	265	395	525	800	1,175	—	—	—
PR35	4¢	gray black	Unused NGAI	320	470	700	1,050	1,750	—	—	—
PR36	6¢	gray black	Unused NGAI	425	650	1,000	1,450	2,000	—	—	—
PR37	8¢	gray black	Unused NGAI	475	750	1,100	1,500	2,250	—	—	—
PR38	9¢	gray black	Unused NGAI	550	800	1,200	1,675	2,250	—	—	—
PR39	10¢	gray black	Unused NGAI	675	1,025	1,500	2,000	3,000	4,750	—	—
PR40	12¢	pale rose	Unused NGAI	750	1,100	1,600	2,150	3,150	4,500	—	—
PR41	24¢	pale rose	Unused NGAI	1,025	1,525	2,250	3,150	4,500	—	—	—
PR42	36¢	pale rose	Unused NGAI	1,350	2,050	3,000	4,000	5,850	—	—	—
PR43	48¢	pale rose	Unused NGAI	1,750	2,650	4,000	5,250	8,000	—	—	—
PR44	60¢	pale rose	Unused NGAI	2,100	3,150	4,750	6,000	9,000	—	—	—
PR45	72¢	pale rose	Unused NGAI	2,050	3,000	4,500	6,250	8,750	—	—	—
PR46	84¢	pale rose	Unused NGAI	2,650	4,000	5,750	—	—	—	—	—
PR47	96¢	pale rose	Unused NGAI	4,500	6,650	10,000	12,000	15,000	—		
PR48	$1.92	dark brown	Unused NGAI	11,250	17,000	22,500	25,000	30,000	—		
PR49	$3	vermilion	Unused NGAI	25,000	32,500	42,500	—	—			
PR50	$6	ultramarine	Unused NGAI	70,000	85,000	110,000	—				
PR51	$9	yellow orange	Unused NGAI			350,000					
PR52	$12	blue green	Unused NGAI	225,000	—	—	—				
PR53	$24	dark gray violet	Unused NGAI	500,000							
PR54	$36	brown rose	Unused NGAI	400,000				one exam			
PR55	$48	red brown	Unused NGAI	—	—	—					
PR56	$60	violet	Unused NGAI	—	—	—					
1879 American Bank Note Issue (Soft Paper)											
PR57	2¢	black	Used	11	17.50	25	32.50	45	110	—	—
			Unused NG	12	16	30	32.50	37.50	45	—	—
			Unused OG	27.50	40	75	85	110	160	—	—
PR58	3¢	black	Used	15	22.50	32.50	40	50	100	—	—
			Unused NG	15	20	35	37.50	42.50	60	—	—
			Unused OG	30	45	85	100	125	225	—	—
PR59	4¢	black	Used	15	22.50	32.50	40	50	100	—	—
			Unused NG	15	20	35	37.50	42.50	60	—	—
			Unused OG	30	45	85	100	150	250	—	—

SCT#	DENOM	COLOR	CONDITION	F 70	F-VF 75	VF 80	VF-XF 85	XF 90	XF-SUP 95	SUP 98	GEM 100
PR60	6¢	black	Used	25	40	55	70	90	160	—	—
			Unused NG	27.50	37.50	50	55	70	100	—	—
			Unused OG	60	85	125	160	210	425	—	—
PR61	8¢	black	Used	25	40	55	70	90	160	—	—
			Unused NG	30	42.50	55	62.50	80	115	—	—
			Unused OG	65	90	135	160	300	650	—	—
PR62	10¢	black	Used	25	40	55	70	90	160	—	—
			Unused NG	30	42.50	55	62.50	80	115	—	—
			Unused OG	65	90	135	160	275	500	—	—
PR63	12¢	red	Used	97.50	140	210	260	325	675	—	—
			Unused NG	115	145	210	235	275	445	—	—
			Unused OG	225	325	500	650	875	1,650	—	—
PR64	24¢	red	Used	97.50	140	210	260	325	675	—	—
			Unused NG	115	145	210	235	275	445	—	—
			Unused OG	225	325	500	650	875	1,650	—	—
PR65	36¢	red	Used	250	375	525	625	800	1,500	—	—
			Unused NG	250	330	475	525	675	1,100	—	—
			Unused OG	450	700	1,000	1,500	2,100	3,500	—	—
PR66	48¢	red	Used	220	350	475	575	750	—	—	—
			Unused NG	225	310	450	500	650	—	—	—
			Unused OG	450	700	1,000	1,400	2,100	—	—	—
PR67	60¢	red	Used	190	325	450	550	725	—	—	—
			Unused NG	285	380	550	600	800	—	—	—
			Unused OG	550	850	1,250	1,750	2,500	—	—	—
PR68	72¢	red	Used	325	475	700	850	1,150	—	—	—
			Unused NG	365	485	700	750	950	—	—	—
			Unused OG	700	1,000	1,500	2,250	3,500	—	—	—
PR69	84¢	red	Used	230	400	600	725	1,000	—	—	—
			Unused NG	300	400	575	625	800	—	—	—
			Unused OG	575	825	1,250	2,000	2,850	—	—	—
PR70	96¢	red	Used	200	325	500	625	950	—	—	—
			Unused NG	375	475	700	800	1,000	—	—	—
			Unused OG	700	1,000	1,500	2,150	3,000	—	—	—
PR71	$2	pale brown	Used	110	200	290	365	525	—	—	—
			Unused NG	120	150	225	250	325	—	—	—
			Unused OG	255	365	550	750	1,150	1,500	—	—
PR72	$3	red vermilion	Used	140	230	325	425	625	—	—	—
			Unused NG	125	170	250	275	375	—	—	—
			Unused OG	280	425	625	850	1,300	—	—	—
PR73	$6	blue	Used	350	475	700	925	1,300	—	—	—
			Unused NG	200	265	400	450	600	—	—	—
			Unused OG	470	700	1,050	1,450	2,000	3,200	—	—
PR74	$9	orange	Used	260	390	550	675	1,075	—	—	—
			Unused NG	165	220	325	350	425	2,400	—	—
			Unused OG	365	550	800	1,000	1,750	2,700	—	—
PR75	$12	yellow green	Used	260	380	525	675	1,025	—	—	—
			Unused NG	165	220	325	375	500	—	—	—
			Unused OG	385	575	850	1,150	1,750	—	—	—
PR76	$24	dark violet	Used	350	475	675	900	1,300	—	—	—
			Unused NG	150	200	300	325	450	—	—	—
			Unused OG	360	525	800	1,000	1,650	2,600	—	—
PR77	$36	indian red	Used	400	575	775	1,025	1,375	—	—	—
			Unused NG	175	240	350	375	450	—	—	—
			Unused OG	350	550	850	1,050	1,650	—	—	—
PR78	$48	yellow brown	Used	525	725	1,050	1,375	2,000	—	—	—
			Unused NG	175	240	350	375	450	700	—	—
			Unused OG	390	600	900	1,150	1,700	2,400	—	—
PR79	$60	purple	Used	450	625	900	1,200	1,800	—	—	—
			Unused NG	175	240	350	475	700	1,100	—	—
			Unused OG	375	575	850	1,100	1,600	2,500	—	—
			1883 Special Printing of the 1879 Issue								
PR80	2¢	intense black	Unused NGAI	875	1,175	1,750	2,150	2,850	—	—	—

SCT#	DENOM	COLOR	CONDITION	F 70	F-VF 75	VF 80	VF-XF 85	XF 90	XF-SUP 95	SUP 98	GEM 100
1885 American Bank Note Issue											
PR81	1¢	black	Used	8.75	14	22.50	36.50	57.50	145	—	—
			Unused NG	21.50	27.50	42.50	57.50	80	135	—	—
			Unused OG	40	62.50	95	130	200	425	—	—
PR82	12¢	carmine	Used	22	35	52.50	82.50	130	275	—	—
			Unused NG	42.50	57.50	85	97.50	130	215	—	—
			Unused OG	95	135	200	275	375	675	—	—
PR83	24¢	carmine	Used	22	35	52.50	82.50	130	275	—	—
			Unused NG	47.50	65	95	110	145	225	—	—
			Unused OG	105	150	225	310	425	750	—	—
PR84	36¢	carmine	Used	45	65	95	130	210	425	—	—
			Unused NG	72.50	100	145	175	225	400	—	—
			Unused OG	160	230	350	475	650	1,150	—	—
PR85	48¢	carmine	Used	55	85	125	165	260	575	—	—
			Unused NG	90	125	180	210	280	500	—	—
			Unused OG	185	275	425	625	1,000	1,800	—	—
PR86	60¢	carmine	Used	85	120	175	245	350	725	—	—
			Unused NG	130	175	260	290	375	650	—	—
			Unused OG	275	400	600	900	1,250	2,000	—	—
PR87	72¢	carmine	Used	90	130	190	280	400	875	—	—
			Unused NG	130	175	260	290	375	650	—	—
			Unused OG	275	400	600	900	1,250	2,000	—	—
PR88	84¢	carmine	Used	165	290	425	600	975	1,800	—	—
			Unused NG	180	230	350	410	550	900	—	—
			Unused OG	400	575	900	1,225	1,600	3,000	—	—
PR89	96¢	carmine	Used	125	225	325	390	550	1,125	—	—
			Unused NG	150	200	300	350	450	775	—	—
			Unused OG	350	500	750	1,000	1,400	2,500	—	—
1894 First Bureau Issue (Unwatermarked)											
PR90	1¢	intense	Used	5,000	—	—	—	—	—	—	—
		black	Unused NG	80	110	160	185	250	410	—	—
			Unused OG	185	280	400	575	775	1,375	—	—
			Mint NH	400	575	900	1,300	1,800	3,400	—	—
PR91	2¢	intense	Unused NG	82.50	125	190	215	270	400	—	—
		black	Unused OG	210	310	450	600	875	1,450	—	—
			Mint NH	470	700	1,075	1,575	2,200	4,000	—	—
PR92	4¢	intense	Used	—	—	13,500	—	—	—	—	—
		black	Unused NG	105	140	210	235	275	475	—	—
			Unused OG	240	360	550	725	1,000	1,800	—	—
			Mint NH	575	825	1,275	1,875	2,650	4,800	—	—
PR93	6¢	intense	Unused NG	950	1,250	1,900	2,250	2,800	—	—	—
		black	Unused OG	2,000	3,000	4,500	6,500	9,000	—	15,000	—
			Mint NH	—	—	11,500	—	—	—	—	—
PR94	10¢	intense	Unused NG	280	370	550	600	775	1,350	—	—
		black	Unused OG	650	925	1,400	1,850	2,600	4,500	—	—
PR95	12¢	pink	Used	4,500	—	—	—	—	—	—	—
			Unused NG	550	750	1,100	1,325	1,750	—	—	—
			Unused OG	1,175	1,775	2,600	3,500	5,000	9,250	12,500	—
PR96	24¢	pink	Used	8,000	—	—	—	—	—	—	—
			Unused NG	925	1,225	1,850	2,000	2,500	—	—	—
			Unused OG	1,700	2,500	3,750	5,500	8,000	13,500	—	—
PR97	36¢	pink	Unused NG	—	—	—	—	—			
			Unused OG	50,000	—	—	—	—			
PR98	60¢	pink	Used	16,000	—	—	—	—			
			Unused NG	—	—	—	—	—			
			Unused OG	40,000	—	—	—	—			
PR99	96¢	pink	Unused NG	—	—	—	—	—			
			Unused OG	35,000	50,000	—	—	—			
PR100	$3	scarlet	Unused NG	—	—	—	—	—			
			Unused OG	35,000	50,000	—	—	—			
PR101	$6	pale	Unused NG	—	25,000	—	—	—			
		blue	Unused OG	35,000	50,000	—	—	—			

SCT#	DENOM	COLOR	CONDITION	F 70	F-VF 75	VF 80	VF-XF 85	XF 90	XF-SUP 95	SUP 98	GEM 100

SCT#	DENOM	COLOR	CONDITION	F 70	F-VF 75	VF 80	VF-XF 85	XF 90	XF-SUP 95	SUP 98	GEM 100
1895 Second Bureau Issue (Unwatermarked)											
PR102	1¢	black	Used	67.50	125	180	260	425	750	—	—
			Unused NG	45	60	90	100	120	170	—	—
			Unused OG	105	150	230	300	425	750	—	—
			Mint NH	200	325	500	800	1,200	2,450	—	—
PR103	2¢	black	Used	67.50	125	180	260	425	750	—	—
			Unused NG	45	60	90	100	120	170	—	—
			Unused OG	105	150	230	300	425	750	—	—
			Mint NH	200	325	500	800	1,200	2,450	—	—
PR104	5¢	black	Used	215	300	425	600	875	1,600	—	—
			Unused NG	55	82.50	125	140	160	225	—	—
			Unused OG	145	200	300	425	600	1,000	—	—
			Mint NH	250	400	650	1,000	1,550	3,250	—	—
PR105	10¢	black	Used	475	600	900	1,125	1,600	2,500	—	—
			Unused NG	115	160	240	270	310	450	—	—
			Unused OG	265	405	600	850	1,250	2,250	—	—
			Mint NH	500	875	1,300	2,000	3,200	5,000	—	—
PR106	25¢	carmine	Used	500	650	975	1,350	1,750	3,000	—	—
			Unused NG	150	200	300	340	400	575	—	—
			Unused OG	350	500	750	1,050	1,450	2,600	—	—
			Mint NH	650	1,075	1,650	2,500	3,850	6,250	—	—
PR107	50¢	carmine	Used	550	800	1,075	1,400	2,100	3,750	—	—
			Unused NG	440	600	875	975	1,100	1,375	—	—
			Unused OG	1,300	1,800	2,750	3,250	4,250	6,000	—	—
			Mint NH	2,600	4,250	6,250	8,500	12,000	16,500	—	—
PR108	$2	scarlet	Used	800	1,100	1,550	2,100	2,900	4,250	—	—
			Unused NG	430	575	850	925	1,075	1,850	—	—
			Unused OG	1,050	1,475	2,250	3,000	4,500	7,000	—	—
			Mint NH	2,000	3,250	5,000	7,000	11,000	17,500	—	—
PR109	$5	ultramarine	Used	1,750	2,250	3,000	3,750	5,000	8,000	—	—
			Unused NG	425	550	850	925	1,050	1,600	—	—
			Unused OG	1,050	1,550	2,250	3,100	4,500	6,750	—	—
			Mint NH	1,800	2,850	4,500	7,000	11,000	—	—	—
PR110	$10	green	Used	2,000	2,750	3,750	4,750	5,250	10,500	—	—
			Unused NG	450	600	900	975	1,150	1,750	—	—
			Unused OG	1,100	1,675	2,500	3,250	5,250	7,500	—	—
			Mint NH	2,200	3,400	5,250	7,750	13,000	—	—	—
PR111	$20	slate	Used	2,500	4,000	4,500	5,500	7,000	10,000	—	—
			Unused NG	600	800	1,200	1,350	1,600	2,400	—	—
			Unused OG	1,400	2,050	3,250	4,250	5,750	10,000	—	—
			Mint NH	2,750	4,250	6,750	9,750	16,000	—	—	—
PR112	$50	dull	Used	950	1,100	1,500	2,150	3,250	—	—	—
		rose	Unused NG	525	700	1,050	1,200	1,425	2,000	—	—
			Unused OG	1,250	1,825	2,750	3,500	5,250	9,250	—	—
			Mint NH	2,600	4,150	6,250	9,500	15,000	—	—	—
PR113	$100	purple	Used	7,000	11,000	15,000	—	—	—	—	—
			Unused NG	700	925	1,400	1,525	1,700	2,500	—	—
			Unused OG	1,600	2,300	3,500	4,750	6,500	11,500	—	—
			Mint NH	3,100	4,500	7,250	11,500	—	—	—	—

SCT# DENOM	COLOR	CONDITION	F 70	F-VF 75	VF 80	VF-XF 85	XF 90	XF-SUP 95	SUP 98	GEM 100
1895-97 Bureau Issue (Double Line Watermark)										
PR114 1¢	black	Used	12	17	25	35	55	110	200	—
		Unused NG	1.40	1.75	2.75	4	7.50	12.50	20	—
		Unused OG	3.75	5.50	8	10	14	22.50	35	—
		Mint NH	8	12.50	20	30	42.50	80	140	—
PR115 2¢	black	Used	12	17	25	35	55	110	200	—
		Unused NG	1.40	1.75	2.75	4	7.50	12.50	20	—
		Unused OG	3.75	5.50	8	10	14	22.50	35	—
		Mint NH	8	12.50	20	30	42.50	75	140	—
PR116 5¢	black	Used	22.50	29	40	60	95	170	400	—
		Unused NG	2.10	2.75	4.25	5.50	9	17.50	27.50	—
		Unused OG	5.75	8.75	13	16	20	32.50	60	—
		Mint NH	11	18	27.50	42.50	60	100	150	—
PR117 10¢	black	Used	12	17	25	35	55	110	200	—
		Unused NG	2.10	2.75	4.25	5.50	9	17.50	27.50	—
		Unused OG	5.75	8.75	13	16	20	32.50	60	—
		Mint NH	11	18	27.50	37.50	50	85	150	—
PR118 25¢	carmine	Used	25	42.50	65	95	130	225	375	—
		Unused NG	3.50	4.60	7	8.50	12	18.50	30	—
		Unused OG	9.25	13.75	20	26	37.50	60	100	—
		Mint NH	18	27	45	65	90	170	275	—
PR119 50¢	carmine	Used	40	50	75	110	150	250	425	—
		Unused NG	4.25	5.75	8.50	10	12.50	20	32.50	—
		Unused OG	11.25	16.50	25	30	40	65	120	—
		Mint NH	22	35	55	70	110	175	350	—
PR120 $2	scarlet	Used	60	82.50	110	160	220	375	625	—
		Unused NG	5	6.50	10	12	16	25	40	—
		Unused OG	13.25	20	30	37.50	50	87.50	160	—
		Mint NH	30	50	75	100	225	500	750	—
PR121 $5	dark blue	Used	92.50	110	175	240	310	550	925	—
		Unused NG	6.75	9	13.50	16	20	30	42.50	—
		Unused OG	18.50	27.50	40	47.50	65	110	190	—
		Mint NH	37.50	62.50	100	130	350	475	650	—
PR121a $5	light blue	Used	250	350	500	725	1,000	1,725	2,800	—
		Unused NG	35	45	67.50	75	87.50	125	200	—
		Unused OG	900	130	200	250	325	475	775	—
		Mint NH	200	310	500	700	975	1,600	2,750	—
PR122 $10	green	Used	87.50	120	175	240	330	575	975	—
		Unused NG	7	9.50	14	16.50	22.50	32.50	45	—
		Unused OG	20	27.50	42.50	52.50	70	110	190	—
		Mint NH	40	65	105	135	210	350	625	—
PR123 $20	slate	Used	100	140	200	290	400	700	1,200	—
		Unused NG	7.50	10	15	17.50	23.50	35	47.50	—
		Unused OG	19	27.50	45	55	75	130	250	—
		Mint NH	42.50	67.50	110	145	210	400	750	—
PR124 $50	dull rose	Used	200	275	400	550	750	1,300	2,000	—
		Unused NG	14	18	27.50	30	35	47.50	70	—
		Unused OG	35	50	75	100	140	250	400	—
		Mint NH	70	105	170	275	400	775	1,300	—
PR125 $100	purple	Used	170	215	300	425	800	1,800	2,750	—
		Unused NG	11.25	15	22.50	24	29	45	75	—
		Unused OG	30	50	65	85	125	190	350	—
		Mint NH	62.50	105	150	210	350	550	1,100	2,000

SCT#	DENOM	COLOR	CONDITION	F 70	F-VF 75	VF 80	VF-XF 85	XF 90	XF-SUP 95	SUP 98	GEM 100

1912-13 PARCEL POST ISSUES

SCT#	DENOM	COLOR	CONDITION	F 70	F-VF 75	VF 80	VF-XF 85	XF 90	XF-SUP 95	SUP 98	GEM 100
Q1	1¢	carmine	Used	0.70	1.15	1.60	9.50	32.50	125	350	—
		rose	Unused OG	1.90	3	4.25	6	12	32.50	47.50	95
			Mint NH	4.50	7.50	12	25	50	225	575	1,400
Q2	2¢	carmine	Used	0.55	0.90	1.25	5.25	22.50	105	325	1,100
		rose	Unused OG	2.15	3.55	5	7.50	12.50	30	60	110
			Mint NH	4.75	8	12.50	25	60	500	950	1,600
Q2a	2¢	lake	Unused OG	2,800	3,750	5,000					
Q2b	2¢	carmine lake	Unused OG	150	225	350	—	—			
Q3	3¢	carmine	Used	2.75	4.25	6	10.50	32.50	130	425	—
		rose	Unused OG	4.25	6.25	9	12	17.50	47.50	85	170
			Mint NH	7.50	15	24	45	85	375	1,050	2,400
Q4	4¢	carmine	Used	1.50	2.15	3	7	27.50	120	400	—
		rose	Unused OG	12.50	18.50	27.50	40	70	150	350	675
			Mint NH	20	42.50	77.50	100	225	875	1,800	—
Q5	5¢	carmine	Used	1.10	1.55	2.25	4.50	27.50	120	375	—
		rose	Unused OG	9.75	15	22.50	30	50	115	190	—
			Mint NH	21	37	62.50	105	175	575	2,000	3,500
Q6	10¢	carmine	Used	1.50	2.15	3	6	25	125	375	—
		rose	Unused OG	15	28	40	47.50	72.50	165	360	—
			Mint NH	30	57.50	90	125	235	800	2,200	4,500
Q7	15¢	carmine	Used	6.25	10	13.50	22.50	75	190	600	1,500
		rose	Unused OG	25	40	60	67.50	82.50	175	325	—
			Mint NH	50	110	170	215	500	925	3,750	—
Q8	20¢	carmine	Used	12.50	18.50	25	42.50	105	250	650	—
		rose	Unused OG	50	77.50	110	125	160	350	575	—
			Mint NH	82.50	150	260	375	600	1,250	4,250	—
Q9	25¢	carmine	Used	3.75	5.75	8	15	42.50	150	425	—
		rose	Unused OG	21.50	35	52.50	62.50	82.50	190	350	—
			Mint NH	42.50	85	145	240	350	850	2,250	—
Q10	50¢	carmine	Used	22.50	32.50	45	67.50	165	375	1,100	—
		rose	Unused OG	95	130	210	250	400	550	1,100	—
			Mint NH	140	260	525	750	1,300	2,350	7,250	14,000
Q11	75¢	carmine	Used	15	24	35	57.50	150	325	1,000	—
		rose	Unused OG	32.50	55	85	100	130	235	450	875
			Mint NH	57.50	95	190	300	500	1,000	2,850	7,750
Q12	$1	carmine	Used	17.50	27.50	40	57.50	140	350	975	—
		rose	Unused OG	130	175	260	320	400	625	1,300	2,250
			Mint NH	230	370	625	800	1,300	2,500	7,500	16,500
Q1-Q12 Set	12 stamps		Used	85.50	130.40	183.60	305.25	845	2,365	7,000	
			Unused OG	385	574.30	860.75	1,043	1,460	2,600	5,065	
			Mint NH	675	1,208	2,134	3,035	5,243	11,825	35,825	

1912 PARCEL POST POSTAGE DUE ISSUES

SCT#	DENOM	COLOR	CONDITION	F 70	F-VF 75	VF 80	VF-XF 85	XF 90	XF-SUP 95	SUP 98	GEM 100
JQ1	1¢	dark green	Used	1.80	2.80	4	9	27.50	125	375	—
			Unused OG	3.75	5.75	8	11.50	16	27.50	47.50	100
			Mint NH	7.50	12.50	22.50	37.50	75	250	500	—
JQ2	2¢	dark green	Used	8	12	16	27.50	67.50	225	625	—
			Unused OG	25	42.50	60	75	97.50	190	300	—
			Mint NH	52.50	100	160	260	400	825	1,500	—

SCT#	DENOM	COLOR	CONDITION	F 70	F-VF 75	VF 80	VF-XF 85	XF 90	XF-SUP 95	SUP 98	GEM 100
JQ3	5¢	dark	Used	2.10	3.25	4.50	9.50	30	120	375	—
		green	Unused OG	4.20	5.75	9	13.50	20	37.50	62.50	—
			Mint NH	9	12.75	24	45	100	350	700	—
JQ4	10¢	dark	Used	20	30	40	65	150	550	1,000	—
		green	Unused OG	50	70	110	150	225	400	650	—
			Mint NH	100	175	290	420	700	1,500	2,650	—
JQ5	25¢	dark	Used	2	3.15	4.50	11.50	35	175	475	1,000
		green	Unused OG	32.50	52.50	70	87.50	120	200	375	—
			Mint NH	60	115	185	290	450	900	1,900	3,500

1925-29 SPECIAL HANDLING ISSUES

SCT#	DENOM	COLOR	CONDITION	F 70	F-VF 75	VF 80	VF-XF 85	XF 90	XF-SUP 95	SUP 98	GEM 100
QE1	10¢	yellow green	Used	0.70	1	1.50	4.50	15	52.50	190	—
		wet printing	Unused OG	1.50	2.10	3	4.50	12.50	20	40	—
		"special" bklt paper	Mint NH	2.10	3.40	5.25	8	20	45	190	190
QE1a	10¢	green	Used		0.85	1	10	20	45		—
		wet	Unused OG	1	1.40	2	10	17.50	45	—	—
		printing	Mint NH	1.85	2.80	4.25	15	22.50	60	160	400
QE1b	10¢	light	Used		125	150	—				
		green	Unused OG	2.50	3.60	5	7.75	20	40	95	—
		dry printing	Mint NH	4.25	6.50	10	14	35	82.50	175	—
QE2	15¢	yellow green	Used	0.70	1	1.50	4.50	15	52.50	190	—
		wet printing	Unused OG	1.35	2.15	3.25	6.50	15	30	60	—
		"special" bklt paper	Mint NH	1.90	3.10	4.75	10	22.50	45	165	—
QE2a	15¢	green	Used		0.75	0.90	—				
		wet	Unused OG	1	1.45	2.25	3.50	9	20	40	—
		printing	Mint NH	2	3.10	4.75	7.50	15	35	160	—
QE2b	15¢	light green	Used		125	150	—				
		dry	Unused OG	2.50	3.60	5	7.75	20	40	95	—
		printing	Mint NH	4.25	6.50	10	15	32.50	60	200	500
QE3	20¢	yellow green	Used	0.70	1	1.50	3.75	12.50	45	135	—
		wet printing	Unused OG	1.90	2.50	3.75	7.50	15	40	85	—
		"special" bklt paper	Mint NH	3.50	6	8.75	12.50	25	60	190	425
QE3a	20¢	green	Used		1	1.50	—				
		wet	Unused OG	1.90	2.50	3.75	7.50	15	35	75	—
		printing	Mint NH	3	5	7.75	12.50	22.50	50	140	400
QE3b	20¢	light green	Used		125	150	—				
		dry	Unused OG	3.50	5.25	7.50	11	20	45	110	—
		printing	Mint NH	6	10	15	22.50	45	95	240	425
QE4	25¢	deep	Used	1.80	2.50	3.75	11	20	75	175	—
		green	Unused OG	9.50	14	20	22.50	27.50	45	100	—
			Mint NH	15	25	37.50	45	60	170	360	1,400
QE4a	25¢	yellow	Used	10	15	22.50	37.50	60	140	425	—
		green	Unused OG	7.50	11	16.50	19	25	35	55	—
			Mint NH	14	22.50	30	40	55	140	325	800

HUNTING PERMIT (DUCK) STAMPS

SCT#	DENOM	COLOR	CONDITION	F 70	F-VF 75	VF 80	VF-XF 85	XF 90	XF-SUP 95	SUP 98	GEM 100
RW1	$1	blue	Used	95	135	175	185	210	260	425	—
			Unused NG	105	150	175	190	220	245	425	—
			Unused OG	150	210	300	325	360	425	—	—
			Mint NH	275	600	775	850	1,125	2,100	4,600	—

SCT#	DENOM	COLOR	CONDITION	F 70	F-VF 75	VF 80	VF-XF 85	XF 90	XF-SUP 95	SUP 98	GEM 100
RW2	$1	rose	Used	97.50	125	160	180	200	275	425	—
		lake	Unused NG	100	145	175	185	200	225	340	—
			Unused OG	190	270	375	390	420	460	600	—
			Mint NH	300	500	700	825	1,000	1,500	4,150	10,000
RW3	$1	brown	Used	47.50	80	100	115	135	170	250	—
		black	Unused NG	35	70	90	95	105	125	160	—
			Unused OG	82.50	120	150	160	180	210	300	600
			Mint NH	165	230	325	375	500	900	1,550	4,500
RW4	$1	light	Used	27.50	47.50	65	75	90	130	175	—
		green	Unused NG	40	62.50	85	97.50	115	130	190	—
			Unused OG	70	110	140	155	175	250	365	—
			Mint NH	125	200	300	425	550	875	3,000	—
RW5	$1	light	Used	37.50	60	75	87.50	105	120	170	—
		violet	Unused NG	40	62.50	85	97.50	115	130	190	—
			Unused OG	100	125	200	215	245	285	425	—
			Mint NH	145	260	425	575	1,000	1,800	4,650	—
RW6	$1	chocolate	Used	28	37.50	50	57.50	67.50	90	150	—
			Unused NG	32.50	47.50	60	67.50	80	105	170	—
			Unused OG	55	77.50	115	125	145	200	275	—
			Mint NH	100	180	250	280	325	800	1,600	4,500
RW7	$1	sepia	Used	28	37.50	50	57.50	67.50	90	150	—
			Unused NG	32.50	47.50	60	67.50	80	105	170	—
			Unused OG	55	77.50	115	125	145	190	250	—
			Mint NH	100	180	250	280	325	700	2,250	—
RW8	$1	brown	Used	28	37.50	50	57.50	67.50	90	150	—
		carmine	Unused NG	22.50	35	45	50	60	72.50	140	—
			Unused OG	45	65	95	105	120	135	200	—
			Mint NH	90	160	225	270	350	625	1,250	3,250
RW9	$1	violet	Used	25	35	45	52.50	62.50	75	140	—
		brown	Unused NG	25	35	45	50	60	75	130	—
			Unused OG	45	65	95	105	120	160	200	—
			Mint NH	90	160	225	280	375	850	2,000	4,650
RW10	$1	deep	Used	17.50	24	35	40	50	62.50	100	—
		rose	Unused NG	20	28.50	35	40	52.50	65	87.50	—
			Unused OG	27.50	42.50	55	61.50	72.50	92.50	150	—
			Mint NH	42.50	72.50	120	140	190	400	900	2,600
RW11	$1	red	Used	14	22	35	40	47.50	57.50	90	—
		orange	Unused NG	20	27.50	35	42.50	52.50	65	87.50	—
			Unused OG	22.50	35	45	55	67.50	160	200	—
			Mint NH	47.50	72.50	125	160	240	600	2,150	—
RW12	$1	black	Used	12.50	20	25	30	37.50	50	70	—
			Unused NG	17.50	25	35	40	50	65	92.50	—
			Unused OG	20	35	45	52.50	75	100	135	—
			Mint NH	32.50	67.50	100	130	180	475	850	—
RW13	$1	red	Used	6.25	8.75	12.50	15	20	30	55	—
		brown	Unused NG	10	13.25	15	17	21	27.50	50	—
			Mint NH	20	35	50	65	110	210	750	1,400
RW14	$1	black	Used	7.50	10.50	15	17	20	27.50	62.50	—
			Unused NG	12	16	18	20	25	35	65	—
			Mint NH	20	35	55	70	130	190	425	1,650
RW15	$1	bright	Used	6	8.50	12	13.50	16	25	60	—
		blue	Unused NG	10	12.50	15	17	21	30	62.50	—
			Mint NH	22.50	37.50	60	80	150	210	500	1,500
RW16	$2	bright	Used	7.50	11	15	17	20	30	62.50	—
		green	Unused NG	11.50	16	20	24	30	35	50	—
			Mint NH	27.50	42.50	70	85	135	220	525	1,600
RW17	$2	violet	Used	7.50	11	15	17	20	30	62.50	160
			Unused NG	11.50	16	20	24	30	35	50	—
			Mint NH	40	67.50	90	105	130	210	425	900
RW18	$2	gray	Used	7.50	11	15	17	20	30	62.50	—
		black	Unused NG	11.50	16	20	24	30	37.50	52.50	—
			Mint NH	40	67.50	90	105	140	220	450	1,150
RW19	$2	deep	Used	7.50	11	15	17	20	30	62.50	—
		ultra	Unused NG	11.50	16	20	24	30	37.50	52.50	—
			Mint NH	40	67.50	90	105	140	240	575	1,050

SCT#	DENOM	COLOR	CONDITION	F 70	F-VF 75	VF 80	VF-XF 85	XF 90	XF-SUP 95	SUP 98	GEM 100
RW20	$2	rose	Used	7.50	11	15	17	20	30	62.50	145
		brown	Unused NG	11.50	16	20	24	30	37.50	52.50	—
			Mint NH	40	67.50	90	115	145	260	700	—
RW21	$2	black	Used	7.50	11	15	18	23	30	60	125
			Unused NG	11	16	20	26	30	35	57.50	—
			Mint NH	37.50	65	85	100	130	180	380	1,100
RW22	$2	dark	Used	7.25	9.75	12.50	15	20	27.50	45	120
		blue	Unused NG	11	16	20	26	30	35	57.50	—
			Mint NH	37.50	65	85	100	130	170	330	1,050
RW23	$2	black	Used	7.25	9.75	12.50	15	20	27.50	45	—
			Unused NG	11	16	20	26	30	35	55	—
			Mint NH	37.50	65	85	100	125	160	300	2,750
RW24	$2	emerald	Used	7.25	9.75	12.50	15	20	27.50	45	—
			Unused NG	11	16	20	26	30	35	55	—
			Mint NH	37.50	65	85	100	120	155	300	2,750
RW25	$2	black	Used	7.25	9.75	12.50	15	20	27.50	45	—
			Unused NG	11	16	20	26	30	35	55	—
			Mint NH	37.50	65	85	100	125	175	375	1,450
RW26	$3	multicolor	Used	7.25	9.75	12.50	16	21	32.50	60	—
			Unused NG	22.50	30	45	50	60	75	90	—
			Mint NH	60	95	130	145	170	230	400	825
RW27	$3	multicolor	Used	7.25	9.75	12.50	16	21	32.50	60	—
			Unused NG	21.50	25	30	32.50	35	37.50	50	—
			Mint NH	40	75	95	110	125	160	325	1,150
RW28	$3	multicolor	Used	7.25	9.75	12.50	16	21	32.50	60	—
			Unused NG	15	21.50	30	32.50	35	37.50	60	—
			Mint NH	47.50	70	95	110	140	190	350	875
RW29	$3	multicolor	Used	7.25	9.75	12.50	16	21	32.50	60	140
			Unused NG	17.50	25	35	37.50	42.50	50	75	—
			Mint NH	55	77.50	110	125	150	225	375	1,150
RW30	$3	multicolor	Used	7.25	9.75	12.50	16	21	32.50	60	140
			Unused NG	17.50	25	35	37.50	42.50	50	75	—
			Mint NH	42.50	65	100	110	135	185	340	825
RW31	$3	multicolor	Used	7.25	9.75	12.50	16	21	32.50	60	—
			Unused NG	17.50	25	35	37.50	42.50	50	75	—
			Mint NH	42.50	65	100	115	140	190	350	—
RW32	$3	multicolor	Used	7.25	9.75	12.50	16	21	32.50	60	—
			Unused NG	20	28.50	40	44	50	57.50	85	—
			Mint NH	42.50	65	100	110	140	185	350	—
RW33	$3	multicolor	Used	7.25	9.75	12.50	16	21	32.50	60	—
			Unused NG	20	27.50	40	44	50	57.50	85	—
			Mint NH	42.50	65	100	110	140	185	350	750
RW34	$3	multicolor	Used	7.25	9.75	12.50	16	21	32.50	60	—
			Unused NG	20	27.50	40	43	48.50	57.50	80	—
			Mint NH	42.50	65	100	115	155	210	400	825
RW35	$3	multicolor	Used	7.25	9.75	12.50	16	21	32.50	60	—
			Unused NG	9.50	14	20	22	25	29	45	—
			Mint NH	30	45	65	80	110	225	525	1,200
RW36	$3	multicolor	Used	4	6	8	10	14	22.50	30	—
			Unused NG	9.50	14	20	22	25	29	45	—
			Mint NH	30	45	65	80	110	225	550	—
RW37	$3	multicolor	Used	4	6	8	10	14	22.50	30	—
			Unused NG	9.50	14	20	22	25	29	45	—
			Mint NH	30	45	65	80	110	190	325	750
RW38	$3	multicolor	Used	4	6	8	10	14	20	30	—
			Unused NG	6	11.25	15	16	17.50	19	22.50	—
			Mint NH	19	32.50	42.50	50	70	100	180	325
RW39	$5	multicolor	Used	3.20	5.25	6	8	12	18	27.50	—
			Unused NG	4	6	8	10	13	17.50	26	—
			Mint NH	13.50	24	30	47.50	80	120	200	400
RW40	$5	multicolor	Used	3	4.75	6	8	11	15	26	—
			Unused NG	3.50	5.25	7	9	12	16	25	—
			Mint NH	9	13.50	18	25	45	55	115	260
RW41	$5	multicolor	Used	2.50	4	5	7	9	12.50	21	—
			Unused NG	4	5	6	8	10	12.50	20	—
			Mint NH	9	13.50	18	27.50	45	70	140	350

SCT#	DENOM	COLOR	CONDITION	F 70	F-VF 75	VF 80	VF-XF 85	XF 90	XF-SUP 95	SUP 98	GEM 100
RW42	$5	multicolor	Used	2.50	4	5	7	9	12.50	21	—
			Unused NG	4.60	5.75	7	9	11.50	15	24	—
			Mint NH	7.50	10	15	22.50	42.50	75	170	—
RW43	$5	green & black	Used	2.50	4	5	7	9	12.50	21	—
			Unused NG	4.60	5.75	7	9	11.50	15	24	—
			Mint NH	6.25	8.25	12.50	17.50	40	60	150	260
RW44	$5	multicolor	Used	2.50	4	5	7	9	12.50	21	—
			Unused NG	4.60	5.75	7	9	11.50	15	24	—
			Mint NH	5	6.75	10	15	25	60	140	375
RW45	$5	multicolor	Used	2.50	4	5	7	9	12.50	21	—
			Unused NG	2.80	4.50	7	8.50	11	15	20	—
			Mint NH	5	6.75	10	17.50	40	55	110	250
RW46	$7.50	multicolor	Used	3	5	6	8	10	13.50	24	—
			Unused NG	4	6	8	9.50	11.50	13.50	25	—
			Mint NH	6.25	8.25	12.50	17.50	40	60	155	400
RW47	$7.50	multicolor	Used	3	4.75	6	8	10	13.50	24	—
			Unused NG	4	6	8	9.50	11.50	13.50	25	—
			Mint NH	6.25	8.25	12.50	19	40	60	140	275
RW48	$7.50	multicolor	Used	3	4.75	6	8	10	13.50	24	—
			Unused NG	4	6	8	9.50	11.50	13.50	25	—
			Mint NH	6.25	8.25	12.50	19	40	60	140	275
RW49	$7.50	multicolor	Used	3.75	5.50	7	8	11	15	24	—
			Unused NG	4	6	9	10	12	15	25	—
			Mint NH	7.50	10	15	22.50	42.50	65	160	325
RW50	$7.50	multicolor	Used	3.75	5.50	7	8	11	15	24	—
			Unused NG	3.25	4.65	7	7.75	9.25	11.50	20	—
			Mint NH	7.50	10	15	22.50	37.50	65	160	325
RW51	$7.50	multicolor	Used	3.75	5.50	7	8	11	15	24	—
			Unused NG	3.25	4.65	7	7.75	9.25	12.50	20	—
			Mint NH	6.25	8.25	12.50	17.50	27.50	50	140	275
RW52	$7.50	multicolor	Used	4	6	8	10	13	18	30	—
			Unused NG	3.25	4.65	7	8	10	12.50	20	—
			Mint NH	7.50	10	15	22.50	37.50	65	155	260
RW53	$7.50	multicolor	Used	4	6	8	10	13	18	30	—
			Unused NG	4	6	9	11	15	20	30	—
			Mint NH	7.50	10	15	22.50	37.50	65	160	300
RW54	$10	multicolor	Used	4	6	8	10	13	18	30	—
			Unused NG	4	5.75	8	9.50	11.50	15	25	—
			Mint NH	8.75	12	17.50	27.50	40	65	130	175
RW55	$10	multicolor	Used	4	6	8	10	13	18	30	—
			Unused NG	4	5.75	8	9.50	11.50	18	25	—
			Mint NH	8.75	12	17.50	27.50	40	65	150	475
RW56	$12.50	multicolor	Used		5.50	8	10	13	18	30	—
			Unused NG		6.50	9	11	14	19	30	—
			Mint NH		16	21.50	30	42.50	60	150	475
RW57	$12.50	multicolor	Used		5.50	8	10	13	18	30	—
			Unused NG		6.50	9	11	14	19	30	—
			Mint NH		15	20	27.50	40	57.50	110	300
RW58	$15	multicolor	Used		5.50	8	10	13	18	30	—
			Unused NG		12	15	17.50	20	27.50	52.50	—
			Mint NH		22.50	30	37.50	60	87.50	175	350
RW59	$15	multicolor	Used		7.50	10	12	15	19	30	—
			Unused NG		11.50	15	16.50	19	22.50	50	—
			Mint NH		22.50	30	37.50	55	160	260	650
RW60	$15	multicolor	Used		6.25	9	11	13	16	27.50	—
			Unused NG		11.50	15	16.50	19	23.50	42	—
			Mint NH		20	27.50	32	37.50	55	115	185
RW61	$15	multicolor	Used		7.50	10	12	15	19	30	—
			Unused NG		11.50	15	17.50	22.50	32.50	45	—
			Mint NH		20	27.50	32	37.50	55	110	175
RW62	$15	multicolor	Used		9	12	17.50	22.50	30	45	—
			Unused NG		12	15	17.50	20	25	45	—
			Mint NH		22.50	32.50	37.50	50	67.50	140	325
RW63	$15	multicolor	Used		9	12	17.50	22.50	30	45	—
			Unused NG		11	12.50	15	19	22.50	40	—
			Mint NH		22.50	32.50	37.50	50	75	145	250

SCT#	DENOM	COLOR	CONDITION	F 70	F-VF 75	VF 80	VF-XF 85	XF 90	XF-SUP 95	SUP 98	GEM 100
RW64	$15	multicolor	Used	9	12	15	20	365	50	120	
			Unused NG	11	15	17	20	24	45	—	
			Mint NH	20	27.50	32.50	40	65	135	325	
RW65	$15	multicolor	Used	16	22.50	27.50	35	50	75	—	
			Unused NG	16	22.50	25	30	37.50	52.50	—	
			Mint NH	32.50	45	52.50	62.50	105	170	275	
RW65A	$15	multicolor	Used	12	15	17	20	30	50	—	
			Unused NG		15	16	17.50	22.50	32.50	—	
			Mint NH		30	35	45	85	130	—	
RW66	$15	multicolor	Used	15	20	23.50	30	45	75	—	
			Unused NG	19	22.50	25	30	37.50	50	—	
			Mint NH	32.50	40	45	55	75	135	275	
RW66A	$15	multicolor	Used	10	12	14	17.50	25	40	—	
			Unused NG		15	16	17.50	22.50	32.50	—	
			Mint NH		30	35	42.50	57.50	105	—	
RW67	$15	multicolor	Used	12	15	18	22.50	30	60	—	
			Unused NG		15	17.50	19	22	25	50	—	
			Mint NH	27.50	35	40	50	80	145	260	
RW67A	$15	multicolor	Used	12	14	17	22	45	85	—	
			Unused NG		17.50	19	20	22.50	32.50	—	
			Mint NH		30	35	42.50	57.50	105	270	
RW68	$15	multicolor	Used	13.50	18	21	26	47.50	70	140	
			Unused NG	15	17.50	19	22	25	50	—	
			Mint NH	22.50	30	33.50	42.50	65	120	200	
RW68A	$15	multicolor	Used	12	14	16	19	22.50	40	—	
			Unused NG		15	16	17.50	22.50	32.50	—	
			Mint NH		30	35	45	65	100	—	
RW69	$15	multicolor	Used	12	16	19	24	37.50	60	—	
			Unused NG	15	17.50	19	22	25	50	—	
			Mint NH	27.50	35	40	50	80	115	180	
RW69A	$15	multicolor	Used	10	12	14	17.50	25	40	—	
			Unused NG		15	16	17.50	22.50	32.50	—	
			Mint NH		30	35	42.50	57.50	100	180	
RW70	$15	multicolor	Used	13	16	19	24	37.50	60	110	
			Unused NG	14	17.50	19	22	25	45	—	
			Mint NH	27.50	35	45	57.50	87.50	145	260	
RW70A	$15	multicolor	Used	10	12	14	17.50	25	40	—	
			Unused NG		15	16	17.50	22.50	32.50	—	
			Mint NH		30	35	45	60	100	—	
RW71	$15	multicolor	Used	12.75	16	19	25	35	65	130	
			Unused NG	13.75	17	18.50	21	25	45	—	
			Mint NH	27.50	35	45	57.50	85	125	200	
RW71A	$15	multicolor	Used	10	12	14	17.50	25	40	—	
			Unused NG		15	16	18	22.50	32.50	—	
			Mint NH		30	35	42.50	57.50	100	180	
RW72	$15	multicolor	Used	13	16	19	25	35	65	130	
		type I	Unused NG	13	16	17	19	24	42.50	—	
			Mint NH	24	30	37.50	50	75	125	210	
RW72b $15 multicolor black signature			Mint NH	1,750	1,950	2,250	2,650	3,250	3,750	5,750	
RW72b $15 multicolor blue signature			Mint NH	—	2,100	2,500	2,750	3,250	3,750	4,250	7,000
RW72b $15 multicolor gold signature			Mint NH	—	2,500	3,000	3,250	3,800	4,500	5,500	—
RW72c	$15	multicolor	Used	13	16	19	25	35	65	130	
		type II	Unused NG	13	16	17	19	24	42.50	—	
			Mint NH	24	30	37.50	50	75	125	210	
RW72A	$15	multicolor	Used	9	11	13	16	22.50	35	—	
			Unused NG		15	16	18	22.50	32.50	—	
			Mint NH		27.50	30	35	50	100	—	
RW73	$15	multicolor	Used	9	11	15	20	30	40	—	
			Unused NG	12.50	15	16	17.50	22.50	40	—	
			Mint NH	20	25	35	47.50	72.50	110	225	

SCT#	DENOM	COLOR	CONDITION	F 70	F-VF 75	VF 80	VF-XF 85	XF 90	XF-SUP 95	SUP 98	GEM 100
RW73b 1signature	$15	multicolor	Mint NH		110	150	170	190	220	300	400
RW73b 2 signatures	$15	multicolor	Mint NH		110	150	175	200	230	310	425
RW73A	$15	multicolor	Used		9	11	13	16	22.50	35	—
			Unused NG			15	16	18	22.50	32.50	—
			Mint NH			25	27	30	45	95	—
RW74	$15	multicolor	Used		9	11	15	22.50	32.50	45	110
			Unused NG		13.50	16	17	18	22.50	40	—
			Mint NH		29	35	45	60	80	120	200
RW74b	$15	multicolor	Mint NH		100	140	150	180	240	325	550
RW74A	$15	multicolor	Used		9	11	13	16	22.50	35	—
			Unused NG			15	16	18	22.50	30	—
			Mint NH			23.50	30	40	55	100	—
RW75	$15	multicolor	Used		9	11	15	22.50	32.50	45	—
			Unused NG		13.50	16	17	18	22.50	40	—
			Mint NH		30	35	45	60	90	120	200
RW75b	$15	multicolor	Mint NH		50	70	77.50	90	140	260	375
RW75A	$15	multicolor	Used		9	11	13	16	22.50	35	70
			Unused NG			25	28	32.50	45	67.50	—
			Mint NH			35	45	60	90	125	200
RW76	$15	multicolor	Used		9	11	13	16	22.50	35	—
			Unused NG			16	17	18	22.50	40	—
			Mint NH			30	40	55	80	110	200
RW76b	$15	multicolor	Mint NH		42.50	60	72.50	95	140	200	300
RW76A	$15	multicolor	Used		9	11	13	16	22.50	35	—
			Unused NG			20	21.50	24	30	40	—
			Mint NH			30	37.50	50	75	100	200
RW77	$15	multicolor	Used		9	11	13	16	22.50	35	100
			Unused NG			16	17	18	22.50	40	—
			Mint NH			30	40	55	82	110	200
RW77b	$15	multicolor	Mint NH		40	55	67.50	82.50	135	225	425
RW77A	$15	multicolor	Used		9	11	13	16	22.50	35	—
			Unused NG			20	21.50	24	30	45	—
			Mint NH			30	37.50	50	75	100	200
RW78	$15	multicolor	Used		9	11	13	16	22.50	35	100
			Unused NG			16	17	18	22.50	40	—
			Mint NH			37.50	47.50	65	100	135	240
RW78b	$15	multicolor	Mint NH		42.50	60	70	85	125	190	325
RW78A	$15	multicolor	Used		9	11	13	16	22.50	35	100
			Unused NG			20	21.50	24	30	45	—
			Mint NH			40	50	67.50	105	145	250
RW79	$15	multicolor	Used		9	11	13	16	22.50	35	100
			Unused NG			16	17	18	22.50	40	—
			Mint NH			37.50	47.50	65	90	125	250
RW79b	$15	multicolor	Mint NH		42.50	60	70	85	125	190	325
RW79A	$15	multicolor	Used		9	11	13	16	22.50	35	—
			Unused NG			20	21.50	24	30	45	—
			Mint NH			40	50	67.50	105	145	250
RW80	$15	multicolor	Used		9	11	13	16	22.50	35	—
			Unused NG			16	17	18	22.50	40	—
			Mint NH			37.50	47.50	65	100	135	210
RW80b	$15	multicolor	Mint NH		57.50	80	95	120	160	210	350
RW80A	$15	multicolor	Used		9	11	13	16	22.50	35	—
			Unused NG			20	21.50	24	30	45	—
			Mint NH			35	37.50	45	65	140	—
RW81	$15	multicolor	Used		9	11	13	16	22.50	35	100
			Unused NG			16	17	18	22.50	40	—
			Mint NH			40	52.50	67.50	110	130	175
RW81A	$15	multicolor	Used		10	12.50	15	18	25	40	—
			Unused NG			20	22	24	30	47.50	—
			Mint NH			40	45	50	80	130	175

SCT#	DENOM	COLOR	CONDITION	F 70	F-VF 75	VF 80	VF-XF 85	XF 90	XF-SUP 95	SUP 98	GEM 100
RW82	$25	multicolor	Used	10		12	14	17.50	27.50	45	—
			Unused NG			25	27.50	29	32.50	45	—
			Mint NH			55	60	70	105	120	175
RW82A	$25	multicolor	Used	10		12	14	17.50	25	35	—
			Unused NG			32.50	35	37.50	40	45	—
			Mint NH			55	60	67.50	85	120	150
RW83	$25	multicolor	Used		12.50	15	20	30	40	65	—
			Unused NG			40	45	50	57.50	70	—
			Mint NH			90	105	120	140	170	240
RW83A	$25	multicolor	Used	10		12.50	14	17.50	25	35	—
			Unused NG			32.50	35	37.50	40	45	—
			Mint NH			65	67.50	75	90	125	175
RW84	$25	multicolor	Used	10		12.50	14	17.50	25	35	—
			Unused NG			25	27.50	29	32.50	45	—
			Mint NH			45	50	60	85	130	190
RW84A	$25	multicolor	Used	10		12.50	14	17.50	25	35	—
			Unused NG			32.50	35	37.50	40	45	—
			Mint NH			40	45	50	65	125	—
RW85	$25	multicolor	Used	10		12.50	14	17.50	25	35	—
			Unused NG			25	27.50	29	32.50	45	—
			Mint NH			55	62.50	70	95	170	—
RW85A	$25	multicolor	Mint NH			50	55	62.50	70	125	210
RW86	$25	multicolor	Used	10		12.50	14	17.50	25	35	—
			Unused NG			25	27.50	29	32.50	45	—
			Mint NH			45	50	60	85	140	—
RW86A	$25	multicolor	Mint NH			45	50	55	65	90	—
RW87	$25	multicolor	Used	10		12.50	14	17.50	25	35	—
			Unused NG			25	27.50	29	32.50	45	—
			Mint NH			37.50	42.50	50	77.50	130	—
RW87A	$25	multicolor	Mint NH			37.50	40	45	52.50	70	150
RW88	$25	multicolor	Used	10		12.50	14	17.50	25	35	—
			Unused NG			25	27.50	29	32.50	45	—
			Mint NH			37.50	42.50	50	77.50	130	—
RW88A	$25	multicolor	Mint NH			37.50	40	45	52.50	75	—